Women and Technological Change in Developing Countries

AAAS Selected Symposia Series

Published by Westview Press, Inc.
5500 Central Avenue, Boulder, Colorado

for the

American Association for the Advancement of Science
1776 Massachusetts Avenue, N.W., Washington, D.C.

Women and Technological Change in Developing Countries

Edited by
Roslyn Dauber and Melinda L. Cain

AAAS Selected Symposium **53**

AAAS Selected Symposia Series

This book is based on a symposium which was held at the 1979 AAAS National Annual Meeting in Houston, Texas, January 3-8. The symposium was sponsored by the Society for Applied Anthropology, AAAS Sections H (Anthropology) and K (Social and Economic Sciences), and the AAAS Office of Opportunities in Science.

All rights reserved. No part of this publication may be reproduced or transmitted in any form or by any means, electronic or mechanical, including photocopy, recording, or any information storage and retrieval system, without permission in writing from the publisher.

Copyright © 1981 by the American Association for the Advancement of Science

Published in 1981 in the United States of America by
 Westview Press, Inc.
 5500 Central Avenue
 Boulder, Colorado 80301
 Frederick A. Praeger, Publisher

Library of Congress Cataloging in Publication Data
Main entry under title:
 Women and technological change in developing countries.
  (AAAS selected symposium ; 53)
  Bibliography: p.
  1. Underdeveloped areas--Women--Congresses. 2. Women in community development--Congresses. 3. Women in rural development--Congresses. 4. Underdeveloped areas--Technology and state--Congresses. I. Dauber, Roslyn. II. Cain, Melinda X. III. Series: American Association for the Advancement of Science. AAAS selected symposium ; 53.
  HQ1870.9.W65   305.4'2   80-21653
  ISBN 0-89158-791-8

Printed and bound in the United States of America

About the Book

Technology, generally considered a positive force that enhances both social and economic development, only benefits a whole population when it permits the productive use of all human resources, female as well as male. Nevertheless, women continue to be a neglected component in planning for technological development. This book considers developmental target areas--health, food, housing and fertility--that concern women as family members and as heads of households and assesses the specific needs of women both in adapting to technological change and as agents of that change.

About the Series

The *AAAS Selected Symposia Series* was begun in 1977 to provide a means for more permanently recording and more widely disseminating some of the valuable material which is discussed at the AAAS Annual National Meetings. The volumes in this *Series* are based on symposia held at the Meetings which address topics of current and continuing significance, both within and among the sciences, and in the areas in which science and technology impact on public policy. The *Series* format is designed to provide for rapid dissemination of information, so the papers are not typeset but are reproduced directly from the camera-copy submitted by the authors, without copy editing. The papers are organized and edited by the symposium arrangers who then become the editors of the various volumes. Most papers published in this *Series* are original contributions which have not been previously published, although in some cases additional papers from other sources have been added by an editor to provide a more comprehensive view of a particular topic. Symposia may be reports of new research or reviews of established work, particularly work of an interdisciplinary nature, since the AAAS Annual Meetings typically embrace the full range of the sciences and their societal implications.

WILLIAM D. CAREY
Executive Officer
American Association for
the Advancement of Science

Contents

About the Editors and Authors xiii

Foreword: Seeing Our Global Economy
Whole--*Hazel Henderson* xvii

PART 1. APPROACHES TO THE STUDY OF WOMEN
AND TECHNOLOGY

1. Overview: Women and Technology--Resources
   for Our Future--*Melinda L. Cain*.................3

   Technology and People:
     Resources for Development   3
   Women, Technology and Development   4
   Choice of Technology   5
   Case Studies: A Starting Point   6
   Notes   8

2. Integration into What? Reflections on
   Development Planning for Women--
   Elise Boulding 9

   Alternatives to Integration for
     Women   25
   Appendix A. A Sampling of Some
     Recent Women's Groups Working on
     Development from a Feminist
     Perspective   28
   Bibliography   31

3. Women, Technology and the Development
   Process--*International Labor Organization (ILO):
   Office for Women*..............................33

   Introduction   33

viii   Contents

    Background   33
      UN Conferences,33; ILO Basic Needs Approach,34
    The Aim of the Paper   34
    Redefining Women's Work   35
    Access to Scientific and Technological Knowledge   36
      Scientific and Technical Education and Training,36; Rural Women and Technological Inputs,38; Technological Change and Occupational Distribution Between Men and Women,41
    Some Conclusions   42
    Future Directions   43
    Notes   43

PART 2. SETTING THE CONTEXT: CASE STUDIES

4 New Technologies for Food-Related Activities: An Equity Strategy--*Irene Tinker* 51

    Biases in Economic Development Theory   52
      Economic Activity in the Informal Sector,53; Women's Contributions to Family Survival,55
    Women and the Food Crisis   56
      New Technologies and Women,57
    Preparation of Food   76
    The Basics of Water and Energy   79
    Conclusion   82
    References   83

5 Impact of Selected Industrial Technologies on Women in Mexico--*Mangalam Srinivasan* 89

    The Impact of Selected Industrial Technologies on Women   91
      The Electronic Industries,93; The Textile Industry,94; Extraction of Petroleum and Refinery Technologies,96; The Impact of Offshore Assembly Plants (the Maquiladoras) on Women,98; Women and Industrial Policies,104
    Notes   107

6 Women and the Development of "Underdevelopment": The African Experience--*Ann Seidman* 109

    The Explanatory Model Proposed   109

Contents   ix

The Evidence	110
Range of Possible Policies	118
References	123

7 Java, Indonesia: The Introduction of Rice Processing Technology--*Melinda L. Cain* 127

Introduction	127
Background	128
Traditional Rice Harvesting	129
The Tebasan Harvesting System and the Use of Sickles and Scales	130
The Introduction of Rice Hullers	131
Choice of Technology and Economic Aspects	131
Impact of the Technology	134
Concluding Remarks	134
Notes	136

8 Baseline Study for Socio-Economic Evaluation of Tangaye Solar Site-- *Grace S. Hemmings-Gapihan* 139

Introduction	139
Description of the Solar Unit	139
Description of Tangaye	139
Labour-Saving Devices and the Cost of Fuel	140
Use of Commercial Mills in the Area	141
Solar Mill and Pump: Labour-Saving Devices for Women and Herders	142

Food,142; Water,143

Management of the Solar Unit	145
Bibliography	148

9 Changing Role of Maya Mothers and Daughters--*Mary Elmendorf*...................149

Action Implications   162
  Infra-structure,162; Health Services,163; Education,163; Economics,164; Community Involvement,165
Appendix A. Population Profile of Chan Kom, 1978   166

Appendix B. Sex Distribution by
  Age and Marital Status, Chan
  Kom, 1978   167
Appendix C. Sex Distribution of
  Unmarried Individuals, Chan Kom,
  1978: Working-Studying/Inside-
  Outside the Village   168
Appendix D. Chan Kom: Workers
  Outside the Village, 1978   169
Appendix E. School Enrollment
  in Chan Kom, 1978   171
Appendix F. Changes in Chan
  Kom, 1971-1976   173
Appendix G. Birth Control
  Acceptors in Module VII of
  the Maternal-Child Health
  and Planning Program of the
  Mexican Ministry of Health   174
Notes   175
Bibliography   177

10 Women's Work in Multinational Electronics
    Factories-- *Linda Y.C. Lim* 181

PART 3. IMPLICATIONS FOR POLICY

11 Technologies Appropriate for Women:
    Theory, Practice and Policy--*Marilyn Carr*....193

    Theory   194
    Practice   196
    Policy   199
    Notes   201

12 The Plight of the Invisible Farmer:
    The Effect of National Agricultural
    Policy on Women in Africa--*Louise Fortmann*....205

    Factors in Women's Agricultural
      Production Excluded from
      Agricultural Policy   207
    Agricultural Policies Imple-
      mented so as to Exclude Women   209
    Policies with Adverse Effects
      on Women   211
    Ensuring that Women Benefit from
      Their Labor   212
    References and Notes   213

13   The Differential Impact of Programs and
     Policies on Women in Development--
     Hanna Papanek 215

        Integrating Research on Women's
           Work in Development Analyses   221
        References and Notes   226

14   Roles of Women: UNCSTD Background
     Discussion Paper--*NGO Task Force on Roles
     of Women, Mildred Robbins Leet, Chairperson* 229

        Women in Science and Technology
           for Development   229
        Conclusion   236

15   Applying Policy Analysis to Women and
     Technology: A Framework for Consider-
     ation--*Roslyn Dauber* 237

        Policy Analysis   237
        Development Theory and Related
           Policy   239
        Communications Strategy: Key
           to Policy Implementation   241
        Change and Policy   242
        Technology and Its Role in
           Development   242
        Technology Assessment   243
        Technology, Women and Employment   245
        Women and Technological Devel-
           opment   247
        The NCAT Plan for Action   248
        Conclusion   249
        References   250

Concluding Remarks--*Roslyn Dauber* 253

Annotated Bibliography--*Melinda L. Cain
and Roslyn Dauber* 257

About the Editors and Authors

Roslyn Dauber, *a writer and analyst concerned with research and development policies and priorities, worked for the Office of Technology Assessment on project definition of appropriate technologies, monitoring the U.N. Conference on Science and Technology for Development, and on proposal generation for alternative U.S. technical assistance programs to developing countries. She has also worked on other projects analyzing U.S. involvement in multilateral science and technology-related activities. She is coauthor of* An Introduction to Future Studies *(with Cornish et al.; World Futures Society, 1977).*

Melinda L. Cain *is a research social scientist at the Office of International Programs, Denver Research Institute of the University of Denver. She has been instrumental in designing a participatory planning technique for organizational planning and program management in developing countries. As director of the Development Training Programs, she has been responsible for workshops in Asia and Latin America as well as in the U.S. for foreign nations. She has also worked on various policy studies for UNCSTD, authored several articles on the socio-economic impacts of technological choice, and is currently involved in research on the efficiency of small scale enterprise in Colombia.*

Elise Boulding *is professor and chair, Department of Sociology, Dartmouth College, and is the U.S. Commissioner for UNESCO. From 1973 to 1977 she co-chaired the research committee on sex roles and society for the International Sociological Association. She has written several books on development, women and the family, including* Women in the Twentieth Century World *(Sage, 1977).*

Marilyn Carr *is an economist for the Intermediate Technology Development Group in London. A specialist in* appropriate technology and rural development, she spent three years as a village technologist with the African Training and Research Centre for Women in Addis Ababa. She is the author of **Appropriate Technology for African Women** *(Addis Ababa: ECA, 1978)* and **Economically Appropriate Technologies for Developing Countries** *(London: IT Pubs., 1976).*

Mary Elmendorf, a fellow of the Research Institute for the Study of Man, is involved in a long-term research project on the behavior of Mayan women in relation to demographic change. She has been a consultant to the World Bank since 1975, working in the Division of Population and Human Research, the Office of Environmental and Health Affairs and, currently, the Department of Energy, Water and Telecommunication. She participated in mission teams to Kenya, Nicaragua and Mexico, and in 1973 she was consultant to the Ford Foundation on the changing role of women in Latin America. Earlier she was chief of the CARE mission in Mexico and consultant to the Peace Corps. Among her many publications are **The Mayan Women and Change** *(Cuernavaca, Mexico: CIDOC, 1972) and* **Nine Mayan Women: A Village Faces Change** *(Wiley, 1977).*

Louise Fortmann is a visiting professor of sociology at Cornell University. Her areas of specialization are rural sociology, law and social organization and change. She is the author of a number of articles and conference papers on women and development.

Grace S. Hemmings-Gapihan is currently a Lewis Farmington Fellow at Yale University and is working on a study of international development and evolution of women's economic roles in rural Upper Volta for the African American Scholars Council. She conducted the Upper Volta baseline socioeconomic study preceding installation of a solar mill and pump designed by Lewis Research Center/NASA and financed by AID. Her interest in West Africa spans two decades, and she has published numerous articles on technology and women's economic roles.

Hazel Henderson is a lecturer, civic activist and author. She is a director of the Worldwatch Institute and of the Council on Economic Priorities and a member of the advisory council of the Office of Technology Assessment. She helped found the Public Interest Economics Foundation, the National Council for the Public Assessment of Technology, and the Environmentalists for Full Employment. She is the author of **Creating Alternative Futures** *(G.P. Putnam's Sons and Berkeley Books, 1978) and a contributor to numerous anthologies and journals, including* **The Saturday Review** *and* **The National Observer.**

About the Editors and Authors

Mildred Robbins Leet *is chairperson of the NGO (Non-Governmental Organization) Task Force on Roles of Women for Science and Technology for Development and a U.S. delegate to the U.N. Status of Women Commission. A consultant on women in development for Leet and Leet and codirector of Hotline International, she has also served as president of the National Council of Women and vice-president of the International Council of Women.*

Linda Y.C. Lim, *assistant professor of economics at Swarthmore College, is involved in on-going research on industries in less-developed countries, especially those industries that employ women. Her area of specialization is economic development and international and political economics, especially of Southeast Asia.*

Hanna Papanek *is a research associate at the Center for Asian Development Studies at Boston University and chairperson of the Committee on Women in Asian Studies (Association for Asian Studies) and of the Committee on Sex Roles in Society (International Sociological Association). She has been active in organizing several of the major conferences on women and development and has lived and worked for ten years in Southeast Asia. She has published numerous articles on women and edited (with Rounaq Jahan)* Women and Development: Perspectives from South and Southeast Asia *(Dacca: University Press, 1979).*

Ann Seidman *is a professor of international development and social change at Clark University and chairperson of the research committee of the Association of Concerned African Scholars. For eight years a scholar and teacher at African universities, she is the author of seven books on economic development in Africa, most recently* Women and Work *(Westview Press, 1978).*

Mangalam Srinivasan *is the associate director of the Technology Policy and Assistance Council, a research associate for the Center for Science Technology, New York University, and consultant to the World Bank. She has been a Fulbright Scholar and a fellow of the Center for International Affairs at Harvard University. An invited speaker at the International Women's Year plenary session (Mexico City), she prepared one of the background papers on women in development for the World Congress of Women. She has published widely in the area of management and development policies and analysis of urban situations, including the U.N. study, "Integrating Women in Agricultural Development."*

Irene Tinker *is director of the Equity Policy Center and a former director of the Office of International Science,* *xvi*   *About the Editors and Authors*

AAAS, *and assistant director of ACTION. She was the first president of the Federation of Organizations for Professional Women, organized the experts' seminar at the International Women's Year Conference (1975), established the Committee on Women in Development for the Society of International Development (1972) and, in 1976, established the International Center for Research on Women. She also served on the U.S. delegation to the U.N. Commission on the Status of Women. She has written on comparative elections, urbanization, technologies and population and edited* Women and World Development *(with M.B. Bramsen; Overseas Development Council/Praeger, 1976).*

The International Labor Organization (ILO), *a specialized agency associated with the United Nations, is active in the formulation of international labor standards and in the study of social and economic trends throughout the world.*

The Non-Governmental Organization (NGO) Task Force on Roles of Women *was formed in 1972 to consider the roles of women in science and technology for development; to explore the possibility of an agenda item related to women for the United Nations Conference on Science and Technological Development (UNCSTD); and to develop recommendations for the UNCSTD World Programme of Action.*

Hazel Henderson

Foreword: Seeing Our Global Economy Whole

This book offers important insights toward an essential reconceptualization of the planetary development process of humankind. The case studies collected here provide evidence of the fundamental flaw of an economics which equates the total social productivity of people, their communities, and the entire ecosystem with the narrow concept of productivity measured in the monetized terms of a cash-based economy.

It is sometimes forgotten, particularly by economists, that human productivity long preceded the brief 300-year era of Western industrialism, as also did the forests in which people have always hunted, the land they have tilled, the waters they have fished and the sun, wind and other resources they have always used. In general, economic theory has recognized only a productivity measured by such monetary estimators as the Gross National Product. I believe that this view and these monetary measures are much too limited, for when we concentrate only on the monetized economic sectors, the cash and exchange transactions, we are working with very poor descriptors of the rich reality of life. We are also working with descriptors which devalue or ignore all of the principal contributions of women to their societies.

As Karl Polanyi has pointed out in The Great Transformation (1), the invention, in 17th-century Britain, of a new resource allocation method based on a national system of "free" markets, instituted by laws which included the enclosure of land, was an unusual event in human history and a significant departure from the past. Until that time, most resource allocation in human societies had been based on two very different principles: reciprocity and redistribution. Markets had always existed, but they had been mainly local and based on barter rather than systematized and based only on cash transactions. In the former, women, even while caring for their children, could participate; from the latter they have been substantially excluded.

Money is easily counted and tracked, so economics and its data-gathering activities focus on money or its equivalents. Yet when one examines the full spectrum of productive activities carried out in societies world-wide, one must acknowledge that most of the production in the world, both before and after the Industrial Revolution, has taken place <u>outside</u> of the cash-based, GNP-measured sector of national economies. Karl Marx perceptively referred to these vast non-market sectors of production as production for <u>use</u>-value and contrasted them with production for <u>market</u>-value.

Today, some theoreticians are re-examining these overlooked use-value sectors in the world's economies. Although invisible in traditional economic theory, they have been written about under various names: the informal economy (2), the household economy (3), the familial economy (4), the socioeconomy (5). These terms clearly indicate the importance of these use-value concepts for women in development. Moreover, similar concepts underlie the research of the past decade on social indicators of development, which focus on health, education, nutrition, housing and political participation, rather than only on averaged, per capita, cash income. (See, for example, Erma Adelman and Cynthia Taft Morris (6).) I have described elsewhere the re-appearance of the use-value economy in the United States and Europe as "the emerging counter-economy" (7).

Why is there now a new awareness of the importance of the use-value economy? Precisely because the view which equates economic growth only with rising GNP is insufficient to explain recent events in <u>all</u> industrialized countries. There is a growing awareness that social costs and impacts, which have hitherto been ignored, must now be taken into account. Traditional economic theory has no way of taking into account the bills for exploitation and resource-depletion, at least not before the fact; but after the fact, these are bills which we cannot avoid paying. These "externalities" have always existed, but now industrial economies are facing problems which are real, substantial, and are the result of ignoring the economic reality which lies beyond traditional money measures. To use Kenneth Boulding's term, these signal the end of "cowboy economics." If properly attended to, I believe these also offer new opportunities for women in development. The path will not be easy, however, and women must become increasingly aware of these problems and the part they can play in alleviating them.

Today industrial economies will find Keynesian pump-priming increasingly ineffective and borrowing from the future and from the planet's nonrenewable resource endowment will become increasingly costly in both human and monetary terms. Cheap energy and cheap raw materials are clearly no longer a part of our present or our immediate future. We also see, in growing currency instabilities, the limits of the price system, of monetary and fiscal management tools and of the ineffectiveness of macroeconomic aggregates as levers of governance and resource allocation.

It is becoming acknowledged that the brief explosion of Western industrial and technological growth was fueled by cheap energy and cheap, often imported, raw materials. But it is generally overlooked that this growth was and is also based in substantial part on the freely given, unpaid work of many women, who have nurtured the young, cared for the old and sick, grown and prepared food, managed the household, transmitted the culture and aided their communities in many other essential ways. This vast base of unpaid--and hence undervalued--work has always existed, and it is this work which has created and maintained the social infrastructure--the cohesion--that has permitted the competitors of the market sector to "succeed." Indeed, in the monetized economy, other less powerful social groups also provide subsidies through exploitation of their labor, a situation in which racial and ethnic discrimination, social hierarchy and caste systems frequently play a part.

We will need many new maps to understand the world's informal economy of use-value, even though it is basic to the economies of all nations. In the papers which follow, we are shown vivid glimpses of its functioning. We are also made aware of how little research or even routine statistical data are available on use-value production. Policy analysts have inevitably been short-changed by the economists' view of production in exclusively monetary terms. Policy-making based only on such data has led to what Elise Boulding terms "the bureaucratization of the world." It has also led to a kind of elitism, for the monetary data are too highly aggregated to be adequate guides to or measures of real world situations. Rather than operational direction, the statistical illusions derived from these aggregations lead us only into embarrassingly vague and monetary-based-- hence unproductive--debates concerning "productivity," "wealth" and "income," not to mention "inflation," "stagflation " and the rest. Ordinary people now sense this mystification of real issues by the fictions of economic jargon.

A "New International Economic Order," if based only on such imprecise and obsolete notions, cannot serve much better than the existing one. The intellectual baggage of traditional development economics—"modernization" (a curiously old-fashioned word); "comparative advantage"; "global economic efficiency" as measured by prices in the "world market"—are all terms being questioned today. Even Western development theorist W. W. Rostow has rethought his Stages of Economic Growth (8) and now criticizes traditional economics in his new book, Getting from Here to There (9). In fact, it has become clear to many insightful political leaders that the Western view of global economic growth as a continuous process is mistaken and that such growth was only a single historical event, specific to those countries which were first on the ladder in an earlier era of resource abundance. Indeed, leaders of many Southern Hemisphere countries are aware—as women have always been—that economics is simply politics in disguise. As the English economist John Stuart Mill noted a hundred years ago, the distribution of the fruits of production is always a political matter (10).

Today we are also realizing that access to the tools of production is a political rather than a technical matter. No clearer example of the inadequacy of the economics of comparative advantage is visible than that of the anomalies of the micro-processor revolution. Over-developed countries are bracing themselves for what the Organization for Economic Cooperation and Development calls the prospect of an era of virtually jobless economic growth due to automation in the 1980s. The developing countries, on the other hand, may face another kind of spector: the further innovations in micro-processor technology may destroy their last form of "comparative advantage"—cheap labor—in spite of a short-term increase in low-wage employment. (See Linda Y. C. Lim and her discussion in this volume of some of these issues as they apply to the new "space-age sweatshops" which assemble micro-electronic consumer goods.)

Other papers in this book illustrate our statistical ignorance concerning women's production, and some document women's exploitation. It is pointed out that the "trickle-down" theories of development, within and between nations, are inadequate in practice, however hopeful their promises. "Technology transfer" has been an elitist misconception. New models in which economic and technical factors are embedded but not controlling are needed to represent and direct the sociocultural development process. Such rethinking is now emerging in Africa, Asia, Latin America and in the industrialized countries as well. One example is the recent establishment in Senegal of the new "Université des Mutants" to examine and test specific cultural mutations. One hopes that it will be one among many sources of new models of sociocultural-technical development.

New models and new modes of behavior are clearly needed. Industrial and developing countries are still bound by paternalistic institutions and customs, poorly assessed technologies disruptive of cultural and ecological stability and simplistic notions of economic "progress." Women must assume their responsibilities to "hold up half the sky," yet most are not free to do so. Until development policies take a clear look at the reality of women's contributions, development will continue to be unbalanced. We must also realize that development is only one facet of a global system based on competition among nation-states, and that the militarism and institutionalized patriarchies of the past do not provide a harmonious basis for world order on our crowded, interdependent planet.

Perhaps a new planetary coalition is in the making and a much broader political constituency is emerging--one comprising the exploited people in all the planet's countries, not only women but all who are denied basic needs and human rights by all forms of discrimination and abuse of power and wealth. Thus the message of this book takes on a special urgency for all who hope and work to see our global economy "whole."

References

1. Karl Polanyi, <u>The Great Transformation</u>. Boston: Beacon Press, 1944.

2. James Robertson, <u>The Sane Alternative</u>. Privately published, 1978. Robertson: 7 St. Ann's Villas, London, SW11 4RV.

3. Scott Burns, <u>The Household Economy</u>. Boston: Beacon Press, 1975.

4. The Vanier Institute, <u>Some Reflections on the Evolution of Canada's Political Economy</u>. Ottawa, Canada: Vanier Institute, 1978.

5. Robert Theobald, <u>The Rich & The Poor: A Study of the Economics of Rising Expectations</u>. New York: Menton/New American Library, 1962.

6. Irma Adelman and Cynthia Taft Morris, <u>Economic Growth and Social Equity in Developing Countries</u>. Stanford, California: Stanford University Press, 1974.

7. Hazel Henderson, <u>Creating Alternative Futures</u>. New York: G. P. Putnam's Sons, 1978.

8. W. W. Rostow, <u>Stages of Economic Growth</u>. Cambridge, England: Cambridge University Press, 1960.

9. W. W. Rostow, <u>Getting From Here to There</u>. New York: McGraw Hill, 1979.

10. John Stuart Mill, <u>Principles of Political Economy</u>. London: John W. Parker & Sons, 1857.

Part 1

Approaches to the Study of Women and Technology

Melinda L. Cain

1. Overview: Women and Technology — Resources for Our Future

The theme of the 1979 annual meeting of the American Association for the Advancement of Science was "Science and Technology: Resources for Our Future." An essential component of a strategy to use those resources is the development or enhancement of human resources and, in particular, women. Therefore, this session organized on women and technology was designed to address an issue of great importance, particularly to developing countries. The utilization of science and technology for development purposes is highlighted by the 1979 UNCSTD*, an international, agenda-setting conference that culminated almost three years of preparation and activities all over the world. Human resources were an important aspect of these preparations also, and it is within this international, agenda-setting framework that women and technology emerge as vital forces that will shape our global future.

Technology and People: Resources for Development

Much discussion has been focused on the use of technology in the development process. A first assumption is that technology has been shown to be a powerful force in promoting social and economic development. However, without careful attention, the positive influence of technology can be undermined by negative externalities and unanticipated or secondary effects.[1]

A second assumption relevant to this issue is that technology is not a neutral or value-free tool; that is, access to and control of technology is an important determinant to the impact technology will have, especially within the context of developmental progress.[2]

---

*United Nations Conference on Science and Technology in Development

"Human power" is, likewise, an important resource for development and a particularly abundant resource in developing countries. A great deal of foreign assistance has been directed--indirectly or directly--towards human resource development, in particular towards the enhancement of productivity. Thus, the complete utilization of <u>all</u> human resources in developing countries is a very obvious, common sense approach to doing development well. That is, to ignore 50 percent of the world's human resources by focusing the use and transfer of technology and other development efforts on men only is an omission that is potentially detrimental to the future of the whole society. Therefore, it is within this context--of mixing technology with human resources towards the betterment of human kind--that the issue of women and technology is addressed.

Women, Technology and Development

The approach to the study of women's roles and status in a development context is not to be viewed as an end in itself but rather as a means to promoting more effective development overall. However, a starting point for this is a better assessment of current contributions by women in order to enhance their roles and participation. The issue of "women in development" has become particularly fashionable in recent years since the introduction of the Percy Amendment that required all U.S. foreign assistance efforts to include women in the design and implementation of projects. Furthermore, since the initial conference of the International Women's Year, marking the beginning of the U.N. Decade for Women, increased international attention has been given to roles and activities of women. The rationale for such attention is that women have been largely ignored both as subjects and objects of development efforts, considered only in the context of "welfare" or social service projects. This bypassing of an essential resource has done much to limit opportunities for many women to engage in fruitful and productive activity.

However, attention to the issue is only a first step, to be followed by practical tactics to implement such proposals. The practical implementation steps are sadly lacking--not often due to intentional efforts to counteract what appears to some to be a "western feminism"--but more due to ignorance or lack of experience in how to go about doing "women in development" in a realistic, practical manner to include women where they have so long been ignored.

Research results are beginning to document the long, arduous work days of African, Asian, and Latin American

Overview: Women and Technology   5

women—15-hour work days that often include miles of walking to gather firewood or find water. Because of the historical failure to consider women as "equal partners in development," much of today's efforts are to regain what the past has taken away from these women; then assistance can help them move forward again.[3]

It is obvious, and common sense, but still necessary to say again that, when technology permits the productive use of all human resources, female as well as male, the betterment of the whole population can be achieved.

Choice of Technology

The initial step in technological use is the need to choose a technology appropriate to the problem or situation. As pointed out in the following paragraph, the choice is a crucial factor in determining the successful use of a technology:

> The choice of technologies is one of the most important collective decisions facing a developing country. It is a choice that affects the whole fabric of economic and social structure. It determines who works and who does not; the whole pattern of income distribution; where work is done, and therefore the urban/rural balance; and what is produced, that is, for whose benefit resources are used.[4]

This, of course, opens the door to the debate on "appropriate" or inappropriate choices and to a Pandora's box of value judgments and philosophical undertones. This book, and indeed, this chapter, does not intend to render a value judgment on what constitutes an "appropriate" choice. What it does wish to convey is that choices should consider an efficient use of available inputs and should consider them within the local social and cultural context. Furthermore, "It is important that a saving of unnecessary arduous labor should not be confused, as it sometimes is now, with a saving of manpower. The latter is not usually desirable in the developing countries, but the former is something which should be attempted whenever possible; we do not need to use a sledge hammer to crack nuts, but we do need to find better ways of cracking them than with our bare hands."[5]

An issue to consider here also is who makes the choices of technology. Those least affected by a choice are often those responsible for determining that choice, while those who will be forced to live with or adapt to the new technology and the changes it brings are least likely to have any say in the matter.

Some development studies have focused on reasons for seemingly less than optimal choices of technology.[6] Such influences include distorted factor prices (where capital subsidizes protective wage legislation and causes factor prices to be out of proportion to their availability, thus biasing the use of capital); irrational biases for sophisticated machinery, enhanced by such bureaucratic influences as risk aversion, strict time schedules and limited sectoral planning; and lack of information or knowledge about the range of technological alternatives.[7] This latter influence is of particular note with respect to women. Rural women have very limited access to information about technology and what it might do for them, not only by virtue for their position outside the mainstream of such information flow but also because of the selective perception of those controlling or choosing technology that ignores technology for women. It is obvious, therefore, that inappropriate choices--for women and society in general--will continue to be made unless an approach is followed that considers the need to mitigate such influences.

The myth that "technology is machinery and is fulfilling of men, not women," is untrue. It is true that cultural traditions in many countries prohibit women from working on or with certain machinery. However, as shown by this book, there are many instances where certain technologies can be immensely useful in lessening arduous tasks done by women when the technologies are designed to adapt to the women's situation, rather than expecting the women to adapt to the technology.[8]

In developing countries, underemployment and unemployment are critical problems. To give technology to women is seen by some to put men deserving of that role "out of work." The issue here is not one of competition between the sexes but rather one of opening access of women to gainful and productive employment in order to add to a family's income.[9]

Case Studies: A Starting Point

Much of the literature on women and technology comes from micro-level case studies that analyze a particular situation where technology has been introduced, assessing the negative or positive impacts. Social impacts are noted such as labor displacement, increased inequality between the sexes, decline in productivity or psychological effects.[10] Little has been done before now to build a conceptual framework for the growing literature of the field. Although case study literature

Overview: Women and Technology   7

produces fragmented data initially, the collection of evidence built by case studies can be instrumental in producing credible generalizations on which to base policy statements.

A major problem arises, however, because policymakers cannot wait for case studies to "fall together." Their decisions and actions tend to be immediate and are hampered by a sensitivity to a wide range of political influences. Therefore, the essential question is how to build a bridge between research and policy; that is, how to make research more policy-related and accessible to policymakers and, on the other hand, how to get policymakers to realize the value of empirical evidence on which to base important policy decisions.

This book attempts to put forth a strong case for such "bridge-building" in the subject arena of women and technology. Society loses by delaying longer. Researchers who choose study topics that are policy-oriented and relevant to current political issues are more likely to receive attention than those who study topics, no matter how challenging, that are outside the mainstream of political concern. Current studies in the women and development field tend for the most part to be policy-relevant, if not directly policy-oriented. It is obvious from the contributions in this book that strong policy lessons can be learned from current studies on women and technology. From this, other new subject areas may take notice and continue the trend.

For the policymaker, an ear to research is warranted, mixed with sensitivity to the "local area plus population" that will be impacted by policy directives. Not knowing where to look or not having the "right" information available are situations that plague a policy person. Furthermore, the oft-cited woe of many development project managers is the requirement of including and reporting on special considerations such as the environment and women. There is no simple crib sheet to instruct managers in how to deal with any and all situations, but enough information is becoming available to help managers respond in the area of women and development.

Thus, the underlying mission in setting forth the issue of women and technology is to recognize the topic of women, technology and development within a research-to-policy perspective. This book draws attention to current research trends in an effort to show that they can be useful to policy people and that policy directives can make an immense difference in dealing with human resources.

Notes

1. Albert H. Teich (ed.), Technology and Man's Future, New York: St. Martin's Press, 1977 (2nd edition); and Frances Stewart, Technology and Underdevelopment, Boulder, Colorado: Westview Press, 1977.

2. Denis Goulet, The Uncertain Promise, Washington, D.C.: Overseas Development Council, 1977; David Dickson, The Politics of Alternative Technology, New York: Universe Books, 1975.

3. Ester Boserup, Women's Role in Economic Development, New York: St. Martin's Press, 1970; Mayra Buvinic, Women and World Development, An Annotated Bibliography, Washington, D.C.: Overseas Development Council, 1976; May Rihani, Development as if Women Mattered, Washington, D.C.: Overseas Development Council, 1978.

4. Intermediate Technology Development Group, Journal of Appropriate Technology, (n.d.) p. 2.

5. Elizabeth O'Kelly, Rural Women: their Integration in Development Programs and How Simple Intermediate Technologies Can Help Them, London, 1978, p. 3.

6. See chapter 4 in Part II, Melinda Cain, "Java, Indonesia: The Introduction of Rice Processing Technology".

7. op. cit., F. Stewart; C. Peter Timmer, The Choice of Technology in Developing Countries, Harvard University: Center for International Affairs, 1975.

8. See Chapter I in Part III, Marilyn Carr, "Technologies Appropriate for Women: Theory, Practice and Policy"; Marilyn Carr, Appropriate Technology for African Women, Addis Ababa; Ethiopia: UN Economic Commission on Africa, 1978.

9. Adrienne Germaine, "Poor Rural Women: A Policy Perspective", Journal of International Affairs, Volume 30, No. 2, 1976-1977, p. 167-168.

10. See entries in Annotated Bibliography, in particular, Irene Tinker, "The Adverse Impact of Development on Women" in Irene Tinker and Michele Bo Bramsen (Eds.), Women and World Development, Washington, D.C.: Overseas Development Council, 1976.

Elise Boulding

2. Integration into What? Reflections on Development Planning for Women

It was Mary Beard (1946) who first pointed out that it was the decline of land as the primary source of capital and its replacement by industrial capital in the post-feudal era that eroded the power base of European women, leaving them dependent and politically helpless by the nineteenth century. That landed power base had operated, particularly for women of the upper classes, from the time of the first cities in the Middle East. Since few wept the passing of the aristocracy, women or men, the significance of the underlying phenomenon of the decline of land and its prerequisites as capital for women in countries of all degrees of industrialization has been missed.

A major feature of the agrarian preindustrial ways of life has been a type of familial division of labor which has left separate and autonomous spheres for women and men. There is no universal pattern for the division of labor -- what women do in one society men do in another, and both do in a third. Often a husband and wife will have separate plots of land, and separate craft and trading enterprises, in the same family. The autonomous spheres principle, with each spouse retaining control of own profits, and giving and receiving credit separately, is very widespread. A careful reading of the Firth and Yamey (1964) study of fourteen preindustrial societies

> makes it clear that in each of these societies women are engaged in the following activities: (1) farming; (2) trade; (3) craftwork; and (4) handling of money, credit transactions, savings and investment activity. In none of these societies do women fail to accumulate and invest capital, whether in the form of land, livestock, gold or other commodities. Some of the capital is in the

form of dowry, or brideprice. While a woman does not necessarily have control over all of the bridal fund, in no case is she left without the possibility of accumulating capital over which she does not have exclusive control.

Marguerite Dupire's (1963) study of the nomadic Fulani women distinguishes between cattle owned jointly by husband and wife and cattle owned exclusively by the women. Women have their own cash income from trade in cattle and dairy products, and all ownership of clothes, tools, and furniture is separate for husbands and wives. The dowry, which "belongs" to the wife and is "cared for" by the husband, is a separate item from her private capital. The dowry is considered as the children's inheritance, held by the husband.

Marilyn Strathern's study of New Guinean women analyzes how money flows in that society revolve around the movements of the women, and the life cycle events of families. The wife becomes the instrument of the flow of wealth between groups. "Women are like tradestores," and "Women walk about and bring plenty of valuables" are revealing folk sayings (1972:99). Interestingly, though the men regard themselves as the decision makers and the controllers of all the significant transactions in the society, with the women as their servant-producers, Strathern discovered that the women think of themselves as independent transactors. A complete analysis of this New Guinean economy from the women's perspective would be very interesting to compare with existing anthropological documentation.

H. J. Simons' book on the legal status of African women in South Africa documents the loss of rights to land and capital that can take place for women once economic dualism becomes strongly established in a country. Women cannot now assert inheritance rights they had under tribal law, yet "many tens of thousands of widows officiate in practice as the heads of the households" (1968: 254). (E. Boulding, 1977:97, p. 8).

The actual holding of land is of minimal importance in many of these societies, since rights are assigned by the tribe or extended family, but the rights to independent accumulation by women and men are very important. Surpluses are carefully "invested" by women in order to pass on as large an

Integration into What? 11

inheritance as possible to daughters (sometimes also to sons). The women of an extended family are a type of female credit association, enabling special ventures to be made in acquiring new livestock, jewelry, etc.

The intrusion of cash-cropping and export agriculture into this type of economy is always an asymmetric intrusion, as Boserup (1970) has shown. The industrialized countries passed through the phase of disruption of the family production partnership several centuries ago, and successfully reorganized production into a predominantly male sphere with auxiliary roles available to women only if they left the homestead and entered the factory at auxiliary wages. The urban migration in Europe had already detached women from their rural means of production. They lived resourceless in urban tenements with children to raise and no means of feeding them - a woman's traditional responsibility ordinarily carried out with the help of her kitchen garden. A husband, if present (and many women migrants to the city had children but no spouse) rarely earned enough to support the whole family in any case. There were periods in the nineteenth century when half the women of some of Europe's cities were unpartnered (E. Boulding, 1976:625-626).

The asymmetry of the spheres of autonomy for women and men in industrial society is very strong, and shows no sign of abating, in spite of the Equal Remuneration Convention adopted by the International Labour Office in 1951, since ratified by 93 countries. Table 1 is from a 1975 ILO report comparing earnings of female and male workers in industrialized countries in textiles and in manufacturing generally. The disparities vary no less than in newly industrializing countries. A report on wage disparities in the textile industry in more recently industrializing countries is based on a different type of computation, but tells the same story (Table 2). Since textiles are a key transition industry in the modernization process, it is particularly interesting to see how women remain in the same wage trap in this industry no matter how industrialized the country. If we move from the oldest modernizing industry of textiles to the newest modernizing industry of electronics, we find terms like "space-age sweatshop" used to describe women working at microscopes in an electronics factory in Malaysia (Nationwide Womens' Program, 1978).

There have been many efforts to improve the position of women, particularly in this women's development decade. In February of 1975 the EEC (European Economic Community) Council issued an Equal Pay for Equal Work directive asking member states to bring national laws in line with that principle (the above-mentioned 1951 Convention having had no effect).

12 Elise Boulding

Table 1. Earnings of female workers in manufacturing and in the textile industry compared with those of male workers in selected countries, 1975

Countries	Earnings of female workers as a percentage of earnings of male workers	
	All manufacturing	Textile industry
Australia	73.4	74.6[1]
Finland	73.1	74.3[2]
Ireland	60.4	61.1
Norway	78.0	83.5
Sweden[3]	84.8	85.5
Switzerland	68.0	68.2
United Kingdom	66.5	71.8

[1] This includes the clothing and shoe industry
[2] The cotton section only
[3] 1974

Source: Women at Work, International Labour Office Bulletin No. 1, 1978, p. 18.

Table 2. Disparity Between Men's and Women's Earnings In Selected Occupations (October 1976)[1]

Type of remuneration, occupation and country	Currency unit	Earnings Males	Earnings Females	Disparity %
Hourly Wages: Spinners (textile manufacture)				
Morocco	Dirhams	1.74	1.50	13.8
Singapore[2]	Dollars	0.98	0.76	22.4
Venezuela	Bolivares	26.12	19.00	27.3

[1] Percentage by which women's earnings are lower than men's.
[2] June 1976.

Source: Women at Work, International Labour Office Bulletin No. 1, 1978, p. 18.

Integration into What? 13

The U.S.A. Equal Rights Amendment has been the focus of a decade-long struggle for ratification, with laggard states still holding out in 1979. In spite of all efforts, statistics continue to show that while women's labor force participation increases, salary levels and administrative roles with very minor exceptions persistently and substantially lag behind those of men, in this very decade. This asymmetry should make us question very strongly the appropriateness of first world development agencies of any kind designing development programs for third world women.

There has been a strong urge to develop such programs because the situation of the third world seems so desperate. We see severely impacted third world societies with men dehumanized by want or greed; landless laborers working for a pittance, farmers converting production to cash crops sold for export while their families go hungry, urban migrants working for a pittance in the cities. We see women working ever longer hours as they must traverse the denuded land for greater distance for firewood and water, and work extra hours in the cash crop fields of their spouses or other men, with little time left for working their own kitchen gardens. They have no time to produce the surpluses that women have traditionally produced to pass on to the next generation. Children bred as helpers are a burden because so few of them live and so much energy goes into fruitless childbearing. There is an assumption that this is how it always was, and that only "development" will save the women. Yet often when data are available on earlier times in specific third world regions, they suggest that the standard of living was higher a century or more ago, sometimes as recently as a generation ago. From an ILO publication:

> It is significant to note that for the first time in the African continent, a shortage of basic food stocks is appearing in countries where earlier there were adequate quantities of food. For example, in the Ivory Coast women have been steadily losing their rights to land for growing food. It was also observed in the river valleys of the Upper Volta that women have left the areas in large numbers after settlement schemes were introduced. In West Africa, retail trade which until recently was controlled by women is now steadily losing out to supermarkets and other such establishments (ILO, 1978:5, 6).

There is evidence that in the past women and men had types of economic partnership that no longer exist. The women know it from their grandmothers.

14   *Elise Boulding*

For most of the women I encountered, change
--whether seen in their lifetime, or as compared to
the lives of their mothers--seems to hold a negative
connotation. In their mothers' time, most of them
said, "life was not as difficult" or "as complicated". We have less to eat than before.

...one change mentioned repeatedly and with dis-
tress, regardless of country or ethnic or religious
identification, was the disintegration of relationships between men and women. Over and over again I
was told: "Men were better in the old times; they took
care of their families"; "There is no trust between
men and women anymore". Older women complained about
lack of communication with their menfolk. Unmarried
girls voiced the hope that their husbands would "talk
with me", "plan with me", or "be understanding" and
spoke of their fear that communication between husband
and wife is rare, if not downright impossible.
(Perdita Houston, Message From the Village, pp. 1-3)

The fear of men by women may be an old fear in urban
societies, where women lost their independent base a very
long time ago, but it is a new fear in many rural societies
and among new migrants to the cities. High rates of alcohol-
ism among migrant men are one source of fear in their wives:
"It's not that he's bad, it's that he got in bad company" the
migrant women will say (Guyot, 1978).

Migrant women, whether in third world cities or industrialized first world cities of Europe and North America, may
be the worst sufferers of all. They have left rural deprivation to experience urban deprivation, and may also lose
their husbands in the process. They must then support children in the slums of an alien land whose language they do not
know. A few move up to secure working class existence. Most
don't.

What we are in danger of doing now is inflicting the
diseased solutions of the first world on the diseased conditions of the third world, and as usual women will get the
worst of both.

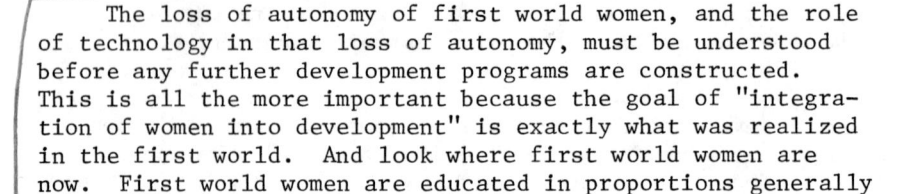

The loss of autonomy of first world women, and the role
of technology in that loss of autonomy, must be understood
before any further development programs are constructed.
This is all the more important because the goal of "integration of women into development" is exactly what was realized
in the first world. And look where first world women are
now. First world women are educated in proportions generally

approximating those of men, they are in the labor force in increasing numbers, and the dollar earnings of women, particularly in the United States, are steadily declining in relation to men's earnings. A 1977 U.S. Department of Labor Report indicates that for every dollar men make, women make fifty-nine cents. Ten decades ago the percentage was higher.

The proportion of women in administrative positions worldwide is 10 percent. In Euro-North America it is 14 percent. Only in the Scandinavian countries are first world women more than 10 percent of the national parliaments. Second world parliaments, in the socialist countries contain roughly one-third women; in third world countries rates range from one-third to zero. Integration has meant systematic marginalization, accomplished so effectively that the majority of first world women must enter the paid labor force to maintain their household according to the standards modernization rhetoric has taught them to think of as required. The only work available to them is low-paid, low-status work. Only upper middle class women can command the salaries which the average middle class man can command.

One group of first world women has maintained autonomy throughout the modernization process, primarily because the pre-industrial partnership has continued to remain viable: farm women engaged in family farming on family-sized farms. The women, like the men on family farms, work long hours, and their wellbeing from year to year is subject to the vagaries of nature, but they are the one occupational group who report themselves as happy and satisfied with their work, as not wanting to change it for any other way of life. In a current United States field study of farm women I am finding that the answer of married women to the question, "what do you like most about farming?" is almost uniformly "working together with my husband". For unpartnered women, it is "being my own boss". Both the partnered and the unpartnered women are reflecting a sense of independence, of control over their own lives, of participating in the crucial decisions about how work shall be done. The family farm represents a unique balancing point for women's roles. If the farm sinks too deeply into debt the autonomy is lost. Also expansion and mechanization to the point where the farm is no longer a family enterprise where husband and wife both have the range of necessary skills to handle most of the work and children enter the partnership at an early age, may mean loss of autonomy and a retreat for women into more conventional housework or labor force roles. I say may, because women who have once been partners don't lose those skills, they sometimes find new fields to conquer in an agro-industrial farming situation.

16   Elise Boulding

First world farm women are among the least studied and least understood of the female sectors of modernized economies.

The complex event chain that reduces individual autonomy in industrializing societies does not of course affect women alone. It also affects men. This has to do with the extent of stratification associated with the development of large-scale production systems at least as we have known them in both the capitalist and socialist mode. It has to do with the character of the political, economic, and military bureaucracies associated with these modes of production, and the types of regulatory systems developed to ensure functioning of these large-scale systems according to centralized planning patterns which have not changed very much for 2000 years. As Jacoby has shown (1973) the central control-local autonomy issue was a focus of a struggle in the earliest of ancient bureaucracies, and continues to be a focus of struggle today. What is important here is that those bureaucracies have always been a male world. The initial asymmetry of domain of any bureaucratic system has to be seen in the light of the origins of bureaucratic systems in the authoritarian palace-temple regimes of the earliest city states. Each technological innovation that made new surpluses possible, from plows to irrigation systems to mechanical conveyor systems, was linked to the palace-temple complex. Exclusionary rights to the fruits of the technology was maintained by the military arm of the palace-temple complex.

In a sense, technology was militarized from very early times. The palace-temple-army-technology complex was operated by men, and the kitchen garden-homecraft-childbearing complex was operated by women. Care of humans of all ages at the family level is highly labor-intensive. In a home-based production system the personal care can be shared out and combined with other tasks. Once the other tasks have left the home, care-giving by simple definition becomes more specialized. It becomes harder for women to enter into the capital-intensive production realm of the technological complex, and they do not have the bargaining power they had in the homestead production situation. That the biological specializations of reproduction and lactation should become the basis for other role assignments to a more pronounced degree with industrialization than had been true before is one of the many ironies of industrialization.

The military capabilities always associated with the technological complex, at least in historical experience as we have known it, reenforce the basic tendency of the bureaucracy to dominate by physical force when necessary. Force remains irrelevant in the tasks of nurturance in the kitchen

Integration into What? 17

garden-homecraft-childbearing complex, reenforcing the tendency for the skills of nonviolent persuasion to remain familistic skills. In industrially advanced societies, when women enter the capital-intensive technological domain they bring their little-valued skills of nurturance with them, and are thereby made to appear compliant with the system they enter. When men enter the labor-intensive family domain it is typically in an administrative way as "head of household". Physical violence also enters the family domain predominantly, though by no means exclusively, through the male. Thus each set of skills distorts the domain of the other.

Technological advance has never stood free of the palace-temple-army complex in any society. There has been no independent drive in any society to place technology "in the hands of the poor" or "in the hands of women". But there has been a drive from within bureaucracy itself ever to expand, ever to improve its tools, increase its power. As Jacoby (1973) describes it, the bureaucratization of the world has occurred over the centuries as men have surrounded themselves with logistical networks of ever greater complexity to deal with the craving for protection and authority. The consequences are alienation, loneliness and insecurity for everyone. What Jacoby does not note is that the only domain left in which alienation, loneliness and insecurity are faced directly is the family. Dealing with that loneliness and insecurity is in the hands of the powerless: women.

It is one of the cliches of the present era that the household domain has shrunk drastically in the past century. Industrialization has taken resources out of the household and as a consequence women have been forced to work at the lowest paid jobs in the market sectors to maintain life. Industrialization has given women some fairly elaborate domestic technology in return. This technology is however not for the poor. In its most elaborate forms it is used by middle and upper income women as toys. Industrialization has also forced women to organize and pay for the child care they can no longer give as part of their own productive services, thus ensuring that, as a class, women will not only shoulder the burden of the lowest-paid work in the market sector, but also the cost of creating the enabling conditions that permit them to enter that labor force.

To integrate women at the lowest wages into a world economy which spends more than $400 billion yearly on the production of arms is the ultimate in abandonment of autonomy for women. The rehumanization of the world cannot take place through such means.

What are women to do? To cooperate with being integrated into the present international order is to destroy all hope for a different future. The new international economic order does not promise to be very different from the old--not for the poor, least of all for women. It only offers the opportunity for more third world women to become marginalized labor in the modern sectors of their world economies, or continue as rural landless laborers (which most of them already are) at slightly higher wages. The bureaucratization of the world will increase under the new international economic order, for more centralized planning on a grander scale than in the past, will be required. Special programs under the label "basic needs strategies" will be devised to build small rural factories that women can work in to increase their marginal incomes. Packaged appropriate technologies containing all the recommended small incremental improvements of food storage facilities, wheelbarrows, food dryers, flour mills and high-protein multi-vitamin food supplements will be sold to them by multinational corporations. Whatever cash surplus their wage increases might have generated will thus be quickly absorbed by the external economy. Yet these are all things that women, particularly intellectual women concerned with development, have asked for. (Few people have any idea what village women might ask for.) If third world women get packaged appropriate technologies from the first world, we may all be the losers, for the dependency of women may be only further increased.

It is time to learn from third world women what they want, and to find out what they know how to do already. We in the first world have lost our autonomy. Many of them still have the memory of the autonomy of their grandmothers and many of the grandmothers' skills. When even the most meager resources beyond mere subsistence are available, they know how to generate surpluses and to develop credit and insurance systems among themselves. It is this approach, building on existing skills and the tiny surpluses at the bottom rather than on imported resources decided upon from above, that will bring women into development as partners with independent bargaining power and autonomous social goals. The grim alternative is for women to remain as dependents piteously hoping for assistance in mitigating their hardships.

The words de-coupling, de-linking, withdrawal, are often used to describe certain radical third world strategies for breaking the dependency patterns of the old international economic order. According to this strategy third world nations will trade with each other, share skills with each other, strengthening their economies by their own resources

Integration into What? 19

until they feel strong enough to re-enter relationships with more industrialized nations. Oil wealth in the third world has made this strategy less attractive, since oil-rich nations feel strong enough to trade as equals with the first world, and even to invest heavily in the first world. The 77 have thus opted for the next international economic order at once, with no period of withdrawal. It is, of course, a strategy of the male world, tightly linked to the world arms race.

Women have not struck oil. They are poorer, more marginalized than before. Over against the few with comfortable incomes are the one third of all women with household responsibilities who are single, widowed, divorced or abandoned, and their married sisters, who daily scrape the bottom of the family food kettle while hunger stalks the kitchen unassuaged. There are also those we call children, tired old women at seven years of age because they are already working as hard as their bodies will let them to help their mothers get more food.

Is a decoupling strategy possible for women? Lysistrata scenarios make good theater but poor social tactics. Women cannot and will not eject the men from their households around the world en masse, with the promise of reentry if they will stop playing war-cum-development games. Furthermore, men don't know how to stop playing such games. That is why disarmament is so difficult in spite of the best knowledge base in history to work with.

Women don't know how to stop the war games either, although the women's peace movement keeps trying. Women do have skills of self-sufficiency, of resourcefulness, of capacity to endure hunger and pain. These are resources that come into play only when there is a perception of the need to draw on them. In the United States and Europe, these skills are going into the establishment of all-women's workshops of all kinds, and of all-women's communes where children are reared without violence. Every week the various journals that report the alternative future movements around the world announce new all-women's enterprises (printing presses, factories, consultant firms), new communes, new networks, new newsletters for women only. (See Appendix I for a listing of some examples.) The women's self-help health movement, the women's banks, women's cooperative and credit associations, child care communities, all are essentially movements of strategic separatism on behalf of a new future. They are not "anti-male", but rather have a strong task orientation to helping women. For many western women such movements appear new and threatening. There is a considerable self-consciousness, even hostility concerning them, particularly among

20   *Elise Boulding*

successful women who have made it in the man's world. The lesbians are the least apologetic. They have simply lost interest in the man's world.

These movements are not new however. They belong to a one hundred year western tradition of women's self-help organizations, among which the earliest were the Women's Christian Temperance Union and the Young Women's Christian Association. Both YWCA and the WCTU identified with the problems of women in the industrial slums of Europe and North America before they extended their concern to women in the cities of China, India, Japan, and what we now call the third world. The fifty or so officially recognized international women's organizations active on the world scene today (Table 3) range from radical to conservative in political views and social roles, and some have grown stale in their original purpose, but they do represent a set of autonomous women's

Table 3. Women's International Nongovernmental Organizations[1]

Initials	Organization Name
AAWC	All African Women's Conference
ACWW	Associated Country Women of the World
AI	Altrusa International
EUW	European Union of Women
FAWA	Federation of Asian Women's Associations
GB	Girls' Brigade
GFWC	General Federation of Women's Clubs
IA	International Association of Lyceum Clubs
IAPWSGW	International Association of Physical Education and Sports for Girls and Women
IAW	International Alliance of Women
IAWHPJ	International Association of Women and Home Page Journalists
ICJW	International Council of Jewish Women
ICM	International Confederation of Midwives
ICSDW	International Council of Social Democratic Women
ICW	International Council of Women
ICWES	International Conference of Women Engineers and Scientists
IFBPW	International Federation of Business and Professional Women
IFHE	International Federation for Home Economics
IFMW	International Federation of Mazdaznan Women
IFWHA	International Federation of Women Hockey Associations
IFWL	International Federation of Women Lawyers
IFWLC	International Federation of Women in Legal Careers

voices in the public arena. If they are by and large the voices of privilege, that is neither good nor bad in itself, only a factor to note. They do represent a series of worldwide networks with varying capabilities for autonomous action. (See Boulding, 1977, for an analysis of their network capabilities.) New perceptions form new alliances. The International Feminist Socialist women's group, with a looser organizational format than the groups listed in Table 3, nevertheless also has a long history and is exhibiting considerable vitality both in its socialist and anarcha-socialist forms.

In the third world the women's domain has always been organized on a basis of strategic separatism. The tradition of individual accumulation by women, not only of property but also of rights to services and perquisites, to pass on to her children led to a degree of autonomy, however limited.

Table 3. continued

Initials	Organization Name
IFUW	International Federation of University Women
IIW	International Inner Wheel
IULCW	International Union of Liberal Christian Women
IUWA	International Union of Women Architects
IWCA	International Women's Cricket Association
MWIA	Medical Women's International Association
NNF	Northern Nurses Federation
ODI	Open Door International
PAMWA	Pan-American Medical Women's Alliance
PPSAWA	Pan Pacific and Southeast Asia Women's Association
SIA	Soroptimist International Association
SJIA	St. Joan's International Alliance
WAGGGS	World Association of Girl Guides and Girl Scouts
WAWE	World Association of Women Executives
WEGN	West European Group of Nurses
WFMW	World Federation of Methodist Women
WIDF	Women's International Democratic Federation
WILPF	Women's International League for Peace and Freedom
WIZO	Women's International Zionist Organization
WMM	World Movement of Mothers
WUXWO	World Union of Catholic Women's Organization
WWCTU	World's Women's Christian Association
ZI	Zonta International

[1] From Boulding, 1977, p. 191, based on listings in the Yearbook of International Organizations for 1973 and 1974.

A study of non-market activities of Moroccan women by Vanessa Maher (1974) uncovers a vast network of economic activities neither visible to nor countable by economists.... Vertical links of interdependence, both those of kinship and of simulated kinship (patron-client relations), provide the opportunity for poorer women to render services through their own activities or those of their husbands. These kin and pseudo-kin networks become the channels for market wealth to enter the traditional economy. Sometimes the vertical relationships are temporary, as when migrant women seek to gain a foothold in the town. Others are more or less permanent, feudal-type relationships. Maher gives examples of poor but enterprising women who provide a variety of home services, from nursing to cooking and party-arranging, for richer women who are either relatives or who originate in the same rural district. Their payment would be goods in kind, sometimes gifts of money, sometimes jobs for husbands or sons. A particularly enterprising poor woman could utilize this service network to find wives for the men of her family, and husbands, education, and perhaps even job opportunities for her daughters.

The fact that women so frequently need help both in the recurring life-cycle circumstances of birth, marriage, and death, and in family crises of illness, unemployment, or movement of a household from one location to another (all of which events place on the women additional labor burdens not shared by the men of a family), has something to do with the ease with which women outside the market economy can enter the margins of the market world via service to its households and carry needed goods and cash back to their own subsistence sector. If we add to this patron-client relationship the opportunities that women have to interact and match skills and needs around the public oven, the water tap, and the bathhouse, we can see that the redistribution of resources outside the market economy is substantial even in a strongly purdah-keeping society. (Elise Boulding, <u>Women in the Twentieth Century World</u>, pp. 98,9.)

Third world organization by women for self-help purposes is possibly the most highly developed in Africa. There the traditional women's councils provided the soil that today nurtures the All-African Women's Conference, with the most highly developed inter-linkage system with other women's organizations around the world of any of the liaison-type

Integration into What? 23

organizations (Boulding, 1977:215-217). New associations of third world professional women are forming to take hold of development thinking for themselves and prevent a new colonization of the women's domain by well-intentioned first world women. The African Women's Association, The Pacific and Asian Women's Forum and the Latin American Association of Women Social Scientists were all three independently formed in meetings in different world regions in December of 1977. An Arab Women's Association is currently in formation. In each case the intention is to form an independent base from which to deal with men, with the West, and with development planning generally. There is not infrequently contempt for first world women veiled beneath the polite interaction with the West. Western women are after all "lackeys"--at least in one view. At the least, western women are the handmaidens of bureaucratization.

Bureaucratization, with its universalistic standards, works against the humanizing, individualizing process that goes on in the women's domain. Furthermore, "integrating women into development" means providing women with so many helping services that they become dependents of the modern nation state. The socialist vision, like the capitalist one, is a firmly integrationist vision. The image of women working side by side with men in an all-adult egalitarian world while all child care and family maintenance is done in segregated state-maintained centers may seem like utopia or a bureaucratic nightmare depending on one's understanding of the potentialities of transforming bureaucracy in a socialist state, and one's attitudes toward the role and place of children in society. The concept of social transformation itself underlies most twentieth century visions of the future, secular or religious; capitalist, socialist, anarchosocialist or apolitical. Transformation is a widely shared goal. As the Italian women's movement motto states, "Tutta la nostra vita deve cambiare." Everything must be changed. But changed to what?

Mistrusting our capacity for large-scale social design, and valuing a society where persons of all ages mingle freely and have control over their own spaces, I prefer to opt for a strategic separatism that frees up the potentials of women for economic and social experiments on a small scale, outside the patriarchal social order. These experiments are and will continue to be carried on both by partnered and unpartnered women. It builds on what women already know how to do and removes them from the position of being pawns in someone else's development scheme. What makes this different from what women have always done to humanize their lives under oppressive conditions? The new world information order may make it different.[1] Never have social movements had such instant access to each other around the globe. Because many women have, for good reasons, gravitated to journalism and various communication media, there is a journal-newsletter-radio-TV network of women now that can be used to create a multiplier effect for every experiment that is worth sharing. The IFN, the International Feminist Network that grew out of the 1978 International Tribunal on Crimes Against Women, and ISIS, the resource and documentation center set up in Geneva and Rome in 1974 to serve the new international women's movement, are just two examples out of many new functioning networks created since 1970. The IWY Tribune Newsletter created in 1975 is another; WIN, the Women's International Newsletter, is another; and the International Roster of Women Professionals still another. None of these are women's organizations in the traditional nineteenth and early twentieth century sense. They are all networks, functioning with minimum organization and maximum flexibility. The regional women's organizations mentioned above are part of this movement. The parallel structures in the bureaucratic world include national development agencies and the 32 United Nations Agencies all of which have some concern for women in development, and the regional and international United Nations Research and Training Centers for Women now in formation. These organizations will have an interesting time learning to relate to and dialogue with the strategically separatist women's organizations. The older women's nongovernmental organizations may play a mediating role, or opt for one side or the other. It is too early to tell.

What all these developments mean is an end to privatism for women. It is now possible to imagine a separate autonomous sphere for women that is public, from which new forms of economic and political organization can evolve. What the two

---

[1] The telematics revolution which will give information storage and retrieval and two-way communication facilities to ordinary citizens around the world is not yet evident in the daily lives of citizens of the West. The capabilities are there, but it will take another five years for newspapers and television programs as we know them to be superseded, and for computer access to cease to be a monopoly of the intelligentsia. If anything, the third world is more aware of the new world information order than the industrialized world, and more eager to use it. It offers an opportunity to break down the information monopoly that currently resides in the first world. It also presents opportunities for severe abuse in authoritarian and security-conscious societies, however, both in the first and third worlds. The path to the new world information order may be a long and rocky one.

Integration into What? 25

recent "voices" books and others like them have done (Voicing Migrant Women's Concerns, Guyot et al., 1978, and Voicing Rural Women's Situation, Huston, 1978) is to show that when women not accustomed to speaking begin to speak, a new social reality becomes visible. In the most unlikely settings, women can begin to plan jointly how to improve their lives in their own way. African women have a particularly strong history of collective public action. The number of rural collective farms and enterprises started in the past decade by rural African women as reported in United Nations and development publications suggests a new type of social momentum.[2]

In the Underside of History (1976) I documented how women over and over again through the centuries have done the invisible work of reconstruction and repair for warring male societies. There are times coming for the human race when none of the old large-scale techno-bureaucratic solutions will work. Runaway military disasters, a range of chemical pollution disasters already under way of which nuclear pollution is only a tiny part, shortage of quickly substitutable alternative energy sources, climatic changes that will alter the agricultural productivity map of the planet and possibly its shorelines - along with the simple inability of existing administrative mechanisms to handle and regulate the developmental infrastructures of industrial or industrializing societies - add up to an urgent need for local ingenuity, local problem-solving. The information society can keep working, even while the administrative society breaks down.

Alternatives to Integration
for Women

What kind of a world do women want? That is the question to be asking, not How can women be integrated into development? Women have only very recently been asking what they want, because they have been so busy adapting to what men want. We get some clues in science fiction written by women, as a recent study of this science fiction reveals (See the Fall 1977 issue of Frontiers, a journal of Women's Studies, on Fantasies and Future, particularly Carol Pearson's "Womens' Fantasies and Feminist Utopias"). There is an amazing convergence of images by women writers about the future in the direction of a more localist society, using technology in sophisticated but careful ways to ensure humanized societies, interactive, nurturant, nonbureaucratic. Catherine Madsen's (n.d.) delightful story, "Commodore Bork and the Compost (a homily)" suggests how women run a space

---

[2] See for example issues of the UNICEF quarterly, Carnets de l'Enfance for 1976, 1977 and 1978 for recent accounts of such enterprises.

ship society. It would be ecologically sound, scientifically
based, yet informal, spontaneous, warm-hearted, and rather
untidy, with lots of room for individuality in space colony
personalities. The Commodore from the tight and tidy male
space ship that visits the women's space ship cannot believe
what he sees - most of all, he cannot believe that it works.

We know very little about how women would develop and
organize technology for human needs because they are rarely
in design or decision-making positions. Perhaps it is time
for women to stop scurrying around trying to get into key
positions in existing development programs, and to organize
themselves instead to think what women might want - and
beyond that, what might be good for human beings on this
planet, women, men, children and the elderly. What we need
are dialogues going on around the world between rural and
urban women, between middle class and working class women,
between craftworkers and headworkers, the old and the young,
about what "development" might mean for human beings. How
might things be, how do the many "we's" of women in different
regions visualize the good life for themselves and for the
human race? It has been clear since the Mexico Women's Conference during International Women's Year that first world
women cannot be voices for third world women about development. Perceptions and felt-needs are very different, and
first world women have had a very special conditioning
because of their educational systems and their socialization
to being handmaidens of male-defined technological progress.
Third world women, precisely because the majority of them
are illiterate, are thinking on the basis of their experience
and not on the basis of formulations in books.

Women are continually being coopted into male settings.
When they are given a chance to speak, it is no longer in a
context where new and original thinking even makes sense.
The attention given to women's needs at the upcoming UN Conference on Science and Technology in Development, will be in
the context of developmental plans already guaranteeing continued dependency on technologies that will come from an
alien hand, packaged by alien organizations, administered by
alien bureaucrats, even if these are fellow nationals.

I propose a mobilization through all the women's networks mentioned in this paper and many more not here identified, to carry on dialogues within and between women's groups
about what the very concept of development means, and how it
can be furthered in the societies we now have. Which technologies do we want to reject, which accept, and what new
ones are needed? What changes do we want in our social institutions?

New social formations that break down the atrophied but still powerful institutional apartheid structures that separate women from men, children and the elderly from middle years persons, family and nurturance from work and from community decision-making, will be needed. So will far greater fluidity in movement of persons and roles, and in working schedules (e.g., flexitime) than we now experience. Nineteenth and twentieth-century fossil-fuel-based technologies will have to be replaced by a different and more careful use of the earth's resources, by a new generation of technologies involving more humanistically oriented and labor-intensive practices in production processes in factory and field. In the factory we can see this foreshadowed in the redesign of the Volvo plant in Kalmar, Sweden, where the assembly line has been discarded in favor of worker teams who assemble a car from start to finish. On the farm we can see it foreshadowed in the rapid growth in the United States of IPM, integrated pest management. This movement has brought labor-intensive involvement of farmers with their crops to the point where pesticide use is drastically decreased and farmers have become familiar with the plant/soil/surrounding ecosystem. Instead of massive spraying there is now a set of individualized responses to plant conditions which help the plants ward off pests. Both examples, from factory and field, incidentally typify precisely the ways in which women have always produced, in home workshop and on family farm. Overall productivity apparently stays high with these "new" labor-intensive approaches. The concept of appropriate labor intensivity has yet to be adequately worked out in the society of the future. So has the optimal orchestration of lifespan birthing-partnering-working-learning-playing-dying rhythms in interaction across generations. So has the de-coupling of human welfare and security from massive military systems. All the really important problems lie ahead of us. We have for too long been mesmerized by a feeling of having produced earth-shaking accomplishments, of having experienced radical discontinuities, in the recent era of scientific-technological-industrial revolutions. In truth these accomplishments are far too firmly rooted in the old temple-palace-army formulae of the past few thousand years to hold any promise for the future. The real discontinuities lie ahead. Women, who have been marginal to all historic power structures, represent a unique resource and expertise available for the construction of new social formations, new approaches to human productivity and welfare. Cooptation into existing power structures continually mutes their potential contribution to the future. The least that can be attempted in the next two decades is serious reflection, on a global scale, among women on what they want to build for the future and how.

28   *Elise Boulding*

Appendix A

A Sampling of Some Recent Women's Groups Working on Development from a Feminist Perspective[1]

CEFRES   55 rue de Varenne 75007 Paris, FRANCE. The Centre Europeen Feminin de Recherche sur L'Evolution de l'Societe (CEFRES) was established 11 March 1977 by a meeting uniting members of 16 nationalities. CEFRES promotes and coordinates research on the future role of women in Society.

DELEGATION A LA CONDITION FEMININE   31, rue Maxenod 63003 Lyon, FRANCE. Among the groups organizing a "Vth Conference of Women Engineers and Scientists" (September 8th in Rouen). More than just a promoter of women scientists and engineers, the annual conference considers the purpose of industrial production, technology transfer, the responsibility of scientists and the women scientist view on a broad range of technological topics.

INTERNATIONAL CENTER FOR RESEARCH ON WOMEN   2000 "P" Street, N.W. #403, Washington, D.C. 20036. ICRW is a project of the Federation of Organizations for Professional Women. These 110 organizations are banded together to promote their common goal of equality for women. They exchange information, promote legislation as well as conduct research on the potential of women.

INTERNATIONAL WOMEN'S TRIBUTE CENTRE   (IWTC)   345 E. 46th Street, Room 815, New York, New York 10017. A group concerned with supporting women's groups in the Third World especially through the compilation of resource books. Regions for which directories have been produced include the Caribbean, Asia and Pacific, and the South Pacific. They have also put together a global directory called "Where on Earth are the Women." They support a newsletter in English and Spanish, Nos. 7 (July 1978) and 9 (early 1979) on the subject of Women and A.T.

---

[1] From the Fall 1978 issue of TRANET, Newsletter of the Transnational Network for Appropriate/Alternative Technologies; ISIS, Bulletin of the international women's liberation movement, Winter 1977-78 issue and Fall 1978 issue. Regrettably, these are all based in Euro-North America, although many of them include third world women, and minority and working class women. Third world based networks are much harder for first worlders to identify.

Integration into What?

ISIS   Via della Pelliccia 31, 00153 Rome, Italy; Case Postale 301, CH-1227 Carouge, Switzerland. ISIS is a resource and documentation center in the international women's liberation movement. It was set up in 1974 by a collective of women to gather materials from local women's groups and the feminist movement and to make these resources available to other women.

The quarterly ISIS International Bulletin reproduces theoretical and practical information and documentation from women's groups and the women's movements around the world. It includes resource listings, reports and notices to help pass on information about what is going on in the movement in other countries and continents and to help in the exchange of ideas, contacts, experiences and resources among women and feminist groups.

Projects in Process:

> RESOURCE GUIDE ON WOMEN IN DEVELOPMENT (in preparation). This Guide raises questions about the concepts of the "integration of women in development" and presents a picture of what women themselves think of development, using material coming directly from women in developing countries.
>
> RESOURCE GUIDE ON WOMEN'S HEALTH (in preparation). This guide will give a variety of factual information on self-help health maintenance for women.

NATIONWIDE WOMEN'S PROGRAM   American Friends Service Committee, 1501 Cherry Street, Philadelphia, PA 19102. This group has organized its first conference on Women and Global Corporations to initiate communications among women concerned with the conflicts between global corporations and individual rights and human development.

PARTI FEMINISTE UNIFIE   Rue des Aduatiques 74, 1040 Bruxelles, Belgium. This group, together with the French movement CHOISIR, appeals to all European women to join with them in presenting feminist candidates for the European parliament elections.

WIN NEWS   Women's International Network, 187 Grant Street, Lexington, MA 02173. Vol. 4 No. 3 Summer 1978 shows most impressively the extent and growth of the worldwide movement for women's rights in the last four years. Forty tightly packed pages list thousands of groups and reports covering the wide range of issues from "Women and the U.N."

through women and violence, rape, abortion, family size and agriculture.

WIRES (The Women's Information Referral Service), 32 Parliament Street, York, ENGLAND.

A WOMAN'S PLACE, 42 Ealham Street, London, WC2, ENGLAND.

WOMEN'S LIBERATION WORKSHOP, 160 Foutain-Bridge, Edinburg, SCOTLAND.

WOMEN IN SCIENCE, 234a Blyth Road, London, WI4, ENGLAND.

WOMEN'S ENGINEERING SOCIETY, Gouberte Place, London, WI, ENGLAND.

WOMEN IN MANUAL TRADES, Ginny, 23 Bridge Avenue, Mansions, W6, ENGLAND.

WORK PLACE NURSERIES, Kingsway Hall, 72 Kingsway, London, WC2, ENGLAND.

ZERO c/o Rising Free, 182 Upper Street, Islington, London, N1, U.K. An anarchist/Anarcha-feminist monthly, containing articles, lists of events, publications and anarcha-feminist groups and contacts.

Bibliography

Beard, Mary. Women as a Force in History. New York: MacMillan. 1946.

Boserup, Ester. Women's Role in Economic Development. New York: St. Martin's Press. 1970.

Boulding, Elise. The Underside of History: A View of Women Through Time. Boulder: Westview Press. 1976.

_____ Women in the Twentieth Century World. New York: Halstead Press. 1977.

Dupire, Marguerite. "The Position of Women in a Pastoral Society" pp. 47-92 in Denise Pauline (ed.), Women of Tropical Africa. London: Routledge and Kegan Paul. 1963.

Firth, Raymond and B. S. Yamey (eds.). Capital, Saving and Credit in Peasant Societies: Studies from Asia, Oceania, The Caribbean, and Middle America. Chicago: Aldine. 1964.

Guyot, Jean, et. al. Migrant Women Speak. London: Search Press Limited. 1978.

Huston, Perdita. Message From the Village. New York: Epoch B. Foundation. 1978.

ISIS International Bulletins. Rome, Italy and Carouge, Switzerland. Numbers 1-9, 1976-78.

Jacoby, Henry. The Bureaucratization of the World. Eveline L. Kanes (trans.) Berkeley: University of California Press. 1973.

Madsen, Catherine. "Commodore Bork and the Compost Heap." n.d.

Maher, Vanessa. Women and Property in Morocco. London: Cambridge University Press. 1974.

Nationwide Women's Program. "Women and Global Corporations," mimeographed conference report. Philadelphia: American Friends Service Committee. 1978.

Pearson, Carol. "Women's Fantasies and Feminist Utopias," pp. 50-61 in Frontiers. Vol. II, No. 3, Fall 1977.

Simons, H. J. <u>African Women: Their Legal Status in South Africa</u>. Evanston: Northwestern University Press. 1968.

Strathern, Marilyn. <u>Women in Between: Female Roles in a Male World, Mount Hagen, New Guinea</u>. New York: Seminar Press. 1972.

<u>Yearbook of International Organizations</u>. Brussels: Union of International Associations. 1973.

_____ Brussels: Union of International Associations. 1974.

<u>Women at Work: An ILO News Bulletin</u>. "Geneva." International Labour Office. No. 3, 1977 and No. 1, 1978.

International Labor Organization (ILO): Office for Women

3. Women, Technology and the Development Process

Introduction

The subject title of this paper suggests inter-relationships among three separate components: women, technology and development.[1] While "women and development" has received considerable attention both inside and outside the UN system, "women" and "technology" as subjects have only recently surfaced in discussions on development strategies having remained "invisible" for a long time. There exists some evidence--fragmentary though it is--on the place and position of women cutting across all sectors of the economy in the processes of development. But women and technology as a dimension in the development process has remained virtually an unexplored territory.[2] That the subject is important as an "issue" may be gathered from the fact that for the first time this item is appearing on the agenda of a preparatory UN meeting, with a view to further investigation at the UN Conference on Science and Technology for Development (UNCSTD) in 1979.

Background

UN Conferences

The point of departure in this paper is the mid-seventies, which could be considered as a landmark in the history of ideas when almost simultaneously women and the developing countries made new demands for restructuring economies and societies. Both the Declarations and the Plans of Action of the New International Economic Order[3] (NIEO) and the Mexico Conference[4] emphasized somewhat similar goals, the core of which was the urgent need to create new equitable relationships between the industrialized and the developing countries in international economic relationships and between men and women in internal relationships. Their coincidental eruption on the world scene and the fact that the time distance between these two important UN conferences was only about a year (Mexico following NIEO), is highly significant. In the main, the conclusions of both conferences spelled out the means to achieve the goals of equal access to all resources in international relations and to work towards strengthening national economies. The similarity, however, ends there, as the discussion on means and goals necessarily overlaps. The question, however, remained! How to recognise, reward, and revalue the contribution of women in the development process and in what manner is women's role related to technology? The former is outside the scope of this paper, but an attempt is made to raise some major questions regarding the latter.

ILO Basic Needs Approach

Following closely the two UN conferences mentioned above, the World Employment Conference in 1976 set out to consider the mechanism by which the developing countries could satisfy their basic needs[5] for essential goods and services. Within this broader framework, the report[6] to the Conference analyzed the policy measures that would be necessary for the family and the community to obtain adequate food, shelter, public transport and health and education facilities, etc. The main instrument to achieve these aims, according to the report, is to create "adequate employment" defined as "more remunerative and higher productivity employment". The precise manner to which women could participate in the formulation and implementation of the basic needs strategy, however, has been omitted from macro-discussions. But the report recognizes the contribution of women in providing the essentials of life and briefly deliberates on the significance of full utilization of women's labour in an economy.

The Aim of the Paper

The modest purpose of this paper is to delineate the significant elements of what appears to be inequalities of access to technical education and technological know-how between men and women in society and to indicate the need for specific policy measures to improve the technological level of women for higher productivity in employment without which the development process (no matter how defined) is likely to encounter serious difficulties.

This paper is divided into four sections: the first section puts together available information on the subject, while the second attempts to examine existing inequalities between men and women as regards access to scientific and technological education and training. The third examines the impact of technological change on productive employment. The final section puts forward some suggestions for taking women and technology a step further in international discussions (especially during UNCSTD 1979).

As mentioned earlier, there does not exist as yet adequate research or empirical evidence on issues directly relating to women and technology either in current concepts of development or in different approaches to basic needs strategies. However, by extending the analogy of interrelationships between the industrialized and the developing world, it is possible to surmise certain core issues which provide a useful starting point for discussions on this subject. During the last few years, three different aspects of women and technology--without interlinkages--have been considered in a few selected studies and reports. These aspects mainly relate to lack of access of women to scientific and technological knowledge in a society. The key points of this unequal access concern (i) scientific and technological education; (ii) rural activities and technological inputs; and (iii) the impact of technological change on occupational distribution between men and women in the modern sector. The significant features of each of these points are briefly considered below.

Redefining Women's Work

If the official definition of labour force were to be employed with the existing economic and social indicators, a world profile of women reveals one-half of the world population and one-third of the official labour force. On the other hand, if a total range of women's actual economic activities were to be taken into account, a different picture of social reality begins to emerge. For example, using simplified assumptions[7], the table on the next page presents the world distribution of work-hours[8] by sex and by market and non-market activities.

The table confirms what has been found in time-budget studies and common sense observation in current literature on the world of work of women: that across economic and social organization and geographical regions, women work longer hours; in market and non-market activities; in industrialized countries and the urban sector of developing countries and more obviously in the rural areas of Asia, Africa and Latin America. It is the nature and type of their work and the global performance of work-hours which raises fundamental economic and social issues. These issues are related to the stage of technological development of an economy as

Table 1. World Distribution of work-hours by sex and coverage in the labour force.

	Percentage Distribution		
	Market	Non-Market	Total
Included in labour force			
Male	66%	10%	44%
Female	34	28	32
Not included in labour force			
Male	--	--	--
Female	--	62	24
TOTAL	100	100	100

Source: The estimates give only order of magnitudes for illustrative purposes, ILO, Womanpower (Geneva, 1975).

well as the existing division of labour between men and women in society.

Access to Scientific and Technological Knowledge

Scientific and Technical Education and Training

During the last decade there has been a veritable educational explosion in the developing countries, including the majority of countries in the African continent. While literacy and numeracy remain a formidable barrier to improving the status of women in developing countries, it should be noted that there is an increasing number of "school enrollments"[9] of girls everywhere. At the same time, more girls continue to drop out[10] of schools than boys at all levels. The first hurdles of primary, secondary and higher level schooling, their access to scientific and technical jobs (in fact, to all jobs) encounter intangible barriers. In fact, several studies have emphasized that there is an inherent bias in the existing education structure of many countries (including developed countries) which pre-selects women into Arts and Humanities away from scientific and technological subjects.

An ILO report pointed out that in most developing countries few girls are enrolled in technical and vocational education (those who are enrolled learn sewing, dressmaking, housecrafts, child-care and embroidery) and few girls are to be found in vocation training outside the school system.

> There is sometimes a failure to distinguish clearly between home economics and vocational training outside the school system. . .although measures are now being taken to bring girls into agricultural schools, colleges and into extension work and services. Some governments (e.g., Egypt, Lebanon, Chile) are making special efforts to encourage the training of girls for some modern occupations such as laboratory technicians and industrial designers and to encourage their subsequent employment.[11]

The principle is generally conceded that women and men should have the right <u>on the same terms</u> (italics added) to receive education and training for highly qualified jobs and should enjoy equality of opportunity and treatment for career advancement. However, international data (scanty though they are) indicates that with the exception of some of the Eastern European countries and the USSR, the proportion of women in most countries in "scientific professions"[12] is particularly low.[13] On the whole, women are employed in research rather than in production and management, in specialist and advisory posts rather than in positions of authority and in the public rather than the private sector.

Outside the formal schooling system and in the agricultural extension programmes, projects and training schemes, the inequalities of access of women to learning continue. On this point, the existing information is unequivocal.

> In nearly all countries, agricultural training at low, middle and high levels is given to men only. This of course produces exclusively male instructors - instructors who, in turn, address themselves to the male farmers, overlooking and disregarding women, even in cases where the wives, daughters and hired female labour are doing the work.[14]

The reasons for this neglect seem to lie in attitudes and beliefs that agriculture with female labour is backward and that female labour should if possible be replaced by male labour when agriculture is "modernized." In Africa, where women account for a large share of the labour force in agriculture, the failure to teach modern farming methods to women results in adverse effects on agricultural productivity and rural incomes.

Rural Women and Technological Inputs

More recently since the choice of technologies[15] in developing countries became a subject of debate, a few studies, particularly in Africa, have focused their attention on rural activities of women and their relationship to basic technologies.[16] The conclusions of these studies concern three basic issues: (i) the introduction of mechanization in agriculture and its impact on women's work; (ii) the unequal division of labour between men and women; and (iii) the desirability of introducing basic technologies to improve the conditions of work and life of women.

(i) <u>Mechanization in Agriculture</u>. Several papers[17] from developing countries have pointed out that mechanization in agriculture is seen mainly in men's work, while women's work in both on- and off-the-farm (including household) tasks has remained predominantly manual. The line of reasoning here is based on the fact that certain technological choices are not only labour specific in that they might use or dispense with units of labour, but that they were <u>female labour specific</u> in that they absorb male labour and at the same time disemploy female labour.

This generalization appears to apply to multiple agricultural tasks (such as weeding, harvesting and carrying operations), food processing[18] and a wide range of construction activities. For example, women's jobs and incomes from home-brewed traditional beer in some African countries are threatened by the introduction of large-scale breweries and in Indonesia, following the introduction of rice mills in Java, 12 million work-hours of women were lost, depriving women of their only source of income. Similarly, in a study in Jammu and Kashmir (India)[19] it was shown that with the introduction of machines to spin yarn, the livelihood of 20,000 women was seriously affected.

(ii) <u>Division of Labour</u>. While the relationships of women to production and distribution in the traditional sectors remain significant and relevant, women seem to have no or limited access to technological inputs at all levels. Thus the output of their productive labour has either remained constant or has decreased in contrast to that of men who have access to factors of production. The direct result of this unequal access between men and women is that the work input of women proportionately increases in various agricultural tasks without giving them any control on their output. What emerges from this situation in many countries is that women work longer hours in almost all rural activities with the aid of only their muscle power. Table 2 provides a breakdown of activity between men and women in percentage of total work-hours.

The unequal division of burden of daily work appears to be a common feature not only of the African continent but also of Asia and Latin America. For example, a comparative study of Nepal and Indonesia (1972-1973)[20] points to the same conclusion. The daily workload of rural population by age and sex shows consistently that in rural areas of both countries women work longer hours (the differentials vary from 6 to 16 additional hours) than men in all age groups. In many societies, age over youth and male over female predominate in making decisions on distribution of work. Irrespective of the mode of production in any society, what appears to be a general feature of developing countries is that unequal division of labour on the farm is further reinforced by unequal division of labour inside the households.[21]

(iii) Basic Technologies.[22] After devoting attention to the energy consuming and frequently underproductive work of women in producing and processing staple foods, hoeing and weeding, in providing fuel and water, a large number of studies[23] have come forward to propose technological solutions. It has been suggested that there are considerable advantages in selecting and maintaining simpler devices and equipment for the use of rural women. Several new tools and devices have been minutely examined and tested and these include thin-walled cement tanks, simple hand-pumps, mud-brick stoves and simply better containers for food. Furthermore, harnessing of solar energy, wind power, biogas rather than commercial sources of energy had been considered more desirable in the rural areas of developing countries.

The essence of this sequence of thought is that rural women have been simply bypassed by the whole process of industrialization of which modern and imported technologies are an important part. It has been argued that the introduction of basic needs technologies rules out ipso facto the products produced by imported technologies, raises the incomes of the rural women, their productivity of the resources employed and simultaneously increases the quantity of resources at their disposal. By adopting the solution involving the use of basic technologies, it has been stated that rural women will not only increase their productive capacity but could be helped to help themselves to produce goods and services for minimum needs.[24]

Table 2. Division of labour between men and women: rural Africa.

Activity	Percentage of Total Labour in Hours	
	Men	Women
Cuts down the forest: stakes out the fields	95	5
Turns the soil	70	30
Plants the seeds and cuttings	50	50
Hoes and weeds	30	70
Harvests	40	60
Transports crops home from the fields	20	80
Stores the crops	20	80
Processes the food crops	10	90
Brewing	10	90
Markets the excess (including transport to market	40	60
Trims the tree crops	90	10
Carries the water and fuel	10	90
Cares for the domestic animals and cleans the stables	50	50
Hunts	90	10
Feeds and cares for the young, the men and the aged	5	95

Source: ILO, A Research Note, Technology and Rural Women, page 2.

Technological Change and Occupational Distribution Between Men and Women

Turning to the modern sector the profile of women workers does not change fundamentally. There too, the introduction of mechanization has produced somewhat similar results. Studies and reports written a decade ago and those published recently point to the same direction: Technological progress has the dual effect of widening women's employment opportunities and at the same time pushing them into less skilled and less mechanized occupations. This was recognized by the ILO Panel of Consultants on the Problem of Women Workers as early as 1957.[25] The Panel underlined the positive features of technological developments which reduced the physical effort in a great many jobs, but also noted that wherever employment opportunities for all workers were in short supply, women workers were more likely to suffer the adverse consequences in the transitional period (emphasis added).

In 1967 when, at the request of the UN Commission on the Status of Women, the ILO undertook a preliminary survey to analyze the impact of scientific and technological progress on the employment and conditions of work of women in selected industries, the conclusions were again similar. The analysis of various industries such as metal trades, textiles, clothing, leather and footwear, food and drink and printing and allied trades indicated that there is a consistent pattern in the employment of women. A common thread runs through each of the industries and that concerned the introduction of new machinery or equipment. It tended to displace women workers from previously held jobs to low productivity and low wage occupations. To take an example from the textile industry which is a very large employer of women in many countries, an ILO report found that when a new machine is installed, the tendency on the whole was to "substitute male workers for women workers and to keep women workers on the older and non-automatic machinery."[26] More recent investigation confirms this view.[27] It appears that even in newer industries such as electronics, also a large employer of women in several countries, including Norway and Singapore, the dynamics of technical change continually displace women into low-skill occupations.

Based on comparative analysis of many countries on the employment of women in postal and telecommunication services, an ILO report states that rationalization measures made possible by the introduction of new technical equipment often entail the abolition of temporary or part-time posts. Automation in telecommunications does away with operators' jobs; computers eliminate much clerical or bookkeeping work. "Such posts are frequently occupied by women, it is the female staff who are the most affected by the adoption of new techniques. . ."[28]

While there does not exist any empirical evidence on measuring the actual technological gap between men and women's jobs, it appears that through various stages of the introduction of advanced or sophisticated technology, the wage differential (between men and women) also proportionately widens. Various reasons have been put forward for this phenomenon. Women workers are generally less skilled than men, or to put it another way their skill qualifications are lower than those of men, from which it is concluded that women are not able to carry out highly complex and technical tasks. In a reply to a UN questionnaire,[29] it was suggested that women are not in a position to take up work in the heavy industries

> . . .involving changes in science and technology, as they are not as yet physically and psychologically equipped for such work. . .mainly because of the lack of facilities for scientific training and research. But being deprived of such additional technological knowledge equally results in widening the skill and wage gap between men and women.

Some Conclusions

Three sets of problems have been alluded to above. First, reference has been made to the unequal access of women to the formal education and training, especially in scientific and technical skills in the modern sector, reinforced by the omission to incorporate women in agricultural training programmes, projects and training schemes. Secondly, some evidence has been examined from the multi-dimensional activities of rural women, especially in food production which indicates that women continue to "manage" the subsistence economy (with or without skills) with "traditional" techniques (new technology frequently aiding men's work). Finally, it has been shown from examples of some industries--modern and traditional--that the introduction of new techniques, in a shifting occupational hierarchy, continues to displace women in low skill, low productivity jobs. This process deprives them of the opportunities of upgrading their skills and acquiring technological know-how. The most significant feature that emerges from the above discussion is the profile of inequality of women workers in relation to technical training, inputs and know-how.

Future Directions

Technology plays a decisive role in the process of development. Discussion of technology "issues" at the international level has been a subject of controversy[30] and there are different approaches and solutions. At the national level, the majority of developing countries continue to make "technological choices" and take decisions which affect seriously their internal division of labour (particularly relationships of production between males and females). There does not seem to be a balanced approach between the transfer from abroad and the development of national "technological capabilities"[31] to take national decisions in the national interest. There are "external and internal constraints" on the transfer, choice and utilization of technologies.

Turning to the "national interest," there appear to be other constraints which may be called "internalized," which play a decisive role in the existing division of labour within an economy and within the household. These are directly and indirectly related to modes of production, "models" of industrialization, and land tenure systems. These "obstacles"--a complex package of economic and social factors--seem to create and perpetuate "technological dependence" of women in relation to scientific initiative, finance, technological control and skill. Since "dependence" cannot be easily quantified, it may be suggested that the indirect cost of women's dependence in technology could be heavy in terms of "unutilized" or "untapped" human resources to the economy and society as a whole and may well adversely affect productivity and employment. The current problems in processes of development may have some direct relation to the fact that inadequate attention has been paid to the role of women in technology.

Notes

[1] An ILO contribution to the African Regional Meeting on UN Conference on Science and Technology for Development (UNCSTD), Cairo, 24-29 July 1978.

[2] The reasons for this neglect are too complex to analyze here. But it may have some connection with the general bias of the social scientist on subjects relating to women. For example, in a recent meeting to consider women and technology as a subject of research, the following view was expressed:

> As an UNCTAD or UN issue, it is just a non-starter. Better to leave it to the World Council of Churches,

whose terms of reference are more in line with this kind of work.

[3] UN, Declaration on the Establishment of the New International Economic Order and Programme of Action, General Assembly Resolutions 3201 (S-VI) and 3202 (S-VI), May 1974.

[4] UN, Declaration of Mexico on the Equality of Women and their Contribution to Development and Peace, 19 June- 2 July 1975, E/Conference/66/34.

[5] ILO, Tripartite World Conference on Employment, Income Distribution and Social Progress and the International Division of Labour, Employment Growth and Basic Needs, Geneva, 1976.

[6] There are several definitions of basic needs and equally a number of approaches to basic needs strategies. Suffice it here to say that the "satisfaction of basic needs" is one of the basic aims of development.

[7] The assumptions are: (i) labour force: 1,050 million males and 550 million females, out of which (ii) 420 million females are of working age and actually work, but their activities are not in the market and therefore not included in the labour force; (iii) male labour force work 50 hours per week of which five are non-market activities and (iv) female labour force work 70 hours a week of which 25 are in non-market activities; and women not in the market also work for the same number of hours (70).

[8] The current terminology in social sciences related to work reflects different concepts of reality. For this reason, here the expression "work-hours" rather than man-hours is employed.

[9] The total number of girls in schools of developing countries has increased in absolute numbers during the last decade. See, for example, UNESCO, Women, Education, Equality, the UNESCO Press, Paris, 1975.

[10] The main reasons for the higher drop-out rate of girls appear to be economic necessity and social preference of boys.

[11] ILO, Equality of Opportunity and Treatment of Women Workers, 60th Session, Geneva, 1975, Report VII and ECOSOC, Access of Women to Education, Resolution 1327 (XLIV), 31 May 1968.

[12] The ILO report defines "professional workers" as primarily including scientists, engineers, higher level technicians and managerial staff, Compendium of Principles and Good Practices Relating to the Conditions of Work and Employment of Professional Workers, Geneva, November 1977.

[13] In 1976, 40 percent of all scientific research workers in the USSR were women. A recent estimate in the United States indicates that only 10 percent of women are in scientific professions. For comparative analysis, see G.F. Schilling and M.K. Hunt, Women in Science and Technology, US/USSR Comparisons, The Round Paper Series, Santa Monica, June 1974.

[14] UNDP (E. Boserup and C. Liljencrantz), Integration of Women in Development: Why, When, How, May 1975. Several agricultural training schemes including Botswana and Liberia are directed towards training males. FAO, Planning Family Resources for Rural Development, Nutrition Information Document Series, Rome, 1972.

[15] For a very good summary, see Hans Singer, Technologies for Basic Needs, an ILO (WEP) study, Geneva, 1977.

[16] For simpler definitions and a summary of rural development vocabulary, see J. McDowell and V. Hazzard, "Village Technology and Women's Work in Eastern Africa," Assignment Children, UNICEF, October/December 1976, No. 36.

[17] Gelia Castillo, "The Changing Role of Women in Rural Societies: A Summary of Trends and Issues," Seminar Report, The Agricultural Development Council, February 1977, No. 12.

[18] For more factual information, see ILO "Technologies for Rural Women," Women at Work, 3/1977.

[19] Devaki Jain, "Are Women a Separate Issue?" Populi, Journal of the UNFPA, 1978. Vol. 5, No. 1.

[20] Ibid., p. 3. It has been suggested that higher daily workload of women could be a causal factor in the decline of life expectancy. In Zambia, the average hours of daily work were estimated to be 16 of women compared to 10 of men, while in Latin America, it was found that the wife of an agricultural tenant works 14 to 16 hours compared to 8 to 10 hours of men.

[21] For these reasons, these economies have been sometimes called "patriarchal."

[22] More recently, "adequate technologies" and "basic needs technologies" are becoming more current as expressions.

[23] On this question the ILO has formulated a research project which examines various aspects of this issue, see A Research Note on Technology and Rural Women, Geneva, April 1978. See, in particular, ILO, Appropriate Technologies for Employment Generation in the Food Processing and Drinks Industries, World Employment Programme Research, Geneva, September 1977 (mimeo); G. Macpherson and D. Jackson, "Village Technology for Rural Development," International Labour Review, February 1975, Vol. III, No. 2. Also, "The Politics and Problems of Appropriate Pumps," World Environment Day, The Environment Liaison Centre, London, 5 June 1978, and I. Ahmed, "Rural Women and Technologies," Women at Work, March 1978.

[24] Elizabeth O'Kelly, "Appropriate Technology for Women," Development Forum, June 1976.

[25] Cited in ECOSOC, Commission on the Status of Women, Economic Rights and Opportunities for Women, report by the ILO, 6 December 1967, E/CN.6/500.

[26] ILO report, op. cit., pp. 10 and 13; and ILO The Effects of Structural and Technological Changes on Industry, Eighth Session, Geneva, 1968, General Report and Training Requirements in the Textile Industry in the Light of Changes in the Occupational Structure, Tenth Session, Geneva, 1978. Effects of Technological Changes on Conditions of Work and Employment in Postal and Telecommunication Services, Joint Meeting on Conditions of Work and Employment in Postal and Telecommunication Services, Geneva 1977.

[27] The ILO Industrial Committee on Textiles has published a series of reports and studies dealing with various aspects of employment and conditions of work.

[28] ILO, Report on Employment in Postal and Telecommunications Services, op. cit., p. 25. Also report by the U.S. Department of Labor suggests that with the over-all expansion of computerization one large group of women clerical workers, telephone operators had been greatly affected by the installation of direct dialling. . .in factories mechanization has caused virtual elimination of some of the unskilled manual jobs performed by women. Women's Bureau, Wage and Labor Standards Administration, Automation and Women Workers, Washington, 1970.

[29] Questionnaire sent out in accordance with Resolution 1328, ECOSOC, *Repercussions of Scientific and Technological Progress on the Status of Women Workers*, 31 May 1968.

[30] ILO, *Employment, Growth and Basic Needs*, op. cit., pp. 141-142.

[31] UNCTAD (V), *Transfer of Technology* (Item 12 - main policy issues), Nairobi, May 1976.

Part 2

Setting the Context: Case Studies

Irene Tinker

4. New Technologies for Food-Related Activities: An Equity Strategy

The world's food supply has become a topic of international diplomacy. The World Food Conference in Rome in 1974 focussed the attention of the world on the increased demand of the growing world population on food resources. Generally there is optimism concerning the ability of the scientific establishment to respond to the food crisis with the new technologies capable of keeping food production ahead of consumption.[1] <u>The World Food and Nutrition Study</u>, completed by the National Research Council in 1977, emphasizes that

> The most important requirement for the alleviation of malnutrition is for the developing countries to double their own food production by the end of the century. We are convinced that this can be done given the political will in the developing and higher-income countries.[2]

The basic strategy for rapid agricultural development, as outlined in the Rockefeller Foundation study <u>To Feed This World</u> is to increase both productivity and farmer's income. "Each agricultural development effort should have income generation through increased productivity as a primary objective."[3] The importance of income in formerly subsistence economies increases as more and more crops and services become part of the monetary economy. It is widely recognized that increasing production is only part of the solution to world hunger; to provide food for the world it is necessary to reduce extreme poverty so that the hungry have money with which to buy food.[4] Since the greatest concentration of poverty is among the rural people in the developing countries who have little or no access to land, there is increased attention to developing rural enterprises related both to the agriculture and to infrastructure.[5]

More recently, a third strategy has been added to the effort to alleviate world hunger and malnutrition: to reduce postharvest food loss. Conservative estimates indicate that 10 percent of durable crops such as cereal grains and grain legumes are lost between harvest and consumption; a comparable figure for nongrain staples such as yams or cassava and for other perishables including fish would be 20 percent or more.[6] Technology applied to the storage, processing, and preservation of various foodstuffs should be able to reduce losses by 50 percent, automatically increasing available food on the world market by 10 percent.

These three strategies--increased production, greater income-producing activities, and a reduction in postharvest food losses--are widely accepted among development planners as solutions for meeting the world food crisis. All three strategies start from the need for putting a platform under poverty, and for ensuring that basic human needs of the world's poor are met. *Yet nowhere in these prestigious works is there an acknowledgment that over half of the agricultural labor in the developing countries is provided by women, or that women do most of the postharvest food processing and preservation.*

Further, food consumption is also related to nutritional value of foods available, methods of cooking, and ability of those doing the cooking--almost always women--to find time and personal energy to fetch the water and fuelwood, grow, forage, or buy food, and cook.[7] While the growing and processing of food are increasingly recorded in national economic statistics, there is a widespread reluctance among economists to list home food preparation and its attendant chores as ecomomic activity.[8] This disregard of the economic value of food preparation reenforced the tagging of food-related issues as women's work, and has had disastrous effects on the field of nutrition, according to Margaret Mead: "Hence, before U.S. training, distribution, preservations, processing, and consumption are disseminated further around the world, the dangers of this type of segregated occupational training should be recognized and corrected."[9]

BIASES IN ECONOMIC DEVELOPMENT THEORY

There are two unexamined biases in contemporary economic development theory which throw up psychological roadblocks to the inclusion of women as equal partners in development. The first is the continued perception of a dichotomy between the modern and the traditional sectors, between the economic activities done for money and those done as volunteer or citizen, between productive work and welfare activities. Statistics still tend only to reflect activities in the modern monetary economy; activities outside those boundaries are not considered productive, and hence not work. Clearly the role of an economic development planner is to modernize the country, to bring the agricultural sector into the modern sphere by crop specialization, surplus production, improved marketing facilities, and mechanization. An increase in the Gross National Product, it was argued for years, would bring a higher improved standard of living for everyone by trickling down. Now the argument includes income-generation at the bottom as well; but the basic tenets of the theory go unquestioned.

The second bias, the irrational stereotypes of appropriate roles for women which many men carry around with them, interrelates with and is reenforced by definitions of economic activity. Essentially, in this view, women don't "work", or if they do, they shouldn't; keeping women dependent on men is a boon to the male ego. Thus a draft of an AID agricultural policy paper done in 1977 could suggest that a measure of development would be reducing the number of women working in the fields. Almost anyone, male or female, would prefer less arduous work than weeding or harvesting in the hot sun, but only if alternative family income were provided either through new jobs for the woman or through doubling of the man's income. With neither alternative a part of the policy plan, the statement clearly reflected a bias about suitable occupations for women: caring--non-economically--for husband and children.[10]

Economic Activity in the Informal Sector

These two unexamined biases have combined to skew development for poor men as well as poor women. First this emphasis on recording statistics only for the modern sector has obscured all activity in the informal sector. Thus planners for Africa were given data which tells them that only 5 percent of the women work. It is too easy to forget that such a figure applies only to the modern sector and then to obliterate, for planning purposes, the fact that 60 to 80 percent of the agricultural labor is done by women in Africa, or that women dominate the marketing and processing of agricultural produce.

Men, too, find employment in this informal sector of the economy. Somehow that is seen, for men at least, as a transitional phase. Post-industrial societies are not supposed to have an informal sector. It took the National Institute of Mental Health to recognize the existence of an "irregular economy" in the United States and to fund studies of what the authors call "economic terra incognito." The concluding section of this study, "Potential Significance and Implications" notes

> This study is clearly related to the alienation of groups, neighborhood-based, from larger structures of the society--in this case from the conventional production and distribution systems. Partly, the irregular economy arises from a lack of institutional response to a misallocation of goods and services, i.e., to a failure of the distribution and pricing systems to adjust and serve areas of unmet needs. In the main, the study attempts to identify these unmet needs and analyze the conditions under which neighborhood-based coping patterns develop.[11]

These comments clearly beg the question "what is work?" Kathleen Newland in her new book The Sisterhood of Man records how differently different countries define which activities are included in national income accounts. She describes the long work days of Iranian nomad women who, in addition to the care and feeding of the family,

> ...haul water into the camp on their backs. They milk and shear the animals, mostly sheep and goats. They collect such edible plants, berries, roots and fungi as the surroundings afford. They churn butter, make cheese and yogurt, and refine the left-over whey into the daily beverage. They spin the wool and goat hair into thread or press it into felt and make clothes, tent cloths, and carpets for their families' use. From each tent-household of an extended family a woman goes daily to collect firewood from the brush; on the average, she spends half a day at the task, plus another hour at the camp breaking the torn-off branches of thorn-bush into pieces small enough for the cooking fire.

> In the national economic accounts of Iran...the only portion of the nomad woman's work that will show up even as subsistence production is her output of woolen textiles and dairy products. If she lived in the Congo Republic instead of Iran, the accountants would also include her food-processing activities in calculating the Gross Domestic Product, but they would omit her production of handcrafted articles. Taiwan's bookkeepers also would leave out handicrafts; they would, however, assign

economic value to the woman's water carrying and
wood gathering. But in Nigeria, it would be argued
that, in rural areas, wood and water are free
goods, like air, and so are the human efforts that
make them useful.[12]

The inconsistencies of the present method of income accounts is increasingly apparent in the United States today. With the rise of two-income families, nearly half of the food consumed in America is eaten outside the home. Suddenly the effort to feed the family has been moved from an invisible category to economic activity. Many of the services to the sick and infirm which were formerly undertaken by compassionate volunteers, predominantly women, must now be paid for. While many women, as well as men, are anguished over the decline in volunteering, no one should be surprised. Money is the measure of success and status in the United States; nonproductive activities are seen as peripheral and marginal--at least until they begin to disappear.

Women's Contributions to Family Survival

A second factor largely ignored is the importance of the woman's economic activity to family survival. Among the poor, every family member that is able must contribute to the family support. Such support becomes even more crucial as modernization pushes the poor family to the margin. Ann Stoler has analyzed women's economic activities in Java in relationship to the family budget and finds that the women in landless and near landless families earn one-third of the household's total income, a much larger share than contributed by wives from larger landholding classes.[13] In Mexico the contribution of women to their families' budgets varies by cultural group as well as class.[14] Not only do women contribute to family income, but because of their responsibilities to the family they often are more adaptable in crisis situations.[15]

Particularly in Africa, the persistence of sex segregation both in occupation and responsibilities means that every woman is expected to provide food, clothes, and education for her children and food for her husband from her own separate budget. During the Sahelian drought, many observers noted that if the sauce to the millet gruel had only a single piece of meat, that was the share of the husband who of course ate first. Peace Corps volunteers urged women to grind the meat so that some protein might be left for the children; they did not presume to suggest that the man contribute money to buy the food. As men's earnings have increased through cash crops or urban employment, they often feel no obligation to increase their share of child support. Recently a Kenyan woman sued her urban-dwelling husband in District Court for school fees for their son. His defense was that he had provided her with a piece of land; she was responsible for the care and schooling of the children. Surprisingly the judge found for the woman who had argued that the size of the land made it impossible for her to save enough money for fees; besides, the husband was well-employed.

Because African women provided the bulk of family support, modern industry and plantations were able to siphon off the men without paying them wages sufficient to provide for the entire family. A recent UN report comments this "functional relationship between the subsistence and the modern sector" in Lesotho, South Africa, provides 95 percent of the cash earned in Lesotho. At any given time, close to 40 percent of the working-age male population resides in South Africa, thereby leaving the villages with a substantial numerical predominance of women. Since the men's earnings are not sufficient, the subsistence output provided by women is necessary for family survival.[16]

The pressures on the family of such migration patterns have clearly contributed to the increased numbers of women-headed households around the world. Economic development policies which have left women behind in the subsistence economy while pushing men into the modern sector encourage the disintegration of the family.[17] Today between 25 and 33 percent of all households are de facto headed by a woman due to divorce, death, desertion, long term migration, or because she never married. These female-headed households constitute the poorest group in every country.[18]

Poor women, whatever their living arrangements, must work to survive. Being invisible to development planners, and being the poorest of the poor, they have as a group been most adversely affected by development.[19] Perdita Huston quotes their own words in her book Third World Women Speak Out: "Life is more difficult than before."[20]

WOMEN AND THE FOOD CRISIS

The three major strategies for meeting the world's food crisis--increased production, greater income-producing activities, and a reduction in postharvest food losses--are also strategies for aiding the rural poor women. Women in Asia and Africa provide between 60 and 80 percent of agricultural labor; they produce 95 percent of the village food supply in Kenya. Indeed, poor women everywhere work in the fields, though such labor is often denied because of the status implications.[21] Women's participation in processing, preserving, and preparing food is even greater than their participation in production. Women's responsibilities to help feed their families are becoming harder to fulfill as modernization restricts traditional activities which enabled women to grow or earn food. Greater income-producing activities for women will have a more immediate impact on providing basic food and health to the poor than similar activities aimed only at men.

In order for the food crisis strategies to accomplish their goal of feeding the world, women must not only be included in planning, they must be central to it. Since development is essential to the introduction of new technologies, women must be consulted in the selection of new technologies, trained in their use, and given means to control those most related to their spheres of economic activity.

Below I will review the impact of current development policies and new technologies on women's work in the production, processing, preservation, and preparation of food, emphasizing positive change while noting cases where women's traditional activities have been undermined. Because the fetching of wood and the drawing of water are necessary to carry out many of these food-chain acitivites, I will also discuss household energy needs and the requirements of a safe water supply. Many technologies have long been available to increase the efficiency of these activities, even to providing surplusses for sale. I will argue that the low priority assigned to them is directly related to the two unexamined biases under discussion.

New Technologies and Women

Almost universally, new technologies for food-chain activities have been introduced to men regardless of women's contributions. Technology, because it is modern, is somehow assumed to be appropriate and understandable only for men, not women. Besides, rural poor women are usually illiterate, and so presumed unable to alter custom to adopt new technologies. Further, rural credit is scarce enough, and seldom is extended to women because they lack assets for collateral. Land is the major rural asset, and colonial governments registered communal land in the man's name.

Women's uncertain access to land, credit, and education prevents their access to and control of new technologies which might help them out of the mire of poverty so that they could afford land, credit, and education. This vicious circle had intensified women's dependency on men in rural areas and undoubtedly encourages urban migration. With fragile marriage patterns the rule rather than the exception, women have little incentive to improve their use of land either for production or for fuel-gathering. Given their incredibly long workdays, poor rural women have almost no spare time which they might use to learn new processing or preservation techniques. Living at the margin, fearful that any change would further reduce their ability to feed their families, women are rightly suspicious of new technology. Interventions must not only reduce the workday, but must also provide sufficient income to buy the food or services which the woman stops providing, and to pay for the cost of the technology.

To date, most new technologies introduced into agricultural production have had a deleterious effect on poor rural women. Small machines for processing agricultural products and new techniques for improved preservation have had mixed impacts. Technologies to relieve the drudgery of collecting wood and refuse for cooking are only now being seriously considered as the environmental impact of current usage patterns becomes apparent. The provision of water for cooking and other household use has taken second place to water for irrigation regardless of the Water for Peace campaign in the 1960s and the more recent agreements at the UN Water Conference of 1977 on clean water for everyone by 1990.

I will briefly discuss each of these elements in the food chain: _production_, _processing_, _preservation_, and _preparation_, illustrating the types of impact that new technologies have had on women as differentiated from men. These various activities are part of a continuous process; successful intervention in one area can trigger change in another. Often the spark vital for the first change came from new access to credit, or land, or training frequently made possible through women's networks or organizations. Strategies for increasing women's access to and control of new technologies will be presented in the final section along with a discussion of delivery systems. Where possible I will note the varying impact which technology has had on different classes of women as modernization contributes to increased social stratification. My focus, however, is always on the rural poor women. Yet even among this group distinctions are appearing.[22] Thus while I argue throughout this paper that women as a group are bypassed by modernization and technology, I wish to stress the importance of refining the target groups whenever projects are undertaken to ameliorate their position.

Production

Women play a major role in all developing countries in the different aspects of agricultural production: subsistence crops, cash crops, market gardens, and small animal and fish culture. The greatest impacts of technology in agricultural production have been on cash crops such as bananas, cotton, pineapples, rubber, tea, coffee, sugar cane, peanuts, and sisal. While many of these crops are edible, they are seldom part of the local diet. Even where eating peanuts was traditional, for example, the demand on the international market has pushed up the price to a point where local consumption has dropped. The nutritional consequence of exporting this high protein source has been widely noted. In fact, both Asia and Africa are net exporters of high-protein foods and net importers of high-carbohydrate foods.[23]

Cash crops have competed for land and labor with food crops. Until recently little research went into improving food crops. Only as wheat and rice became exchange commodities in the international market have there been concerted attempts to improve production. The resultant green revolution has affected rice and wheat, but other major subsistence crops such as yams and millet have yet to respond to research efforts. Market crops and small animal breeding have received little research attention, underscoring again the perceived dichotomy between the modern commercial sector and the traditional subsistence sector.[24]

The impact of the new technologies both on subsistence and on cash crops varies both by major crop and by farming systems. Ester Boserup in her landmark book on <u>Women's Role in Economic Development</u>[25] relates women's status to the need for her labor in subsistence food crops or animals. Thus the technology of the plow contributed to a loss in status historically; similar impacts are recounted below when the introduction of the sickle in Indonesia or new crops in the Sudan lowers women's utility and hence their status.

Africa

The change in women's status as a result of modernization can be seen most clearly in Africa. In the traditional societies, women held fairly independent and equitable positions in both the nomadic and settled agricultural communities. Such societies were also characterized by little social stratification. Women did the bulk of farming work among the settled agriculturists. The major impact of technology, being focussed on non-subsistence crops, has been to draw off land and labor from the food crops. Women continue to grow and control food crops, but because this sector has not been monetized, they must seek money from other activities. The specifics of this impact vary from one society to another:

> --men migrate to urban areas or to mines in search of income;
> --women work cash crops in addition to subsistence crops;
> --women's land is taken away for cash crops;
> --new settlements ignore food needs and thus women's productive activities.

The culmination of these trends, discussed in more detail below, is to increase the work of poor women while lowering her status vis-a-vis men. Women from the growing elite classes have tended to move out of food production, although some have become extension workers or bureaucrats in development agencies.

--cash and subsistence crops

Growing the subsistence crop has been increasingly left to African women as men migrate to cities. Statistics show that one-third of farm managers in Africa south of the Sahara are women, with even higher percentages recorded in some countries: 54 percent in Tanzania and 41 percent in Ghana. Algeria reported female participation in agriculture had more than doubled between 1966 and 1973.[26] Yet women's crops and women's work continue to be largely ignored by extension services.

Most cash crops in Africa are grown on small holdings. Thus, women are being asked not only to work their subsistence crop fields, but also to contribute their labor to cash crops. This added burden reinforces the inequity and inefficiency of the present practices, according to Louise Fortmann in her study of Tanzanian agriculture.

> The inefficiency arises from the fact that women... have limited access to...information and land which would allow them to become more productive. This differential access is based...on accepted social norms and customs. Similarly, the heavy work load already imposed on women often prevents them from adopting improved technology that requires additional labour inputs. Thus the present village and household organization of labour limits the potential for increasing production.

Food-Related Activities: An Equity Strategy 61

> [W]omen bear a disproportionately large share of the work (of export crop cultivation)...Because of traditional rules of land tenure relatively few women are able to undertake cash crop production in their own right. Those who work on their husbands' cash crops rarely receive a proportionate share of the proceeds.[27]

Because women get few rewards from the production of cash crops, it is no surprise that whenever there are competing demands between food and cash crops, they work on the food crops.[28] In the Gambia, where women receive the proceeds from the sale of onions they grew, over 4,000 willingly work on this cash crop.[29] The success of this onion scheme was such that the men farmers asked for assistance in planting this crop, and the government complied. The women, however, refused to work on their husbands' onion crop though they continued to grow traditional crops on their husbands' land. Apparently the mens's onions withered.

--plantations

Plantations are less common in Africa than in Asia, but women in both continents have provided cheap labor. This source of income is diminishing on the coffee and tea plantations in Uganda and Kenya. The introduction of insecticides and fungicides have reduced the need for weeding by as much as 85 percent.

> Thus, technology has been used in a way that has had detrimental and paradoxical consequences for African rural women. While, on the one hand, the technological changes in the modern agricultural sector have deprived women of employment, the shortage of simple technological improvements in food-processing, energy and water supply, on the other hand, has left the rural women overburdened in their daily tasks.[30]

Both national governments, eager for foreign exchange and agricultural experts, using the US as a model, have tended to view the use of land for subsistence crops as inefficient. According to one expert, writing in 1970, "...parts of upland Kenya could be devoted to vegetables, tea, dairying, and so on, but instead they are used by housewives for grains that take 9 to 11 months to mature."[31] Pressures to grow the more profitable export crops have reduced acreage allotted to food crops. Such changes have resulted in women losing their traditional rights to grow their crops on communal land. In

Upper Volta, a foreign development scheme for swamp rice essentially turned the crop over to men through male extension agents working directly with men in the villages. In the Cameroons, women were forced off the cleared land near the village. Land near the village is nearly all taken up with coffee and cocoa plantations.

> Food fields are anywhere from one to ten kilometers from the village with three to six kilometers most often cited. This distance implies a one-half to one and one-half hour walk to the food fields over rough forest paths, often with slippery stream and marsh crossings. The worst aspect of the trek comes during the return--a woman is often carrying the daily food supply of cassava, plantain, and corn, plus firewood, and often her baby as well. The weight is anywhere from 30 to 80 pounds. Injuries from falls or scrapes are common, and much spontaneous abortion and persistent backache is blamed on this aspect of women's work.[32]

--new settlements

New settlement schemes have had a particularly deleterious effect on women. In Nigeria the government provided five hectare plots for the growing of soybeans for sale. Corn could be grown for personal consumption, but amounts were limited by the seeds provided. No garden plots were provided, thus depriving women of land to grow food for the family which they had done, with the exception of corn, before joining the resettlement program. Income from the cash crops was given to the men; women received no wages for their labor. Further, those activities normally done by men, the clearing and ploughing, were mechanized, but not women's activities of planting, weeding and harvesting.[33]

The Mwea irrigated rice scheme in Kenya did allocate small garden plots to the women, but these were small because it was assumed that rice from the irrigated plots would be added to the diet. Women in fact did receive some rice in return for her labor on her husband's land, but since the men refused to eat rice, women had to sell it and buy traditional food at increasingly high prices. Women on the scheme did not have time, nor land, to raise enough food for their own consumption. Thus they worked longer hours than before but could not provide as much food for their families as they had. In addition, they often had to buy firewood for cooking since fuel was scarce in the resettlement area, and women's time was less. Thus while the total income of the families in the scheme has gone up, and visible wealth in the form of transistor radios and bicycles is in evidence, nutritional levels nonetheless have fallen.[34]

The new Halfa Agricultural Scheme involved the settlement of the nomadic Shukriya. The independent production these women traditionally enjoyed came from their ownership of animals and their rights to milk from all the animals they cared for.

> Since the Scheme concentrated on cash crops, men's work acquired a new value: money. The only opportunity women have to make money on the Scheme, being deprived of their animals and not owning tenancies, is cotton picking. But since they can work on immediate family tenancies, the monetary value of that labor is very slim...Poor Shukriya women are the most likely to benefit from cotton-picking on other people's tenancies since being so poor exempts them from behaving according to the dominant social norms.[35]

--nutritional levels falling

A recurring theme in all these studies of new technology for cash crops is that while cash income may have increased, nutritional levels tend to fall. The primary reason for this seemingly contradictory phenomenon is the fact that this income belongs to the man. Men use this money for improving homes, throwing "prestige" feasts, buying transistor radios. In the Cameroons men do use their income to pay school fees, unlike Kenya. Men often spend their money on liquor, gambling, or women, while their wives lack money to buy food they cannot raise.[36]

A second major problem in ensuring that increased income is translated into improved nutrition is the marketing system. The fragmented nature of the present marketing system in Africa means that traditional subsistence crops are not widely available.[37] Market crops cannot be shipped any great distance because of the spoilage problems and inefficient transport. Staples in many areas are sold only by one merchant; in the Cameroons the price of salt and sugar, sold only through the Zapi project store, rose with the availability of cash.[38] As areas urbanize, and markets include a greater variety of food, cash becomes even more important since in smaller markets it is still possible to barter. This fact, and the cost of getting to the central market, limited the ability of Shukriya women to obtain additional food.[39]

--projects which increase food supply

Agricultural technology has clearly not worked in favor of African women. Subsistence crops and market crops have generally been ignored both by researchers and extension workers. Cash crops and farm machinery were considered appropriate only for men. Little concern has been directed at improving breeds of small animals. There are signs of change. The Integrated Farming Pilot Project in Botswana which was started in 1976 for male farmers to improve their dryland farming and livestock management techniques has recently expanded its program to include 100 women. Week-long courses will stress vegetable gardening and poultry keeping. Further, agricultural extension agents will organize special field days to demonstrate new techniques to women.[40] Scattered efforts have been made by Peace Corps volunteers to encourage the raising of bees, poultry, or rabbits, but there is little evidence that these new productive activities were incorporated into the local economy.

The Peace Corps efforts in introducing or improving fish culture in Africa have had a more lasting impact, particularly in Northwest Cameroons. Because this is a new activity in much of interior Africa, there is no cultural reason for introducing this potentially important income-producing activity only to men. However, only since 1978 have any of the "fish" volunteers been women. The current program in Zaire features the tilapia, which is vegetarian. Fingerlings are introduced into shallow ponds which have been built with a plug so that water can be drained for easy harvesting. While men dig the ponds, women carry the agricultural and animal wastes on which the fish thrive. In six months there can be as high as a two hundred percent return! At present the fish are sold and eaten so quickly that preservation is not a problem. There needs to be immediate attention to marketing before problems arise. Given the divided use of money within an African family, improved nutrition will happen faster if the ponds and the fish marketing are developed within the woman's economic sphere.

--income-producing projects

The most successful African program for income-producing gardening and pigs is in Kenya. Its growth seemed almost spontaneous. While the government is now assisting in marketing, they played very little role earlier. It is instructive that the women expanded their gardens and small animals once they had time to do so. Every study of African women speaks about their overwork. How can women so close to survival dare to stop doing any one of the daily chores that keeps her family alive?

The mabati movement in Kenya gave women time. Tin roofs mean that rainwater can be saved and stored, releasing women from the daily chore of fetching water, a chore that takes two to ten hours per household.[41] The women used the traditional rotating credit societies to accumulate cash to buy the tin roofs.[42] Each woman puts so much money in a communal pot; each woman wins the pot with the turn drawn by lot. With the time saved by available rainwater, and often with cash earned by selling some of the water, the women increased their production of vegetables, chickens, and pigs for sale in the urban markets.

This project would seem to corroborate the assumption that the major stumbling block for increased production of food among African women is their present time overload. Yet population pressures have meant that both water and fuel are harder to find, so that the time women spend in the traditional support for the family is increasing. Children can help the mother in these tasks. Thus concern for improved water and energy supplies not only would release women for more productive activity, but would also alter the present incentives for large families.

Asia

--the green revolution increases poverty

The green revolution has tended to increase unemployment and contribute to the maldistribution of income in rural areas.[43] More recently, studies have disaggregated the impact on women and on men. In India the overall impact has been a reduction of employment opportunities for women, a trend reported in the Census of 1951. A study in Punjab, India, noted that while displaced men were given an opportunity to take the training necessary to operate new machinery, women were left to work on the increasingly scarce unskilled jobs.[44] This "pauperisation caused by the disappearance of their traditional avenues of employment" has pushed many poor women into the cities.[45] Nutritional levels are so low among landless women that they lose twice as many children as women from landed households.[46] Children that survive are malnourished, with the worst cases observed among female children.[47]

Such poverty has made plantation work attractive to many poor Indian families, both in India and in neighboring countries. On tea plantations in India and Sri Lanka, women make up over half the labor force; on Indian and Malaysian coffee estates, they make up 44 percent of the labor force, while their participation in rubber estates is only somewhat less. A major reason for this growing female labor force is the wage differentials between males and females: women are paid about 80 percent of male wages for the same work. As production costs rise there is greater incentive to utilize new labor-saving technologies and to increase the percentage of women being paid reduced wages in the labor force.[48]

The differential impact of the green revolution on women of different classes has also been noted in Indonesia, where the intensive farming system has traditionally supported a more equitable society than the plough farming system of South Asia. The new high-yielding varieties of rice have triggered a change in the traditional harvesting patterns. Because of the high investment in the new varieties, particularly in fertilizer, landlords wanted an increased return from the crop. Further, population increase has multiplied the number of harvesters, who are traditionally women. Women use a small knife, the ani-ani, for cutting individual stalks of rice. Leaning from the waist, the women might leave as much as 10 percent of the rice in the fields--a practice which provides a sort of social security for the poorest in the village. The harvesters divide the rice stalks, not evenly, but rather by levels of obligation which may reflect class. Between 12 and 15 percent of the crop goes to the harvesters under this system. Thus traditional harvesting patterns mean that the available rice is only about three-fourths of the rice in the fields.[49]

The new harvesting pattern involves a new technology: a hand sickle. Gangs of men are hired by a middle-man to complete the harvest; with the sickle, little rice is left in the field. Further, the men are paid by weight rather than by rice stalks. Total "cost" of the harvest is therefore only between 6 and 8 percent of the rice in the field. This change in harvest practices automatically showed an increase in rice production, has drastically reduced female labor, especially among the landless, and has effectively abolished the gleaned rice for the poorest.

--income producing activities on and off the farm

Population pressures and technological change have also reduced work opportunities for the poor males, thus increasing the importance to family survival of female income from trade and handicrafts.

It is men, in fact, who have a smaller set of viable alternatives to agricultural labor. Women are, in a sense, better equipped to deal with the situation of increasing landlessness and can manipulate a more familiar set of limited options...[50]

The multiple strategies which poor rural families use for survival can be illustrated with two cases from the wet zone of Sri Lanka.

> One household with 13 members had seven sources of income: (1) operation of 0.4 acres of paddy land by the adults, (2) casual labor and road construction by the head and eldest son, (3) labor in a rubber sheet factory by the second son, (4) toddy tapping and jaggery making by the head and his wife, (5) seasonal migration to the dry zone as agricultural labor by the wife, eldest son and daughter, (6) mat weaving by the wife and daughter, and (7) carpentry and masonry work by the head and eldest son. Another household with 11 members had six sources of income, mostly agricultural: (1) home garden by the family, (2) a one acre highland plot operated by the wife, (3) labor on road construction on weekdays and on the plot on weekends by the head, (4) seasonal migration to the dry zone as agricultural labor by the daughter and son, (5) casual labor in a rice mill in the dry zone by the eldest son, and (6) casual agricultural labor in the village by the head and his wife.[51]

The economic contribution of women to family survival is evident in the study of two Philippine villages, one Muslim and one Christian, near Davos on Mindanao. The Muslim women grow, harvest, and sew nipa palm for house shingles, while the major occupation of the Christian women relates to fishing.

> All the women...worked for money at some point in their lives. All control the family budget, and all but one continue to contribute to the family income. Throughout the Philippines, and indeed all of Southeast Asia, women play an important entrepreneurial role. Traditionally, such activity was not considered particularly high status; perhaps for that reason it was left to women...It is clear that these women, even though they live in a village economy that is often referred to as subsistence could not live without money to buy food. Even their basic diet of vegetables and salted or dried fish must be purchased in the market.[52]

A major factor which encourages women to increase their economic activity in the monetized economy is the ability to

68   Irene Tinker

keep control of their earnings. The success of the Korean Mother's Clubs is a case in point. Based on historic cooperation of women in supporting each other in providing expensive ritual festivals for marriage or death, the Mother's Clubs were set up to facilitate the distribution of birth control pills. Three-quarters of the Mother's Clubs organized Mother's Banks. Encouraged by financial resources of their own, women in many villages started projects to earn money with which to build schools, run stores, improve village services. While the groups have now branched out into a variety of income-producing activities, market production including gathering of nuts for sale was frequently the first income-producing activity.[53] Women are also employed in public works projects, but at lower wages than men, a fact that reiterates Korean women's low, if improving, status.[54]

Studies of women's roles in agriculture in the Muslim countries of North Africa and West Asia have been inhibited more than elsewhere by cultural norms that encourage undernumeration. In Thailand the labor force participation rates in the Southern province, where one-quarter of the population is Muslim, for females over 11 years old is 63.9 percent, as compared to a national average of 86 percent. This suggests few Muslim women are reported as actively employed.[55] Studies in Turkey confirm the invisibility of Muslim women in statistics even when they take complete charge of the farms in areas of intensive out-migration of males. Mechanization has contributed to greater social stratification, with resulting leisure available to wives of the larger landowners. Wage-working families continue to pick cotton, hazelnuts, tobacco, and strawberries.[56]

Recent efforts to reach rural poor women in Bangladesh have been impeded by <u>purdah</u> restrictions. Nonetheless, women's cooperatives are successfully marketing fish, bananas, limes, ducks and chickens, and vegetables. Operating solely with capital saved by the women themselves, these cooperatives are seen as models for the rest of the country. Yet of the 13 cooperatives in the country, only two are totally Muslim. Muslim husbands still resist the idea of their wives leaving the compound for weekly meetings.[57]

As men are drawn off to work in Saudi Arabia, Yemeni women are taking over much of the farming. As noted above, the poorest women in the New Halfa resettlement scheme benefitted from greater opportunity to pick cotton. Yet the recognition of women's economic activity is resisted the most in the conservative Muslim areas. Status is attached to seclusion except for the Westernized elite; with the recent revolution in

Iran, even that is subject to change. Nonetheless, it is clear that poor women in all countries, including Islamic ones, must and do contribute to the survival of their families.[58]

Latin America

Women in the agricultural labor force in Latin America, while lower than that in Africa and Asia, is still an impressive 40 percent, according to the Economic Commission of Latin America.

This figure is low, according to Carmen Diana Deere. In her review of women doing agricultural work in Peru, Deere found that 86 percent of the women in peasant households participated in the agricultural work as compared to the 1976 Peasant Family Survey of 38 percent. Self perceptions are partly responsible; if a man resides at home, he is the farmer. "The majority of the women that considered themselves to be agriculturalists were female heads of households with no adult male present."[59]

In Honduras, 13 percent of the rural households are permanently headed by women; the figure rises to 25-27 percent if seasonal migration is included. These women tend to be landless, and must seek wage employment on the cotton and coffee plantations.[60] In the Peruvian highlands, the transition from the hacienda system to _minifundio_ has relieved women of many servile tasks formerly required by the landlord. But it is difficult for a family to live off the small plots of land. As men are forced to seek wage income off the farm, the responsibilities of the women increase, increasing her self-esteem and status.[61]

As landlessness or near-landlessness increases, the poor farmers must increase their wage labor. In Peru and Honduras men migrate seasonally from the mountains to work on large farms. In Northeastern Brazil, the farmers assist with the sugar harvest on the large plantations.

On the small farms, then, modernization has meant an increase in women's labor as the men frequently seek work elsewhere. In addition, manufactured goods in the market have undercut many local handicrafts previously made by women, making them more dependent on income from agricultural production. Women in Mexico who work on commercial crops are paid less than men. The rationale given is that women do not work, they merely help with the farming.[62]

Processing and Preserving

The processing and preserving of home-grown and home-consumed food is not an economic activity which is counted in the GNP.[63] Women's contributions in this area are even more invisible than their work on farm production. Yet it is here that small technologies can have their greatest impact; they can: reduce post-harvest food loss, thus providing more food for consumption or sale; reduce drudgery and so give women the gift of time; form the basis of income-producing activities. The test of any technology introduced at this level must be its <u>social</u> utility. That is to say, the introduction of the technology should improve the quality of life of the people meant to benefit from its introduction. <u>How</u> the technology is introduced, who <u>owns</u> it, and who <u>controls</u> its use are fundamental questions that must be the basis for planning.

Many of the "new" technologies presently being tried around the world have in fact been tried many times before. That is why the major focus today is on process and adaptation. No longer can it be assumed that a piece of equipment or a method of production can be packaged and dropped in a village where, like a genii, it will transform the quality of life. Disaggregating the intended beneficiaries by sex, and also by socio-economic levels, is clearly a necessary step, but not alone sufficient.

Technologies for Food Processing

Technologies which can assist women in carrying out their food-related post-harvest activities fall within two general categories: mechanical technologies which reduce the expenditure of human or animal energy, primarily in the processing of food; and improved methods of preserving and storing food. I shall discuss the policy issues related to the choices of technologies and review present technologies under each category, giving particular attention to the impact of the choices on income-producing activities of women.

Grinding mills for corn, wheat, and millet, as well as rice hullers, are now widespread throughout the developing world. Small presses for palm oil, coconut milk, or sugar cane are widely distributed. Grinders and beaters for making peanuts into oil are also becoming common. Simple, low-cost hand-operated machines can relieve much of the drudgery from these activities while not displacing too many laborers. Preferably, these machines are sold on long-term credit to women's organizations. As early as the 1950s corn grinders were introduced into what is now West Cameroons through the patronage of a respected elderly village woman. Once the technique of drying the corn before grinding was understood, the grinders were quickly adopted through corn mill societies which were formed to pay back the cost of the grinder within a year.[64] These societies became the trigger for other development efforts.

> With the increased leisure that the women now had they turned to other community based projects. They dug roads to their villages so that lorries could come in to take out their produce, they piped water into storage tanks so that the abundant small streams of the rainy season could still provide them with water in the dry, and they built meeting houses in central villages in which they could hold classes throughout the year regardless of the weather. They learned how to look after their children and how to cook and make soap...to read and write and to do simple arithmetic...They fenced in their farms...set up cooperative shops...Above all they learned how to improve their farming techniques...When independence came in 1961 the movement had spread as far as the coast...and the membership exceeded 30,000 women so that it was able to make its voice heard in the community on most matters affecting women.[65]

Yet when the same organizer, Elizabeth O'Kelly, tried to introduce rice hullers in Sarawak, the technology proved inadequate; the hullers were not strong enough to withstand the constant usage by all the women in a longhouse. Yet the intervention from outside was enough to encourage the formation of women's Institutes which focussed their activity on piping water and improving farming. Fourteen years later these Institutes run seminars, organize flood relief, and even run their own radio station. This type of responsive intervention is being tried in many parts of Africa today; the process may be more important than any specific technology as long as the technology is simple and inexpensive enough for the women's organizations to buy and run it.

Marilyn Carr, in her excellent book on <u>Appropriate Technology for African Women</u>, argues that most hand-operated crop processing machines used in Africa have proved more economically efficient than more sophisticated imported machines. A study in Kenya compared four types of corn-grinding; a Nigerian study compared four types of palm-oil presses. "Another study in Nigeria compared two techniques for processing gari from cassava. This found that a locally-generated 'intermediate' technique was far superior to a fully mechanized foreign machine. Among other things, unit costs of production are about 20 percent lower with the 'intermediate technique'."66

In Upper Volta a government program is assisting women's groups to acquire hand grinders. Yet even remote areas have commercial mills powered by diesel oil. During the last round of oil price increases one mill owner near the village of Tangaye raised his grinding fee by 25 percent to compensate for a price rise in oil of 33 percent. "As a result he lost so many customers that he was forced to open the mill twice a week, on market days, rather than every day as he had done in the past...Expenditures for fuel comprise 50-60 percent of the monthly cost of running the mill."67 Currently the government of Upper Volta, utilizing funds from US Agency for International Development, is installing a solar unit in that village to power a grinding mill and to pump water. This photovoltaic system is highly experimental since the present costs of battery storage make the unit very expensive. For the time being, then, hand grinders may still be the most economically efficient method of grinding local grains. But for how long?

In Indonesia the intermediate alternative for rice hulling is a small, relatively low-cost, Japanese-made, machine-powered rubber hull roller. In the four years from 1970 to 1974 the number of these small rice mills exploded until they dominate the market, and can process up to three-quarters of the total rice crop on Java. The original figures were assembled by Peter Timmer "with the intention of demonstrating in simple, clear-cut terms...that the large scale bulk terminals were inappropriate in the Indonesian countryside. The battle to be fought in the planning agency was not hand-pounding versus small rice mills but large bulk facilities versus large and small rice mills. I was nearly laughed out of court for defending the small rice mills."68

This rapid switch to rubber rollers cost over one million jobs on Java alone and 7.7 million throughout Indonesia.69 Estimating that 125 million woman-days were lost by the introduction of the new technology, William Collier concludes that "the total loss in laborers' earnings...seems to be of the order of $50 million annually in Java...This represents a substantial diminution of income for large numbers of households of landless laborers and small farmers. Three million tons of rice (if hand-pounded) would provide wages for one million women every day for four months each year."70

Whether the rice rollers should have been introduced is irrelevant for Indonesia, but is an issue today in Bangladesh. Hand-pounding continues in Indonesia for most domestic consumption, about 40 percent of the crop. The fact that nearly all home consumed rice continues to be pounded underscores the lack of money which village women have to buy food. Not only are the costs for commercial milling extremely low due to the over-capacity of the many new mills on Java, but milling gives more usable rice per weight. While it is true that pounded rice is more nutritious in that more bran remains with the final product, this dietary advantage is more important to the poorest who no longer have a share in the harvest. For them the economists' argument that in fact the new rice mills have lowered consumer costs of rice per kilogram is important--if they have money with which to buy the rice.

Timmer argues that these lowered consumer costs are valued at three times the value of the lost jobs.[71] These figures clarify the debate. Small rice mills using rubber rollers add to national income nine times the value of the lost jobs. But who benefits? Clearly the distributional impact of this change has been in favor of the larger farmers and the owners of the rice mills. The losers are the poor, but it is the women who lost the jobs. The Indonesian government does have public works programs to provide income to their poorest citizens. But where 125 million women-days of wage labor were lost on Java in 1972, the county public works program provided only 43.5 million man-days of employment.[72] Recent reports note that for the first time in Java women in large numbers are now vying for this strenuous job. The impact of rice hullers has clearly been an increase in rural poverty.

Governments should be able to anticipate such impacts, altering tax, subsidy, or pricing policies in such a way that the poor consumers benefit from lower prices and greater volume of grain. But only a job can replace a job; without income, lower prices are irrelevant. Because statistics fail to reflect the actual employment of the poor, especially poor women, economic costs of new technologies in the area of food milling are ignored. The first step is a more accurate accounting of real work in rural areas.

The nutritional dimensions of new grinders must also be considered. Incomplete milling through hand-pounding leaves sufficient bran in the rice to provide needed vitamin B. Husks are fed to chickens, later consumed. What will prevent deficiency if hand-pounding is further reduced? Can new techniques for handling husks prevent their turning rancid and so provide an alternative food, a new breakfast cereal for the poor?

In Bangladesh, government policy could presumable slow the introduction of small rice mills, allowing time to develop alternative economic activities for displaced labor. A hand rubber roller is being considered a halfway measure which may reduce the economic advantage of the power mills. This intervention should be carefully monitored. No one can really argue that the hand pounding is of itself good.[73] But the heavy work must be balanced against no work when evaluating the impact of any new technology.

Technologies for Preservation

Postharvest food losses are enormous. Most observers agree that a 10 percent increase in the available world food supply could be more easily achieved through a reduction of losses than through increased production. Some of these increases may be illusory, as with the increased yield of rice by the use of sickles: the "lost" rice had provided free food as a sort of social security for the poorest in the village.

Improved storage for grains has been a goal of many development agencies including the Peace Corps. Weevils and rodents destroy half the corn stored in rural Cameroon homes[74]; small changes can reduce that loss by half. Rodent baffles, inverted funnels on support poles of the cribs, can be fashioned from old kerosene tins or molded in clay. Metal storage tanks work well in dry areas but cause mildew problems in more humid areas. VITA (Volunteers in Technical Assistance), under contract to Peace Corps, has issued a training manual on storage techniques.[75]

Waxing cassava has reduced losses in Latin America and is being tried on plantains in West Africa. Solar dryers are being touted as a substitute for the habit, widespread in South Asia, of spreading grain on the black tarmac: one car can wreak havoc.[76] Yet buying a piece of heavy black plastic to line a box is out of reach for many poor. Selling such dryers at subsidized prices would seem an important project. In Tanzania an improved solar dryer was demonstrated at a recent workshop; women were taught to make the mud container and the form for the plastic core.[77]

Many traditional methods of smoking or drying fruit, vegetables, fish, and even meat are being studied for improvement and wider dissemination. In Thailand fish pickled by one method frequently produces illness; another traditional method is safe. In Ghana one group traditionally smoked fish until cheap electricity from the Volta Dam gave an advantage to freezing fish; the knowledge is rapidly vanishing.

Canning has not been widely taught, perhaps because of the concern over botulism poisoning. Ester Ocloo, owner and manager of a commerical cannery, said she once came to the United States on her own to learn home canning techniques at a university in order to teach women in Ghana to do their own canning. In 1977 the UNICEF in Dacca brought out an instructors manual on Food Preservation in Bangladesh as part of a project to encourage income-generating activities among women. The emphasis is on canning: chutney is featured in addition to fruits and vegetables. Canning lends itself much more to community enterprise than to individual effort. Finding markets must be a part of the planning, for the glass container itself prices the product out of the reach of the poor.

In Honduras, Save the Children Foundation assisted a remote mountain village to set up a cooperative mango cannery. It has survived many setbacks. The institutional consumers actually bought less than anticipated; the remoteness of the village added greatly to transportation costs; and the resource poor area has made diversification difficult. Attempts to encourage local consumption through a deposit system on the glass jars has worked only in the immediate neighborhood due to the rugged terrain. But local women take advantage of bottle return; they buy the puree and dilute it with water for sale at soccer matches. Attempts are now being made to market the mango puree as dried "fruit leather", a familiar product in Asia--the Bangladesh book calls it "mango dried sheet"--but not well-known in Latin America. Experiments using plastic sheets to wrap the leather produced a product more chemical than natural. In addition, the cooperative hopes to utilize a system of vacuum-packed plastic bags as soon as it is perfected by a similar cooperative in Costa Rica. Meanwhile, the coop members are planting mango trees; they have also contracted with a neighboring village to pickle their excess onion crop.[78]

Despite the difficulties of setting up this women's cooperative in such a poor and remote village, the coop is functioning. The husbands migrate out at least half the year, but they did help with the building of the cannery, and maintain the equipment. Perhaps if the foreign technician had been female, the women might have been taught this skill. The women, working a six-day week during the mango season, earn $1.50 per day or $42 per month. Men in the region earn between $150 and $300 a year, so that the cannery earnings are an important addition to family income.

For shorter-term preservation, solar coolers and refrigerators are being developed. Improved handling of both fresh and dried perishables are expected to reduce losses. Chemical fumigants and insecticides are particularly useful in reducing losses among cereals and tubers. Experiments in biological control of pests through the introduction of predators continue. Resistant species are being developed. Details of the state of the art for reduction of food losses may be found in the 1978 report by the National Academy of Sciences, <u>Postharvest Food Losses in Developing Countries</u>.

The careful scientific language of the report masks the dominant role which women play in postharvest activities. One paragraph in the staff report alone recognized the human element behind technological change: the discussion group "took note of the fact that the subsistent fisherman and fish merchant are generally second class citizens, often living in crushing poverty, with no hope for the future. This fact and the role of women in the society conditions what, how and by whom technology should be offered, how it should be delivered, and what incentives are necessary to convince the people to adopt the remedies."[79]

Such oblique langauge is not sufficient to counteract the biases among developers and planners that technology is for men. Community-based technologies which reduce food losses and so provide surpluses for sale can and should provide alternative incomes for women displaced in the agricultural production activities.

PREPARATION OF FOOD

Selling of cooked foods is an income-producing activity of great importance to the poor woman, though it is seldom recorded in national accounts. Outstanding among the sparse literature on this subject is Emmy Simmons' study of "The Small-Scale Rural Food-Processing Industry in Northern Nigeria."[80] Even among the secluded Muslim women living near the city of Zaria, "It is rare...to find a rural woman who has never set up production in some food-processing enterprise." These women produce a variety of traditional lunch and snack foods from grain, cowpeas, peanuts, and cassava. Most of the women work alone at home in seclusion, sending their daughters or other young relatives out to sell to neighbors or in the market. Their work is sporadic, more an extension of home activities than a commitment to enterprise. Nonetheless Simmons found that all the products, with one exception, produced a return on cash investment of between 6 and 40 percent.

Two major problems threaten the future of this important income-producing activity: (1) the single owner-operator pattern of the industry, and (2) government policy. Working out

Food-Related Activities: An Equity Strategy 77

of their homes, the women mingle family feeding with commercial cooking, confusing the profits. Also such small scale production leads to uneconomic buying of supplies and inefficient distribution of the products. Much of the profit or loss relates to the size of portions versus the price: frequent price fluctuations of ingredients means that the seller must understand the market. Many women have a canny sense of pricing, but others quickly go out of business. A cooperative organization would seem a logical alternative which would improve investment return, make credit easier, and allow intermediate modernization of the industry. Yet Simmons remarks on the apparent unwillingness of the women to work together. Whether this reluctance to organize stems from cultural or religious practices such as seclusion or easy divorce, or whether no appropriate model or collective action has been tried, is unknown.

Currently the single owner-operator pattern remains competitive with products made by larger industrial establishments, both those in the area offering similar traditional products and those which provide competitive European style breads and candy. Government policies favor larger industry through subsidies and taxes. It seems clear that if the women do not join together to become more competitive, their share of the market will inevitably shrink. Simmons summarizes the impact of this decreasing production on the women themselves and on the rural village economy:

> [W]omen's ability to meet social and economic obligations on their own with earnings from their profitable commercial enterprises will be decreased; the village economy will become less self-sufficient as far as producing and consuming local products; and the value added and income generated by the agricultural sector will migrate more directly to the urban sector. Nutrition may be adversely affected...The deprivation of a substantial means for earning income will have the effect of downgrading women's independent and family roles.[81]

Selling of lunch food and snacks is a traditional part of the economic activity of the West African coastal market women. As the Ivory Coast becomes more urban and workers commute further to their jobs, both breakfast and lunch are often purchased from vendors. While western style lunch shops and fast food chains are appearing, their prices are too high for the average worker. Government has begun subsidizing commercial caterers to provide modern pre-packaged meals at offices or on work sites.

Consistent with its pell-mell rush to copy the west, the government of the Ivory Coast celebrates only the modern. Barbara Lewis, in her insightful study of the over-crowded world of petty traders in that country, notes the lack of government support for the organizational efforts of the market women to set up wholesale purchasing and group savings schemes. Indeed, governmental policy, as demonstrated by courses for women offered through Social Centers run by the Ministry of Work and Social Affairs, appears "designed to refocus women's attention away from moneymaking toward homemaking, rather than providing social or technical skills to upgrade gainful productive activities."[82]

In Abidjan the workforce, drawn from all over West Africa, needs cheap familiar food. Experienced and organized market women are being squeezed out of their traditional activities at the same time that more and more women flood into the informal sector. An imaginative program concerned with supplying indigenous food to workers during the day would benefit both the workers and the women in that capital immensely. The biases against women's work are coupled here with slavish imitation of the west, to the detriment of the majority of Ivoreans.

The reluctance of modernizing governments to accept the continued existence of a more traditional sector has been overcome in many Latin American countries. "Local" markets have been funded by AID along with modern supermarkets. This insight has only occasionally been extended to include local industry. A recent review of Mexico's rural industry program noted the complete lack of attention to women's employment. Of the 60 industries studied, only nine related to food-processing; but no mention was made of women's traditional or present role in these industries.[83]

This report reiterated the danger of assistance agencies setting up non-competitive industries through grant programs: once the subsidy runs out, the industry fails. The literature on women's projects is full of such failures. It is imperative that women's projects be fully competitive and economically viable. Small crafts projects to help women earn "pin money" are not only passe, they are almost destined to fail. Such failures reenforce the biases against women's real economic activity. Even well-conceived schemes may fail if they are not totally integrated into the country's national plan. Will the increased production of millet beer by women's organizations in Upper Volta be undercut by the new Heineken beer factory? Both projects have heavy government subsidies.

In India, a number of very successful women's cooperatives provide possible models for rural industry. In Women's Cooperatives and Rural Development: A Policy Proposal, Ruth Dixon discusses both the dairy industry and a dispersed factory system which produces a soft wheat flatbread for later crisp frying at home.[84]

There are several lessons to be learned from these several studies:

--the importance of an organizational base for women's economic endeavors, and
--governmental recognition of and support for the economic parameters of the projects.

There is a tendency to overload women's projects with welfare concerns: health, education, family planning. These often take precedence, and sink the enterprise. As self-sufficiency is preferable to dependency, so economic activities should be given priority over welfare programs. Recognizing the economic role of women is the starting point.

THE BASICS OF WATER AND ENERGY

Rural survival, much less rural industry, depends upon the availability of water and fuel. The time spent scavenging for fuel or fetching water consumes large amounts of the day for rural women, children, and men. Reducing this expenditure of time must be a priority for rural development. Solutions must be appropriate to the need. Too many wells have caused desertification in the Sahel; too much water has caused severe sanitation problems in India. Elaborate schemes for modern water supplies lie on the planners' shelves in many developing countries.

Clean water for all by 1990 is a slogan often repeated. But where are the development plans to accomplish this? Is part of the problem the lack of monetary value assigned to domestic water supply? If water is seen only as welfare, then hardheaded planners, anxious to show an increase in GNP, do not encourage such projects. If clean water were tied to rural industry as irrigation water has been linked to agriculture, perhaps more funds would be allotted to this need.

Similarly, energy for use in the household and for rural agriculture and homecrafts has gone largely uncounted in national energy statistics. This is due to the custom of measuring only "modern" or "commercial" energy: oil, coal, natural gas, hydroelectricity, and nuclear fuels. Yet such an energy-accounting procedure ignores what in many cases amounts to more than <u>one-half</u> the total energy used in many developing countries, exclusive of animal and human power.

Rural areas, where a majority of population in the developing countries still live, are seldom served by electrical power grids. Diesel motors power pumps for irrigation, provide energy for small industries, and run small lighting systems for wealthy enclaves. But most rural people, like the urban poor, are unable to afford commercial energy in any form even where kerosene is subsidized.

Some two billion people continue to rely on non-commercial energy resources to cook, smoke food, heat water and space, or provide light and safety. These resources are primarily firewood, twigs and brush, agriculture residues, and animal dung. Resources for the Future has just completed a study on "Household Energy for Use and Supply by the Urban and Rural Poor in Developing Countries" which underscores the lack of data on these non-commercial fuels. They conclude on the basis of available data that the lowest energy consumption is among rural areas of South Asia; due to heavy deforestation, animal dung provides as much as 50 percent of the total rural energy consumed. As the amount of dung burned increases, food production will fall unless artificial --and energy intensive--fertilizers are substituted.[85]

It would seem that many countries are following India's path toward deforestation. Experts estimate that Senegal will be bare of trees in 30 years, Ethiopia in 20, Burundi in seven.[86] Ninety percent of wood consumed annually in developing countries is used as fuel.[87] Reasons for this alarming increase in the use of forest reserves are largely related to the population increase both directly in increased cutting and indirectly as more land is cleared for agricultural crops to feed the growing populations. Improved health measures have opened up river valleys in Africa and the terai in Nepal to settlers, also reducing forests and exacerbating erosion.

As available resources drop, the time consumed in gathering fuel increases. In India it has been stated that one person in a family of five must spend full-time gathering dung, firewood, and refuse.[88] Even higher estimates apply to Tanzania.[89] Such time requirements encourage larger family size, for children help the family more than they cost.

When one examines the uses of this energy, it appears that some 40 to 50 percent of the total energy consumed in rural areas is used in cooking alone.[90] In the case of India, for example, this leads to the conclusion that approximately one-fourth of the country's total energy budget is used in rural areas just for cooking, while rural Bangladesh uses about 40 percent of that country's total national energy budget just to cook food.[91]

The urban poor must also eat, yet their energy consumption is estimated as lower than that of the rural poor.[92] As much as one-third of the family's budget may go for fuel in the Sahelian countries. One study states that "to obtain the same amount of usable energy which can be purchased in the U.S. for about $1.30, a charcoal burning family in Addis Ababa may have to spend about $8.00." [93]

As the worldwide energy crisis has engendered a new look at renewable energy resources, some interest is being directed toward improving both the supply of fuel and the efficiency of its use. Mud and sand "Lorena" stoves have cut firewood use in half in Guatemala.[94] But experiments in Mali suggest that the traditional three stones and open fire is still the most efficient cooking method for local food. Pressed rice husks are being marketed; improved methods of making charcoal are being developed; biogas is being produced in many village converters.

Reforestation projects are being upgraded and new plant and tree varieties tried. Biomass plantations will be tried in the Philippines; this fuel will go for large electrical installations as well as for local needs. Small hydro plants may reduce the erosion in Nepal caused by overcutting of trees for firewood. Solar water heating can reduce other fuel usage by a third in Gambia. Solar dryers, solar water pumps and purifiers, and solar sprayers are all in various stages of production. Uses for windpower are being expanded as styles and capabilities are the subject of experiments.

Technology turns to the energy crisis. Will development once again have an adverse impact on poor women? Improved access to fuel supplies will certainly lessen the drudgery of daily living <u>if the women can afford the new fuel or the new stove</u>. Economics is not the only determining factor in the adoption of new technology. Taste, ease of preparation, even the sociability of the kitchen, must be taken into account. Yet shortage of fuel has already changed diets in Guatemala, where many families can no longer afford fuel for the long cooking of beans. Such variables can only be learned at the project site. This was recognized by the participants at the AAAS Workshop on Women and Development sponsored by the U.S. Department of State to develop recommendations for the U.N. Conference on Science and Technology for Development meeting in Vienna in August 1979. The Workshop recommended that the

United Nations sponsor worldwide pilot projects, one in each major region of the developing world, focussing on household energy. And because household is clearly a women's issue, women's views and women's groups must be involved at every phase of study and implementation.

A similar recommendation was put forward by the working group on Energy for Rural Requirements, part of a UNIDO International Forum on Appropriate Industrial Technology which met in New Delhi in November 1978.

> [I]t is the women of the developing world who are most concerned with the problems of energy supply and use, because it is they who do the cooking and, in most countries, gather the fuel. Furthermore, it is usually the women who draw and carry the water for domestic use. Thus, although action programmes undertaken to meet the energy problems of rural areas must involve people at the village level during planning and implementation, their impact on women must be taken into account and indeed, should not be planned or implemented without the significant involvement of women at both the planning level and the village level.[95]

CONCLUSION

Women's traditional economic contribution to the survival of their families is being eroded by technology as the control and profit of technologies flow largely to men. In agricultural production, technologies have been concentrated on cash crops and on selected basic grains. Generally the impact of these technologies has been to increase production, concentrate landholdings, and encourage social stratification. In Asia and Latin America the wives of larger landholders have greatly reduced their involvement in the fields. While this release from hard work is to be commended, there is often an accompanying loss of status. In India, a switch from bride price to dowry has occurred in some areas where brides are no longer valued for their economic contributions.[96] In Africa, however, well-off farm women tend to remain in the rural areas managing the farms and often hiring other women to help with the harvests, particularly of cash crops.[97]

Poor women in all the developing countries have had to work harder as a result of these new productive technologies. Women heads of households or wives of men who migrate to wage jobs elsewhere undertake both the traditional male and female agricultural activities. Families with only a garden plot or splintered field must send _all_ adult family members to work as wage laborers. As new technologies reduce the need for unskilled laborers, a few men are trained for the semi-skilled jobs. (Indeed, men left in the unskilled labor pool are perhaps worse off than the women; women's wages are less and so they are displacing men in plantation work.) Women also have traditionally worked at a greater variety of unskilled jobs and so in many countries they are able to survive through market selling or handicrafts. Elsewhere, women have joined the urban migration, working for low wages in industries or as domestics (or even as prostitutes).

The garden plot where the poor women can grow food to enhance her family's nutrition and then sell the surplus emerges as an important factor in survival. Clearly, greater attention to garden crops and to marketing of fresh vegetables and fruits should be a priority in any planning for rural development. Similarly, attention to small animals and fish culture could add immeasurably to the welfare of the poor, if not to recorded GNP.

New technologies can be useful to women: Technology could greatly reduce postharvest food loss, providing additional food for poor families or supporting small food processing industries which can provide much needed income to poor women. Improved methods for processing and preserving food as well as improved access to water and fuel can also free women from back-breaking and time-consuming labor. But without income, the woman cannot try her hand at new economic activities, much less improve the health of herself and her family or attend literacy classes. Moreover, if new technologies continue to be introduced to men only, women are worse off than before. This vicious circle must be broken, and technology is both part of the problem and part of the solution.

REFERENCES

1. See for example Fred H. Sanderson, "The Great Food Fumble" in P. Abelson, Food: Politics, Nutrition, and Research. Washington, DC: AAAS, 1975.
2. National Research Council, World Food and Nutrition Study. Washington, DC: National Academy of Sciences, 1977.
3. Wortmann, S. & R. Cummings, To Feed This World. Baltimore: Johns Hopkins Press, 1978, p. 235.
4. A major theoretical framework for this view may be found in World Bank, The Assault on World Poverty. Baltimore: Johns Hopkins Press, 1975.
5. Current development strategies are reviewed in the World Bank Paper "Rural Enterprise and Nonfarm Employment." Washington, DC, January 1978.
6. National Academy of Sciences, Postharvest Food Losses in Developing Countries. Washington, DC, 1978.

7. For careful exploration into these interrelationships see the proceedings and papers of the International Conference on Women and Food, University of Arizona, January 1978, sponsored by the Consortium for International Development; sponsored by AID, Office of Women in Development.
8. For an exploration of attempts to measure household activity see <u>Les Femmes dans la Societe Marchande</u>, Andree Michel editor, University Press of France, Paris, 1978.
9. "A Comment on the Role of Women in Agriculture", pp.10-11 in Tinker and Bo Bramsen, <u>Women and World Development</u>. Washington DC : Overseas Development Council, 1976.
10. The USA Club of Rome is exploring the issue of male dominance through a project called "Masculine/Feminine Dimensions of World Problematique," under the leadership of Elizabeth Dodson Gray who has written "Masculine Consciousness and the Problem of Limiting Growth," 1973, mimeo. Dorothy Dinnerstein's <u>The Mermaid and the Minotaur: Sexual Arrangements and Human Malaise</u>. NY: Harper & Row, 1977. explores the male rule of our world and argues that the present inexorable creep toward self-destruction is a function of male psychosis.
11. Berndt, Louise E., and Louis A. Ferman, "Irregular Economic: Cash Flow in the Informal Sector." Center for Metropolitan Problems, NIMH, 1977, mimeo. See also Dow, Leslie M. Jr., "High Weeds in Detroit: The Irregular Economy Among a Network of Appalachian Migrants." <u>Urban Anthropology</u>, Vol. 6, No. 2, 1977, pp. 111-128.
12. Newland, Kathleen, <u>The Sisterhood of Man</u>. NY: Norton, 1977, pp. 129-130.
13. "Class Structure and Female Autonomy in Rural Java," <u>Signs</u>, Vol. 3, No. 1 (Autumn, 1977), pp. 74-89.
14. Elmendorf, Mary, "Mexico: The Many Worlds of Women," in Janet Zollinger Giele & Audrey Chapman Smock, <u>Women: Roles and Status in Eight Countries</u>. NY: John Wiley & Sons, 1977, Chapter 4.
15. See, for example, Marilyn Hoskins, "Vietnamese Women in a Changing Society," 1973, mimeo; and Stoler, <u>op.cit</u>.
16. United Nations, "Development and International Economic Cooperation: Effective mobilization of women in development." A/33/238, 26 October 1978, p. 21.
17. For a longer exposition, see Tinker, I., "Development and the Disintegration of the Family," <u>Assignment Children</u>. UNICEF, 36, October-December, 1976.
18. Germaine, Adrienne, "Poor Rural Women: A Policy Perspective," <u>Journal of International Affairs</u>, Vol, 20, No. 2, Fall-Winter 1976-77. Such figures are extrapolated from micro-studies. An attempt to project this data to the national level may be found in Buvinic, M. and N. Youssef, "Women-headed Households: The Ignored Factor in Development Planning," a report submitted to AID/WID, March 1978, mimeo.
19. I have spelled out this process in "The Adverse Impact of Development on Women," in Tinker, I. and Michele Bo Bramsen,

eds., Women and World Development. Washington, DC: Overseas Development Council, 1976.
20. Chapter 2. NY: Praeger, 1979.
21. Dulansey, Maryanne, "Can Technology Help Women Feed Their Families?" Report on the AAAS Workshop on Women and Development, May 1979.
22. See for example Kathleen A. Staudt, "Class and Sex in the Politics of Women Farmers," Journal of Politics. May 1979; or Ann Stoler, op. cit.
23. Ingrid Palmer, Food and the New Agricultural Technology. Geneva: UN Research Institute for Social Development, 1972, p. 70.
24. Wortman, op. cit., chapter 7.
25. London: G. Allen and Unwin, 1970.
26. UN document, Effective mobilization..., op.cit., p. 22.
27. "Women and Tanzanian Agricultural Development," Dar es Salaam, Economic Research Bureau, 1978, mimeo.
28. Jean A. S. Ritchie, "Impacts of Changing Food Production, Processing and Marketing Systems on the Role of Women, Impacts of the World Situation, Proceedings of the World Food Conference, 1976. Ames: Iowa State University Press, p. 133.
29. Elliott R. Morse, et al., "Strategies for Small Farmer Development: An Empirical Study of Rural Development Projects." Prepared by Development Alternatives, Inc. for AID, May 1975, Vol. I, P. 190.
30. Ibid., p. 24
31. Peter F.M. McLoughlin in his edited "African Food Production Systems." Baltimore: Johns Hopkins, 1970, p. 7.
32. Henn, Jeanne K., "Report on Women Farmers and their Relationship to the ZAPI de l'Est." Washington, DC: World Bank, Rural Development Division, March 1976, mimeo.
33. Dulansey, Maryanne L., "Women in Development: A Training Module." Washington, DC: Consultants in Development, 1977, mimeo, p. 5.
34. Palmer, Ingrid, "Rural Women and the Basic-Needs Approach to Development." International Labour Review, Vol. 115, No. 1. January-February 1977.
35. Murdock, Muneera Salem, "The Impact of Agricultural Development on a Pastoral Society: The Shukriya of the Eastern Sudan." Washington, DC: AID, April 1979, p. 54.
36. Wipper, Audrey, "African Women, Fashion, and Scapegoating." Canadian Journal of African Studies, Vol. 6, No. 2, 1972, pp. 329-349.
37. Lele, op. cit., p. 180.
38. Henn, op. cit., p. 6.
39. Murdock, op. cit.
40. "Women in Development." The NFE Exchange, No. 13, L978/3, Institute for International Studies in Education, Michigan State University.
41. "UNICEF/NGO Water Project", National Council of Women of Kenya, n.d.

42. Rotating credit societies are found throughout the world among men as well as women: for example, the *arisan* in Indonesia, *susu* in West Africa, *gamaya* in Egypt, *tanamoshi* in Japan, etc.
43. A classic statement is found in Uma J. Lele and John W. Mellor, "Jobs, Poverty, and the 'Green Revolution'," *International Affairs*. Vol. 48, January 1972, pp. 20-32.
44. Billings, Martin H. and Arjan Singh, "Mechanization and the Wheat Revolution: Effects on Female Baour in the Punjab," *Economic and Political Weekly*. December 26, 1970.
45. Muzamdar, Vina and Kumud Sharma, "Women's Studies: New Perceptions and the Challenges," *Economic and Political Weekly*. January 20, 1970, p. 117.
46. Rosenberg, David A. and Jean G., *Landless Peasants and Rural Poverty in Selected Asian Countries*. Ithaca: Cornell University Rural Development Committee Monograph, 1978, p. 17.
47. Levinson, F.J., *Morinda: An Economic Analysis of Malnutrition Among Children in Rural India*. Harvard-MIT International Nutrition Policy Series, 1974.
48. UN document, op. cit., pp. 25-26.
49. Rosenberg, op. cit., pp. 70-72; Ann Stoler, "Class Structure and Female Autonomy in Rural Java," *Signs*. Vol 3, No. 1 (Autumn 1977), pp. 74-89; Gary E. Hansen, *Rural Local Government and Agricultural Development in Java, Indonesia*. Ithaca: Cornell University Rural Development Committee Monograph, November 1974, pp. 49ff.
50. Stoler, op. cit., p. 88.
51. Rosenberg, "Incidence of Landlessness and Near-Landlessness," op.cit., p. 8.
52. My section on the Philippines in Reining, Priscilla, et al., *Village Women: Their Changing Lives and Fertility*. Washington, DC: AAAS, 1977, pp. 230 and 238.
53. Misch, Marion Ruth and Joseph B. Margolin, *Rural Women's Groups as Potential Change Agents: A Study of Colombia, Korea, and the Philippines*. Washington, DC: George Washington Univ. Program of Policy Studies in Science and Technology, May 1975, pp. 26-58; also Hyung Jong Park et al., *Mother's Clubs and Family Planning in Korea*. Seoul National University School of Public Health, 1974.
54. Soon Young Song Yoon, "The Emergence of the Fourth World: Korean Women in Development," *Korean Journal*. February 1977, pp. 35-47.
55. Oey Astra Meesook, "Working Women in Thailand." Paper prepared for the Conference on Women and Development, Wellesley, Massachusetts, 1976, mimeo.
56. Kandiyoti, Deniz, "Sex Roles and Social Change: A Comparative Appraisal of Turkey's Women," *Signs*. Vol. 3, No. 1, (Autumn 1977), pp. 60-62.
57. Dixon, Ruth B., *Women's Cooperatives and Rural Development*. Baltimore: Johns Hopkins, 1978.

58. For an insightful view of women's present and potential roles in this area see Roxann A. Van Dusen, "Integrating Women into National Economies: Programming Considerations with Special Reference to the Near East," AID Policy Paper, July 1977, mimeo.
59. "The Agricultural Division of Labor by Sex: Myths, Facts, and Contradictions in the Northern Peruvian Sierra," paper for the joint Latin America Studies Association and the African Studies Association, Houston, Texas, November 1977.
60. Gallup, Cynthia B., "Observations on the Role of Women in the Agricultural Sector in Honduras," USAID Honduras, January 1978, mimeo.
61. Deere, Carmen Diana, "Changing Social Relations of Production and Peasant Women's Work in the Peruvian Sierra," paper prepared for the Fourth World Congress for Rural Sociology, Poland, August 1976.
62. Young, Kate, "Changing Ethnic Roles of Women in Two Mexican Communities," paper prepared for the Fourth World Congress for Rural Sociology, Poland, August 1976.
63. The National Academy of Sciences sponsored an International Working Group meeting on Postharvest Food Losses in Developing Countries. One workshop focused on the importance of interventions in the subsistence or non-market sector. "It was observed...that in many places in the developing world there is an increasing trend toward market-oriented agricultural production, and interventions directed toward commercial agriculture are generally quite different from those required at the subsistence level." Staff Summary Report, p. 31.
64. For a delightful account of the problems surrounding the introduction of the first mills, see Elizabeth O'Kelly, *Aid and Self-Help*. London: Chas. Knight, 1973.
65. O'Kelly, Elizabeth, "The Use of Intermediate Technology to Help Women of the Third World." London: ITTG, mimeo, pp. 9-10.
66. Marilyn Carr, advisor to the Intermediate Technology Group of London and to UNICEF, wrote the book for the African Training and Research Center for Women of the Economic Commission of Africa in 1978.
67. Hemmings, *op. cit.*, p. 4.
68. Timmer, C. Peter, "Choice of Technique in Rice Milling on Java," *Indonesian Economic Studies*, Vol. IX, No. 2 (July 1973) reprinted by the Agricultural Development Council, September 1974, p. 20.
69. Cain, Melinda, "Java, Indonesia: The Introduction of Rice Processing Technology," pp. 127-137, this volume.
70. Collier, *et al.*, *A Comment* (on Timmer's article), reprinted by the Agricultural Development Council, September 1974.
71. Collier, Timmer, *op. cit.*
72. Collier, *op. cit.*

73. No one, that is, but Mirabhen, a disciple of Gandhi, in her cattle ashram in Uttar Pradesh, India, who argued that physical labor sweetened the grain.
74. Henn, op. cit., p. 5.
75. Lindblad, Carl and L. Druben, Small Farm Grain Storage. 1976.
76. "Postharvest Food Losses in Developing Countries," Staff Summary Report, National Academy of Sciences, 1978, p. 13ff.
77. Workshop on Food Preservation and Storage, report published by the Government of Tanzania, distributed by the UN.
78. Conroy, Kim, "The San Juan Bosco Canning Cooperative: The Case Study of a Small Rural Industry." 1979, mimeo.
79. Staff report, op. cit., p. 24.
80. Food Research Institute Studies, Vol. XIV, No. 2, 1975.
81. Ibid., p. 160.
82. Lewis, "Petty Trade and Other Employment Options for the Uneducated Urban West African Women," paper prepared for the AAAS Workshop on Women and Development, March 1979, p. 9.
83. Conroy, Kimberly, "Mexico Rural Development Project PIDER: Analysis of Rural Industry Program," The World Bank, Rural Development Division, April 1979.
84. Johns Hopkins Press, 1978.
85. Dunkerly, Joy, et al., A Report to the World Bank, Chapter III, October 1978.
86. French, D., "The Firewood Problem in Africa," Report on the Africa Bureau Firewood Conference, Washington, DC, USAID, August 1978, mimeo.
87. World Bank, Forestry Sector Policy Paper. Washington DC, February 1978.
88. Mahajani, A., Energy Policy for the Rural Third World. London: International Institute for Environment and Development, 1976.
89. USAID, Environmental and Natural Resource Management in Developing Countries, A Report to Congress, Washington, DC, February 1979, Vol. I, p. 13.
90. Pimentel, D., et al., "Energy Needs, Uses and Resources in the Food Systems of Developing Countries," Report of a workshop held at the College of Agriculture and Life Sciences, Ithaca: Cornell University, December 1977.
91. Revelle, R., "Requirements for Energy in the Rural Areas of Developing Countries." In Brown, Norma L., ed., Renewable Energy Resources and Rural Applications in the Developing World. Boulder: Westview Press, 1978.
92. Dunkerly, op. cit., p. 28.
93. USAID, op. cit., p. 12.
94. Evans, Ianto, Lorena Owner-Built Stoves. A Volunteers in Asia Publication, January 1979.
95. UNIDO, Draft Report, Chapter XI, pp. 71-72.
96. Epstein, T. Scarlett, South India Yesterday, Today, Tomorrow. New York City: Holmes & Meirer, 1973.
97. Reining et al., op. cit., p. 89ff.

Mangalam Srinivasan

5. Impact of Selected Industrial Technologies on Women in Mexico

As a theoretical problem, the analysis of the impact of technical change on women in Mexico requires the fullest possible mobilization of every interdisciplinary research attempt undertaken, conceived and planned. In practical terms, there appears not even a case-method of assessing the place of women in industry; neither are there systematically accumulated and researched data. What data there are appears in aggregates in the government publications, while private academic efforts are seriously involved only in the resolution of "international-level" theoretical problems.

Industry, as the mutual link between science and technology has been an important engine of economic growth and change in the country. A very small part of the gain due to industrialization has been shared with the women in Mexico. The women are beginning to seek and find employment in industry, but most of them are still condemned to the "stagnant micro-system"(1) of subsistence production and drudgery.

The industrial sector in Mexico has been helping to offset some of the "low-level equilibrium" in the subsistence _ejido_, traditional craft, and urban informal sectors which produce no surplus economic benefits. Although the infusion of industrial technology has offered a range of alternative employment possibilities, such opportunities are not benefitting women in any significant degree. It is true that several new technologies, through industrial employment, have put more money in the hands of women than have most traditional sources of employment. Whether this situation has helped equitable income distribution is not yet known. Researchers are just beginning to investigate the relations between technology and income distribution through industrial employment. Skill requirements, age of the labor force, regional disparities, sectoral and spatial adjustments and period covered are all variables which determine where, how and in what manner income

Table 1. Republic of Mexico: Rate of Participation by Women[1] in the Labor Force by Branch of Activity, 1960-1970.

Branch of activity	Total	%1960	%1970
Agriculture-fisheries	100	10.74	5.2
Minerals and Quarry	100	6.72	7.51
Manufacturing	100	15.99	20.63
Construction	100	3.45	3.11
Electricity, gas, water	100	9.36	8.83
Transportation and communication	100	5.26	4.71
Commercial	100	27.02	27.90
Services[2]	100	50.24	43.92
Unspecified	100	21.74	31.25

1. 12 years old and older 2. Includes government workers
Source: Direction General de Estadistica de la S.I.C. VIII y. IX Censo de poblacion.

distribution is occurring through industry. A limited analysis of the potential for employment of women in industries shows unrealized capabilities and has provided a basis for establishing a first judgment that the position of the Mexican women in industry (and therefore in technology) is not inconsistent with their low position in family, society and government. Table 1 enumerates the general position of women in the manufacturing industries _in Mexico_ relative to other areas of employment.

The general position of women in industry is determined, other things being equal, by the level of technology, the degree of mechanization, the scale of pay, and the magnitude and intensity of capital, as well as by how tasks are divided. The employment of women in manufacturing is about 20 percent of the total number of persons employed in these industries (2). Most of the women are employed in industries that have some "craft" connection. The idea that women have to work in food, clothing, child care, crafts and home-related tasks is intrinsic to the industrial employment for women in Mexico. Industries that make traditional items--at whatever level of technology--are more willing to hire women than those industries which work with leather, wood, metal, chemicals, iron and steel, heavy machinery, machine tools, and automobiles that have traditionally excluded them. The analysis of the position of women relative to where they are placed within each industry is uncomplicated due to the fact that we find women mostly in the first and last stages of industrial production. Their work mostly involves preparing the raw materials, selecting and arranging items in the first stages, and assembling parts (as in the case of the maquiladoras, or piece-work plant) and packaging the finished goods in the last stages of production. The in-between stages are permeated with technology, which requires technical skills. No matter how modern the technology deployed in the particular industry, women mostly are engaged in nontechnological gathering, assembling, arranging and packaging activities, and therefore technical skills are not being transferred equally to men and women.

In a country where having a job is a privilege, women do not think that they have a right to good working conditions, adequate pay and access to training and skills. In the more capital-intensive industries, women do not find work except in packaging stages (in fat and oil industries) and unautomated stages (vegetables and fruits). Large companies are less likely to have women workers than small companies unless there are sections where tasks are hand-done. However, capital-intensive and high-technology companies pay good salaries to women, even if they are still being paid less than men. Women are underpaid in these high-technology companies not because they are women, but because they happen to be working in labor-intensive sections and tasks. When there is extreme division of labor, women get jobs, and in these factories women are employed instead of men. (See Table 2 for distribution of workers in manufacturing industries.)

Science, technology and their mutual link--industry--have brought benefits to certain sections of the Mexican society, but the benefits are being coordinated by the dominant urban, rich, elite--and male--sections of the country who have assigned disproportionate benefits to themselves at the cost of widening social and economic gaps between urban and rural, rich and poor, and men and women. Technology is a dependent variable--dependent upon the overriding economic and social configurations of the country. Therefore, looking for help through science and technology without giving simultaneous attention to unequal social and economic developments among the various sections of society, or without paying attention to one-half of the human resources, does not promise much in the way of real human development. There is, in addition, the problem of overlapping impacts of technology and the other activities and processes related to economic development; these further complicate our understanding of what has already been accomplished and what still awaits firm commitment.

The Impact of Selected Industrial Technologies on Women

In my work I have studied textile, food, electronic, and oil refinery and related technologies in relation to their im-

Table 2. Republic of Mexico: Distribution of workers within the manufacturing industries by percentage participation, 1970.

Manufacturing Industries	Men %	Women %
Manufacturing Industries Total	100	100
Food and Food Products	16.2	18.8
Beverages and Tobacco	4.8	1.9
Making of Textiles	6.7	4.4
Articles made of Textiles	1.4	2.0
Clothing Manufacture	4.4	29.1
Shoes - Footwear (not rubber)	4.5	3.3
Wood manufacture - cork	5.6	0.8
Articles made with palm materials	1.3	4.3
Articles of furniture except metal	3.3	0.9
Leather-skin-industries-exclusively used in clothing	1.4	0.6
Making of Cellulose	1.3	0.6
Paper and paper products, cartons	0.8	1.2
Printing	3.6	2.9
Vulcanization of Rubber	1.5	0.6
Pharmaceuticals	1.5	2.9
Soaps and detergents	0.8	1.7
Other chemicals	2.5	1.5
Unspecified chemicals and other products	0.5	0.6
Plastic products	1.5	1.6
Clay - modelling products	0.9	1.1
Minerals except metals	6.7	1.6
Iron and steel	3.5	0.7
Non-ferrous metals	0.7	0.2
Machinery and equipment	8.4	2.2
Construction Machinery and equipment (-electrical items)	1.2	0.7
Other construction Machinery, electrical and its products	3.6	5.3
Other products unspecified - related to construction machinery (+electrical items)	0.5	0.3
Building of motorized vehicles	2.9	1.1
Other transport vehicles	0.9	0.4
Other manufacturing industries	2.8	3.4
Insufficiently specified categories	4.3	3.3

Source: Direccion de Estadistice IX Censo General de Poblacion 1970.

pact on women. These vastly different and unrelated technologies from widely separated regions of Mexico were chosen for the following reasons: Textiles, along with food processing, are traditional Mexican industries which have employed and sustained women throughout history. The range of activities in the textile industry extends to every region of the country, both rural and urban, involves nearly every section of the population, and employs a wide range of traditional and modern methods of production and types of technology. In recent years the textile assembly plants (maquiladoras de ropa) have been multiplying both along the border and in the interior. Mexico also has some of the most automated and modern textile industries in Latin America. Women's involvement in this industry ranges from making of a complete item--such as a poncho, dress, shawl, sweater or coat--to putting a dot on a dress for ten hours a day, five days a week for the whole year of working in the maquiladoras. The food processing industries--the other traditional work source for women in Mexico--offers a valuable base from which to judge the impact of technology on women: Between 1960 and 1970 in the eight largest industrial food subsectors, "modern products" gained an additional share equal to the reduction in "traditional products" (3).

The switch to new products is effecting significant changes in overall employment patterns, as well as changing the composition and patterns of demand for food products. The electronic industries and their "offshore sourcing" (i.e., location of assembly plants in countries with cheap and surplus labor by multinational corporations which are headquartered in the developed countries) offer perhaps the most unique opportunity to analyze the impact of technology from the angle of "female over-employment." The "run-away" plants from Texas and California have located themselves inside the Mexican border to court and engage female labor. Lastly, oil and refinery technologies are impacting on women in extraordinary ways hitherto unknown.

All four of these modernizing sectors have been researched and investigated in varying degrees. The data from several previous missions to Mexico have been carefully studied in conjunction with the present investigation, and the results are discussed in the following pages. The vast range of regions, peoples, occupations, technologies, products and issues these industries represent allow for some generalizations as to the impact of technology on women in Mexico.

The Electronic Industries

Electronics is one nontraditional, high technology based industry that hires women in large numbers. This, of course, is the aggregate position. Within the industry, however, there are large areas of work and challenges that are completely closed to women. The most recent data available show that there are 364 establishments registered with the Mexican government under electronics, but of this number, 35, or approximately 10 percent, are involved in building, importing and distributing discs, cassette tapes and auto stereos. Seven establishments are rental service companies. In these establishments, women are involved only as secretaries and bookkeepers. Of the remaining 322 establishments, 63 register themselves as companies whose principal business is electronics, 180 as manufacturers of electrical items and parts, 75 as distributors, and 5 offer technical assistance and sell electronic accessories (4). The electronic industry had 23,677 women on its payroll in 1970. While this is 27.5 percent of the total number of persons employed in the industry, the complex differentiations within the industry will have to be learned and understood to appreciate the real meaning of women's participation. Women are not employed in technical or managerial jobs in the industry. The electronic media, radio communications, and telex employ women in middle- and low-level jobs, and these jobs amount to about 40 percent of the total employment. Of 36,501 persons involved in repair, maintenance, and service operations connected to electronics, only 1959 (5%) are women. These numbers do not include women working with the government or academia. Government departments such as the secretariat of statistics, Petro Mexico (PEMEX), Consejo Nacional de Ciencia y Technologia (CONACYT), and universities are considerably involved in electronic and computer operations. The estimates of women's participation in both sectors are thought to be between 5 and 7 percent.

The largest number of women employed by the electronic industries are employed in the maquiladoras, which number 157, and all of which are located in the border municipalities. Women make up 90 percent of the total employed, and the implications of this situation are discussed in a later section. The reasons for employing women instead of men range from "they work well," "their attention span is longer," "they are patient," "they do not make trouble for the company," to "they have delicate ways of handling minute electronic components with their small delicate fingers"--excellent qualifications for a surgeon also, and the answer is obvious when one wonders why with such advantages women are not functioning as surgeons in any significant numbers.

The Textile Industry

The art of textiles in Mexico has vividly preserved the native talents, sense of color and patterns, and represents

Table 3. Republic of Mexico: Distribution of workers by sex and by percentage participation, 1970.

Type of Manufacturing	Men %	Women %
Textile Manufacturing	85.3	14.7
Articles made of Textiles	72.9	27.1
Manufactures of Clothing	37.0	63.0

Source: Direccion general de Estadistica, IX, Censo General de poblacion, 1970.

the Mexican civilization in all of its most striking aspects: its worship of the sun, its love of nature, its quintessential symmetry and beauty of proportions, and its technological abilities. Today's Mexican textile industry ranges from handmade items painstakingly constructed in the individual homes of the Indians of Mexico to the making of synthetic yarn and clothing in the most automated textile industries. A very high proportion of women find work in textiles, and like the electronic maquiladoras, the textile offshore assemblies prefer women workers instead of men. The employment picture within the textile industries appears in Table 3.

Thirty-six percent of all working women are employed in the textile industry. In this industry the number of women employed is inversely proportional to the increase in automation but directly proportional to the extreme division of tasks. Therefore, we find in modern maquiladoras de ropa (clothing assemblies) a high proportion of women employed and find fewer women in modern synthetic textile factories that are both capital intensive and technology intensive.

According to one Mexican entrepreneur whose factory is considered the most automated textile unit in Latin America, the automated factories usually do not employ women because of the nature of the work place and the type of machines used. Textile manufacturers acknowledge that women are good workers and that they have great abilities for yarn preparation and weaving. According to the employers, however, weaving with synthetic yarn presents special problems because of the high degree of mechanization. The high level of noise (90 decibels, over the standard permitted in the United States), high speed of the looms (6 or 7 operating at the same time), and the high temperature and humidity factors (26°C and 70% relative humidity) inside the factories are unsuited for women. Another entrepreneur commented that his automated factory does not employ women because he is not prepared to finance the yearly pregnancies of the Mexican woman worker. Several of them gave the opinion that the cost of training the women to operate complicated and sophisticated machinery is rather an expensive proposition. The automated industry has less than 10 percent women workers and none of these women work in the technical, mechanical, or managerial operations. Few are in administrative areas and most work as secretaries, bookkeepers and clerks.

Another factor which is worthy of mention is that the intermediate factories of the textile industry are extremely vulnerable to the imports of hazardous machines from the United States--equipment the U.S. companies are gradually replacing because it is considered dangerous to the health and safety of the workers under U.S. laws. In the cotton factories especially, the cotton dust and the high level of noise and humidity of hazardous factory equipment--rejected by the U.S. and imported into Mexico--cause considerable harm to both the workers and the general public.

In many parts of the Mexican countryside, the modern textile technology has yet to make its impact. Here, women from their porches continue to weave, knit, embroider and tie laces as in the old days. The painstaking art is time-consuming and often it takes months to make one item. The incomes derived from these activities are not commensurate with either the quality of the work or with the time required to make the items. In addition, the maker of these items cannot sell them directly to the buyers or take them to towns for better prices. The mestizo middleman in the villages procures the products from the villagers by every means, including the bribing of policemen who in turn take care to see that the women do not leave the village on their own in search of buyers and better prices! By comparison, the women who work in modern factories are assured of fixed pay, regular hours, and fringe benefits.

Extraction of Petroleum and Refinery Technologies

The vast petroleum reserves of Mexico, estimated at about 37 billion barrels crude, are causing considerable industrial awakening in states where oil is being found. Mexico's Program for Science and Technology (1978-1982), issued by CONACYT, discusses present energy consumption, future energy needs, development of needed technologies, etc., and says nothing about the impact of existing technological activities connected to the recovery, processing, refining, and distribution of oil on the people of Mexico and makes no mention of plans to avoid adverse impacts. In the states of Tabasco and Veracruz, PEMEX's activities have brought about considerable unemployment of the local population, social tensions, economic inequalities, extravagant consumer habits, ecological damage to these prime agricultural areas of Mexico and has led to the outmigration of men in search of jobs. In Tabasco, the PEMEX acquired much of its oil land from farmers by paying them below the market value for their lands. PEMEX usually takes its own men and equipment wherever it goes and therefore almost never hires local people--thereby keeping political and technological control.

PEMEX is headquartered in Mexico City with branches, exploration units, and service establishments located in every part of Mexico. PEMEX is now an important part of every economic consideration in Mexico. Inside sources in PEMEX estimate that out of the 100,000 employees working for the corporation, less than 5 percent are women. Most women who work for PEMEX are in secretarial, administrative, and janitorial-type jobs, while few women work as chemists, doctors and engineers. Energy, one of the most vital sectors in economic and social development, receives practically no policy participation from women.

"The annual consumption of energy resources per capita in Mexico," according to CONACYT, is the "equivalent of approximately 7.8 barrels of crude petroleum." (5) While this figure is lower than the corresponding statistics from developed countries, it is considerably higher than that of most developing countries. The growth in energy consumption (between 1965-1977) increased 6.7 percent per annum (6) and therefore the growth in economic development activities (7) has not significantly increased the share of women in the income growth the country is experiencing.

Oil technology is entirely male-dominated, and women are not employed in any activity connected with exploration, extraction, refinement, or distribution. There are a few women working in the petrochemical area, mostly as research chemists and laboratory assistants, but PEMEX has no firm figures on the number of such women.

The most important adverse effects due to the technology required to recover and process oil and natural gas are occurring on sites where petroleum is being extracted and refined. PEMEX admits in its internal studies that these social and economic distresses have occurred, but defends its activities publicly. Recently, the disputes between the people of Tabasco and PEMEX are bringing out into the open several adverse effects of the presence of oil recovery, processing and refining technologies. At the same time, fine deposits of sulphur are accumulating on the face of the awakening oil land, while the effect of the deposits on human health and ecology awaits evaluation.

Despite the claim made by PEMEX and supported by statistics, a spot survey indicated that there had been a drop in female literacy in Tabasco as more children are becoming disengaged from their formerly stable circumstances, as their families are getting increasingly despondent and dislocated, and as more men are leaving the state to look for jobs elsewhere, leaving their families behind. To the proponents of growth through oil, these troubles and distresses have the function of a Greek chorus, with its antiphons and laments on the side, while economic development will emerge as the ultimate truth and at that point all tensions--economic and social--will have been annulled.

The Impact of Offshore Assembly Plants (the Maquiladoras) on Women

The maquiladoras came about as a result of the Border Industrialization Program (BIP) initiated by the government in 1965. The program began functioning in 1971 and had the express objectives of creating new and more jobs, creating better incomes and greater levels of skills among the industrial workers, and of reducing the country's trade deficits.

The industrial expansion has contributed to the considerable population growth of the Mexican border municipalities. The population growth rates in the border cities are higher than the national average (8). (See Table 4.)

Table 4. Population of border states and border municipios: 1950, 1960, and 1970.

Area	Rates of Growth 1950-60	1960-70
Mexican Republic	3.1	3.3
Border States	4.0	3.6
Border Municipios	5.9	4.2

Source: Jorge A. Bustamante, Maquiladoras: A New Fact of International Capitalism in Mexico's Northern Border. March 1976.

The arrival of the assembly plants had adversely affected agricultural and related activities in the border municipios, creating considerable unemployment among older women. In the years between 1950 and 1970 there has been steady decline of the economically active population involved in agriculture, some increase in industrial employment, and considerable increase in service-related activities. In other words, those that have left agriculture on account of one pressure or another, have not found jobs in the maquiladoras, but rather are forced to get into service industries (the particular categories of which are described later at some length). The decrease in primary activities and the increase in secondary and tertiary activities of the border industrial towns are higher than the respective national averages (Table 5).

The maquiladoras hire mostly female labor and in industries such as electronics 90 percent of the employees are women. This special situation offers rather unique insights into the social and economic environment in which women find themselves in rapidly industrializing situations which offer them more than equal opportunities for employment.

Table 5. Republic of Mexico: Percentage of economically active population of border municipios, 1950, 1960, and 1970.

Area	1950 %	1960 %	1970 %
Republic of Mexico	100	100	100
Agriculture	58.4	54.2	39.5
Industry	16.0	19.0	22.9
Services	21.4	26.1	31.8
Unspecified	4.2	0.7	5.8
Border Municipalities	100	100	100
Agriculture	45.4	39.4	22.2
Industry	16.6	20.2	24.5
Services	31.5	37.6	46.1
Unspecified	6.4	2.8	7.2

Source: Jorge A. Bustamante, Maquiladoras: A New Fact of International Capitalism in Mexico's Northern Border. March 1976.

The facts about the plight of women in the maquiladoras are just beginning to emerge. The analysis of the situation is rendered especially difficult due to the lack of any kind of concepts, hypotheses or theories on the question of women in production. Finding a job as well as holding it are in themselves such *fait accompli* that the question of working conditions is never raised by female employees.

Contrary to the great expectations of the host country, the maquiladoras have turned out to be production arms of high-technology companies from across the border producing consumer goods for exportation only. They indulge in little or no dialogue as to the social benefits of any of their projects for Mexico, effect little or no technology transfer, and clearly demonstrate their motives to be financial for being where they are. In other words, they are there merely to take advantage of the wage differentials between the two countries. Many maquiladoras at the border towns pay as little wage as $3 per day as compared to the nearly $30 per day wage paid by the same firm in the United States (9). The fact that women in these plants are reluctant to unionize and are not adequately initiated in the trade union bargaining methods is of very great advantage to the maquiladoras and hence the pre-eminence of women in these factories who are an "exhaustible labor supply at 30 cents an hour" (10).

Nor are the economic impacts those predicted by the government. The government had expected to promote employment through the creation of industrial jobs. Despite the new jobs, in the decade between 1960 and 1970 the border municipalities have suffered from higher unemployment than the rest of the country. Of the total unemployed among the economically active population, 53.6 percent is to be found in Tijuana, Mexicali, and Cuidad Juarez--all border municipios. Both the employed and the unemployed in these regions are mostly migrants who have relinquished their work in the primary sector in favor of work in modern factories.

Women come to the border towns from every state of the union, looking for jobs in modern industrial factories, while men come mostly from Tabasco. This in itself is a very interesting fact, since Tabasco is experiencing a great economic boom through oil activities, and yet the men in that state unable to find jobs with PEMEX are moving northward.

According to the 1970 Mexican census data, in the border municipalities, the share of agricultural workers in the economically active population declined from 45.5 percent in 1950 to 22.2 percent in 1970 and is still declining. In the same years industry's share has increased from 16.6 percent to 24.5 percent, as has the tertiary sector. Men and women have left agriculture for jobs in the assembly plants; not finding them, they turn to service jobs in the commercial, government, and domestic sector rather than go back to their villages. This finding is supported by Uniquel et al. (11) who point out that, unlike the developed countries, in Mexico the increase in service industries indicate unemployment and underemployment as well as marginal employment. While 90 percent of the assembly plant workers are women, there are more of them unemployed and underemployed as a result of the increased migration.

The Mexican women have always worked producing income and goods for the family and the community. In the rural areas, in agriculture and in crafts, women have always worked along with men. The work in modern technology corporations is different. It is competitive, highly specialized without requiring special skills on the part of the women who work, and is organized in a manner in which changes in personnel occur daily. In fact, no one is allowed to acquire any special skills because specialized workers mean better salaries and the employers are not prepared for that.

For the women who left the land because of exploitation, the urban technology work is not any better. The exploiters are different but the exploitation is the same; only the relationship of land to the means of production has changed. New troubles and problems have been substituted for ancient forms of oppression and sufferings. The supportive family and the known and sympathetic community are absent in the new scene; instead, young women often find their neighbors ready to subject them to every type of abuse, including prostitution.

Unlike the other industrialization programs in the country, where technological changes have led to some form of permanent employment opportunities and to raising the level of the technical skills of the local population as well as those of the migrants, the maquiladoras have a gossamer quality to their comings and goings. Dr. Jorge Bustamante has questioned "whether the maquiladoras have the degree of permanency and stability that would generate economic development and absorb the labor force that the industry has attracted to the large industrial centers" (12). The disappearance of Magnavox and Packard-Bell from the border scene is an example of the kind of instability founded on wage differential and partial production processes catering to exportation only. When the plants folded practically overnight and left for home and elsewhere (in search of cheaper labor), most of the people who lost their jobs, and therefore their sustenance, were women. It has been estimated that as many as 5000 women lost their jobs when these two companies left Mexico.

When their employers leave, women find it very hard to locate another job since they find themselves lacking in skills. Specialization of work for them usually means fixing an item in the socket or putting a dot on the dress. This type of specialization is precisely the obstacle to finding new jobs. Bustamante argues that "... no matter how high the level of training obtained in the maquiladora industry, the degree of specialization by the greater part of the piece-work operation makes the recuperation of that type of training very relative, taking into account the technological development that exists in the 'permanent' industry in the rest of the country" (13).

The women are employed in the maquiladoras for specific tasks that involve fine and minute divisions of labor which result in the women doing highly repetitive jobs. The specialization includes no career training and certainly requires no skills, only the ability to recognize items as they come through the assembly line, and after completing the part of the assembly assigned, to send the same for further assembly or for packaging--again jobs done exclusively by women.

The offshore plants are not stable aspects of the Mexican technological and economic evolution since they are always in search of cheaper labor elsewhere. The net effect of sporadic and seasonal demand for women labor through technological changes is a negative sum. The disadvantages stemming from destitution, disorientation, break-up of families and penury of migratory workers looking for jobs and not finding them as well as losing the jobs they get every few months according to the whims and fancies of the runaway maquiladoras far outweigh any financial benefits due to having jobs in these factories. The aggregate net picture for the area is even a more severe negative sum when we consider the extravagant and wasteful consumer habits, the ecological damage due to sudden migratory pressures, male and female prostitution, gambling, and alcohol and drug abuse in the northern cities.

In general terms, finding jobs in modern industries for women has depended on the size of the male labor force and the availability of child-care facilities (14). But in Mexico's northern border-towns, women's employment has not depended on these factors because women are employed instead of men, and the day care of the children is carefully avoided by industries, which prefer to hire unmarried young women and to keep their labor force in the state of perpetual youth by changing workers quite often.

Despite the general ill effects of the maquiladoras, direct investigation has revealed that women in the plants are happy to have their jobs. The young women in these factories enjoy the money they get even though the maquiladoras pay only 30 to 60 cents an hour (which is far above the monthly wages of 500 to 1000 pesos that most of these women were used to making). In traditional textile industries, a woman often spends a whole month making one item, which she then sells for less than 150 pesos. The same woman has the opportunity in the modern textile maquiladoras to make as much as 3000 pesos per month. The peasant women also seem proud to be wearing American-style clothing as well as to be able to live in a way which caters to their fanciful spending. In addition, having a job which is not home-based (15) of course has its own status in a traditional society.

The image of working in a modern technology-based industry is greatly pleasing to the women workers even though the job has all the trappings of a traditional industry without its benefits. The migration to the north and the preference by women for factory jobs in all urban centers in Mexico have had important effects on the domestic service market. The few who remain to be maids are in a better bargaining position and their salaries have increased two-fold in the last five years.

The so-called specialized jobs in the maquiladoras involve no knowledge of what one is doing, no background or scientific information, no technical abilities, no knowledge of process engineering and none of the manufacturing methods. In other words, the labor mostly is unskilled and the workers untrained. If and when women attain some degree of job-specialization, the company makes sure that they are shifted to another job, not for reasons of career development and training, but to avoid paying the higher wages required for skilled jobs.

The working conditions prevailing in these maquiladoras do not correspond to the modernness of their technologies. Despite the century, the bitter realities of technological awakening in Mexico are quite reminiscent of conditions in Victorian England. The "song of speed" heard along the Mexican northern border is not "ringing grooves of change" of better social and economic opportunities for women, because when we ask

> How much intellect represented,
> How much imagination,
> How much learning,
> How much expression of the great
>   progress of the country (16),
> And what sort of contribution to
>   human happiness and self-expression,

the answers tell us negative stories.

The proximity of Mexico to the world's most advanced technological civilization and to its technology companies has unleashed special problems of its own. The Mexican government has objectively allied itself with the technology corporations and uses wage and skill differentials between Mexico and the United States to achieve its employment goals and economic growth. In selling labor the government has forgotten the laborers--the men and women who work in these companies.

Women and Industrial Policies

Few women occupy significant policy positions in industry and government. The reasons for this are to be found in the historic and traditional attitudes toward women, the inadequacies of the educational system, and the lack of role models.

The differential sex roles instilled early in childhood account for the social discrimination prevalent and for the continuing distinctions in education and training for women in Mexico. Despite the increasing proportion of women in employment, careers in science and technology are not considered appropriate and are seen as being in conflict with the women's traditional roles as wives and mothers. The educational programs in Mexico purportedly offer the same opportunities for progress for both men and women. However, there are no specific programs to promote greater participation of women in vocational, technical, and professional education and career training. The primary and secondary schools actively cater to differential achievements by girls and boys. Boys are encouraged to ask questions, explore, analyze, doubt, and expose theories to fact while girls get good-conduct awards for passivity, submissiveness, silence, and for refraining from asking questions. These are of course archetypes and are not clearly delimited in scope since they continue to influence the individuals in the selection of, preparation for, and performance in work, as well as in the ensuing work-relationships. This contention is adequately borne out by the following enumeration of the participation of women in scientific and technological careers in Mexico: Although women's participation in agriculture and related activities has been and continues to be important, only 5 percent of the scientists and technicians working in these areas are women; the number of women mathematicians and physicists make up 7 percent of the total, and in the combined area of medical, biological and social sciences, the percentage approaches 25 percent of the total scientific and technical personnel.

The sun-roused history of Mexico is intricately interwoven with layers of civilizations, cultures, peoples, and religious influences. Despite its total conversion to Christianity, the country's religious psyche has undergone a synthesis of the old and the new, and the native and the occidental. The bleeding Christ on the crucifix and the mother of God--the Virgin of Guadaloupe--arrived in the human world of the gods and goddesses of the Mayans and the Aztecs, and having failed to eliminate them, co-exist with them. The religious archetypes and stereotypes are ever present in the everyday world of life, work, education, social action, and human interactions. Art and science are organized accordingly. In the social scene, the Indians of Mexico, the Spaniards who came, the child of the Indian (the __Mestizo__) and the child of the Spaniard (the __Creole__) are all still present in the minds of the people and are quite distinct from one another despite acculturation. The position of things occidental in the Mexican society is a very important orientation for understanding the role of women in Mexico, because it tells us

> Who is making things happen,
> Who has the intelligence for survival,
> Who is authorized to conceptualize,
> (and therefore manipulate) ideas and tools,
> Who can create, and
> Who can sustain.

The "ideas and tools" in the Mexican culture belong to men, which explains why few women have anything to do with science and technology in that country.

The process of integrating women into the benefits of technology and employment is hampered by the lack of proper policies, by the manner in which policy is formulated, and by the lack of any kind of hypothesis or theories regarding women in industry. The information and issues encountered by public policy concerned with women at the present time are "descriptive" rather than "analytic." Even when there are opportunities for delineating the problem areas in terms of their components, the data appear in aggregates because the forms have not been revised or updated to include women in the light of their increasingly larger role in industry and technology. There is also present the methodological problem of the scale of analysis. The aggregates and averages indicate the existence of trade-offs, but they fail to indicate who is trading what for what or to establish the relationships that are useful for planning purposes. The aggregate and average measures do tell us that shifts are occurring in the female labor market but are unable to define and describe the trends in the interface between industrial, technology-based employment and traditional sources of employment for women. Thus agriculture, a significant domestic and export industry with tremendous possibilities for the deployment of Mexican labor and indigenous technologies and innovation, is increasingly the recipient of residual labor and the utter destitutes who have not been able to outmigrate in search of industrial employment.

Perhaps the most important of all difficulties is the one associated with the process mechanism related to policy itself. At the present time, in Mexico, no mechanism exists that orients the science policy processes toward planned observations, changes in institutional practices, feed-back information, innovative action programs or creative interventions to achieve greater participation by women in matters of science and technology. The few studies that are being undertaken on the effect of industrial work and modern technologies on women are confined entirely to academic research; none have been connected with technology assessment. This kind of inner logic present in the circle of policy analysts has allowed the decision-makers to define development programs in terms of mechanical increases of technology without regard to its impact on women, whether the programs relate to birth control, packaged foods, chemical fertilizers, household appliances, or industrial employment.

Furthermore, the proponents of growth through technology point out that the abject working conditions--namely, the compartmentalization of work, minute subdivisions of tasks, exploitation of labor in general and women in particular, and exclusion of certain sections of the population from industrial work--are not demanded by technology. They argue that the organization of science and technology for research and inventions is different from the way in which industry is organized. Essentially, the factory is not organized to maximize efficiency but to accommodate management, a condition that has nothing to do with technology itself.

Women find making a career in science and technology particularly complicated because of the lack of role models and the limited career training and suggestions that they receive from schools, families, peers, and government. Dr. Tomas Garza, one of Mexico's most distinguished scientists, points out that the problem of so few women in science is an integral part of the overall problem of science in Mexico. He blames the lack of tradition in theoretical and experimental sciences for the lack of scientific and technological advancements in general and for the problems of scientists in particular.

In summary, it can be seen that not only are women far behind in science, they are far behind in technology and industry due to the same lacks: of education, specialized training and support on the one hand, and to the lack of specific policies for the utilization of their individual abilities and specific qualities for their own and the nations's best advantage on the other.

Notes

1. S. A. Kuzmin explains stagnant micro-systems as follows: "These systems are characterized by a kind of 'low-level equilibrium' whose distinguishing feature is that usually no economic surplus worth mentioning is produced." "An Integrated Approach to Development and Employment," in *International Labour Review*, Volume 115, No. 3, May-June 1977, p. 330.

2. Direccion General de Poblacion, 1970.

3. Unger, Kurt, "Food Manufacturing in Mexico and Technological Dimension for Policy Making: Some Observations and Suggestions." El Colegio de Mexico, 1978.

4. Albarran N., A.F., Gil M., J., A. Guardia et al., La Electronica En Mexico: El Sector Privado, National Autonomous University of Mexico, November 1976.

5. Mexico's program for Science and Technology. 1978-1982-- CONACYT, p. 45.

6. *Ibid.*

7. A number of studies have established the dynamic relationship between economic growth and per capita energy consumption. See R. Krishna Prasad and A.K.N. Reddy, "Technological Alternatives and the Indian Energy Crisis."

National Seminar on Energy, March 1976. Also M. Srinivasan, "Shifts in Energy Consumption and Policy for Energy Development," unpublished paper prepared at the Center for International Affairs, Harvard University.

8. According to Luis Uniquel et al., (Desarrollo Urbano En Mexico, 1974): "the growth is the outcome of external rather than internal factors. The authors point out that the border cities, where the tertiary sector is predominant, have recorded the highest rate of growth of 5.23% as opposed to the national average rate of 3.04%.

9. Bustamante, Jorge A., "Maquiladoras: A New Face of International Capitalism in Mexico's Northern Frontier," paper presented at the sixth National Meeting of The Latin American Studies Association held in Atlanta, Georgia, March 1976.

10. Ibid.

11. Uniquel, Luis et al., op. cit.

12. Bustamante, Jorge A., op. cit., p. 17.

13. Ibid.

14. Tinker, Irene, "The Adverse Impact of Development on Women," in Tinker, Irene, and Bramsen, Michele Bo, Eds., Women and World Development, Overseas Development Council, Washington, D.C., 1976.

15. Vladimir Lenin has argued in many of his writings on women's place in world development that so long as women are excluded from socially productive work and are restricted to housework which is private, women can never be emancipated. Lenin generally held cottage industries to be some of the outstanding causes for the lack of progress in women's status in the pre-revolutionary Russia.

16. Dexter, Walter, Ed., Letters of Charles Dickens, Nonesuch Press, 1938. The questions are somewhat taken out of context but they are pertinent questions to ask with respect to any technology.

Ann Seidman

6. Women and the Development of "Underdevelopment": The African Experience

Analysis of experience the world around has exposed a tendency for the status of women to decline with the introduction of new technologies in the process of development. This brief paper will argue that this is an integral facet of the complex interrelated phenomenon which several political economists have identified as the process of development of underdevelopment. The paper will focus primarily on evidence drawn from Africa, where the author conducted research and taught in universities for almost a decade. The underlying explanation, with appropriate modifications in view of the particular historical circumstances and cultural differences, appears, however, to be more widely applicable.1/

The Explanatory Model Proposed

The basic elements of the explanation here proposed may be incorporated into an interrelated set of propositions. Together, these may constitute the beginnings of a model to explicate the way the introduction of modern technology, in the context of the larger development of underdevelopment process, contributes to the declining status of women:

1. Almost a century of colonial rule shaped institutions which functioned to: a) coerce Africans into a low paid labor force to produce crude minerals and tropical agricultural produce for shipment as raw materials for the burgeoning industries of Europe; and b) to undermine pre-existing handicrafts industries in order to open a market for surplus mass-produced goods produced by European factories.

2. The pre-colonial sexual division of labor, prevailing in many parts of Africa, interacted with colonial

ideologies to foster the migration of male labor to work on European owned mines and estates, or as sharecroppers for African cash crop farmers who sold produce at low prices to European trading companies. Women remained in the underdeveloped rural areas, using outmoded technologies-- typically only a hoe and a cutlass -- to produce the family food requirements and raise children.

3. The limited formal educational institutions introduced by colonial regimes were designed primarily to provide a few middle level African administrators, primarily men, and spread the Christian gospel. Few women went beyond the first grades, if they managed to attend school at all. Most never obtained the essentials for mastering the new technologies introduced in the narrow, export-oriented sectors.

4. After independence, marginally-altered colonially-shaped institutions not only perpetuated the inherited, externally-dependent political economies; they also reinforced the sexual division of labor introduced in the colonial era. New governments' efforts to create "a hospitable investment climate" for transnational corporations in this context accelerated the introduction of capital-intensive machinery and equipment, further aggravating unemployment and the deteriorating status of women.

The Evidence

To present fully the evidence available from the almost 50 countries of Africa -- a spreading land area three times the size of the United States -- would require volumes. Instead, the aim here will be to illustrate these propositions, indicate the wider range of documentation that exists, and suggest areas for further research.

Extensive studies have exposed the way the colonial institutions functioned to coerce Africans into a cheap labor force to produce low-cost raw materials for European manufactured goods.2/

The colonialists introduced institutional changes which, while varying from region to region, all aimed to ensure an adequate supply of low priced labor to produce the desired raw materials. The colonial state imposed various hut and poll taxes to force Africans to earn cash, either by selling export crops or working for Europeans for wages. As a colonial administrator explained,

All that needs to be done is for the Administration to... introduce the Native laborer to the European capitalist. A gentle insistence that the Native should contribute his fair share to the revenue of his country by paying his tax is all that is necessary on our part to ensure his taking a share in life's labour which no human being should avoid. 3/

European settlers took over the most productive land near the major transportation routes, carving out vast estates in east, central and southern Africa: seven million acres in the 'White Highlands' of Kenya; 4/ 20 miles on both sides of the railway through the heart of Zambia (then Northern Rhodesia); 5/ and 50 6/ and 87 7/ percent, respectively, of the entire land area of Southern Rhodesia (soon to be Zimbabwe) and South Africa. European-owned mines and estates there required African labor, so colonial marketing and credit systems 8/ discriminated against Africans' efforts to produce and sell export crops. They were given no option but to work for wages to earn the tax.

To prevent competition with imported manufactured goods, as well as to restrict Africans' alternative employment options, colonial laws prohibited ancient handicrafts and industrial pursuits. 9/ The mine companies, settlers and trading firms invested part of the profits they accumulated by their systematic exploitation of African labor, agricultural and mineral wealth, to introduce some of the world's most advanced technologies in the export sectors. 10/ On the one hand, they augmented their African exports to capture increasing shares of the world market, simultaneously chaining African economies securely to its unpredictable fluctuations. On the other, they created an expanding market for the machinery and equipment produced in the metropolitan country factories. But their increased output went, not to better the lives of the low-paid Africans, but to produce copper, oil, seeds, coffee, cotton, tea -- the raw materials needed for their factories back home to raise their living standards to the highest in the world.

This distorted pattern of introducing new technologies not only systematically fostered underdevelopment, low productivity, and growing unemployment in Africa; it also functioned to disadvantage women. The pre-colonial division of labor had tended, in most instances, to leave to women the tasks of raising children and growing food crops. 11/ Men had formerly helped clear the land,

construct irrigation ditches, build and repair houses—
what might be called 'capital investments.' They also
hunted, cared for cattle, and provided protection. This
mutually sharing relationship, growing out of the family
members' struggle to survive against the harsh realities
of nature, had tended to endow women with significant
decision-making powers about what to produce and how to
produce it. Men and women had worked together, using
long-established technologies, to produce iron tools,
salt, soap, textiles. Women worked in the copper mines
in Central Africa centuries before the Europeans even
dreamed of the region's rich mineral wealth. 12/ In West
Africa, women carried their produce to market, some
of them establishing extensive political as well as
economic influence through their resulting trading
connections. 13/

The colonialists brought with them their own beliefs
that women should stay home with the children. They
primarily sought male wage labor to do the heavy work
on their mines and farms. The Europeans' preconceived
perceptions fit nicely with the emerging colonial
pattern in which women stayed home in the rural areas,
using pre-existing technologies to grow the necessary
food and raise the children. This provided a convenient
rationale for paying the men wages barely adequate to
support themselves alone 14/ -- less than the amount Marx
held even capitalist industry must pay: the minimum socially
necessary to cover the cost of subsistence of the workers
plus the next generation of labor power. 15/

Exclusion of women from employment in 'modern' wage
jobs was reinforced by restrictions on their entry into
colonial schools established for lower level African civil
servants and technical personnel. 16/ The few girls who
were admitted to the formal educational system often
learned little more than to read and write -- considered
vital to pass on the Christian message to their children --
and 'women's work' like home economics to make them
better housewives and mothers. The schools taught few
men and almost no women the mechanical skills required
to handle the modern machinery and equipment introduced
into the export sector.

The loss of male labor and their essential 'capital'
inputs led to the deterioration of pre-existing technologies as women struggled alone to maintain food output.
An integrated cattle-grain complex, 17/ for example, had
supported what Livingstone described as a 'land of milk
and honey' in the Barotse Kingdom of Central Africa, back

in the 19th Century. As the men were forced to migrate out of the villages to seek wage employment on the copper mines and line-of-rail estates, the ancient irrigation channels disintegrated. This process became self-perpetuating, for the next generation, unable to regenerate past productive activities, left in ever greater numbers. Today, the region is the poorest province in Zambia.

Though the details differed in other parts of the continent, the overall development of underdevelopment process was similar: 18/ Women, using little more than hoes and cutlasses, struggled to maintain food output on eroded, worn pieces of soil as the colonial institutional structure pushed the best lands and male labor into production of export crops and mineral wealth.

The attainment of political independence by almost 50 African nations in the 1960s and 1970s did little to alter the basic institutional structures shaping the impoverished economies with their distorted sexual division of labor.

New government ministries, now headed by male African elites, 19/ continued as the lineal descendants of the former colonial departments. 20/ They failed to formulate long term development strategies to restructure the inherited, lopsided national economies. In country after country, they pragmatically expanded government expenditures to build new schools, roads, hospitals, ports, bridges, the infrastructure urged by conventional wisdom to attract private investment in productive activities on farms and in factories. Since domestic private enterprise had little capital or 'modern' skills, African governments competed to attract transnational firms by offering generous holidays, tariff protection, and industrial parks.

Marginally-altered colonial institutions, combined with government policies to attract foreign capital, tended to aggravate the inherited sexual division of labor's impact, further disadvantaging women, both in agriculture and in industry.

In agriculture, government development ministries, together with little-changed marketing and credit systems, continued to foster expansion of export crops. The primary difference was the new African governments' emphasis on encouraging African peasants to grow more for export to obtain more foreign exchange to finance the imports on which their externally-dependent economies had come to rely. This fit well with the increasingly evident preference of transnational trading firms for encouraging Africans themselves, rather than European settlers to grow export crops: 21/ The peasants and the national economies bore the risks when world prices dropped. The transnational firms could shop around to buy from the countries offering the lowest prices. Export crops multiplied, but national incomes remained low. 22/

The expansion of peasant export crops, while contributing little to higher national living standards, further undermined the status of women in the rural areas. The extension agents of the new governments, like those employed by the colonial administrations before, were almost always men. They taught rural men, rather than rural women, about new farming techniques. Where landholdings were individualized to foster private incentives to expand output, the title was usually registered in the mens' names, even where women did most of the work. 23/ The banks, even state-owned banks, typically advanced credit only to the male heads of household. 24/ Men almost invariably managed the boards and cooperatives established to market export crops. Sometimes, they alone had acquired the necessary education to handle the books. In other cases, the prevailing ideology dictated that men assume these tasks.

In Kenya, 25/ for example, the government introduced measures to organize a cooperative to acquire inputs and market pyrethrum. Disappointingly, production declined. Closer examination revealed that, although cooperative by-laws specified males, presumably the household heads, as members, the women had actually been producing the pyrethrum. Not surprisingly, the women, on discovering that payment was to be made to the male cooperative members, reduced their output.

The post independence governments did make efforts, especially after the drought and widespread famine of the early 1970s, to encourage expanded food production. But still, the inherited institutional-ideological matrix tended to disadvantage women, although they were the traditional food producers. In Zambia, for example, the agricultural ministry did employ women as extension agents to help women food farmers learn new techniques. 26/ In the Mumbwa area women flocked to newly-available courses, making complex family arrangements to care for their children. But when they sought to borrow funds to finance the necessary new inputs they had learned about, the rural credit agencies persisted in lending money to males as the presumed household heads. Only the more well-to-do male farmers could buy more complicated machinery and equipment,

The African Experience 115

even for food production; and almost invariably they operated it themselves or hired male day laborers.

A contradictory situation emerged in rural Zambia: 27/ The wives of the wealthiest farmers tended to lose all responsibility for production, becoming increasingly dependent on their husbands. Only in the poorer families, still struggling for bare survival with inadequate tools and little or no fertilizer or irrigation water, could women share more equally with men in decisions about production. Gradually, as larger scale farms introduced new technologies, the options of women in poorer families to contribute to the families' needs tended to be reduced. As more successful male farmers acquired machinery and hired labor to expand their output, they tended to monopolize local markets for foodstuffs, ousting women who had previously headloaded their produce, or carried it on local busses, for sale in nearby villages or urban centers. Eventually, it appeared probable that the male members of these marginal farm families would need to leave for the cities in search of wage employment. The women might stay behind, using the inadequate tools they had to scratch what little they could from worn earth to meet family food needs until -- if -- the men found adequately paying jobs. When they followed their men-folk to the urban centers -- and increasing numbers did -- they almost invariably joined the unemployed or underemployed living in illegal 'squatter' compounds, often without even garden plots. Urban population throughout Africa mushroomed at 10 to 15 percent a year, 28/ and shanty-towns sprawled ever more widely at the foot of towering modern skyscrapers that attested the growing wealth of the 'haves.' The women who came to live in them were typically denied any but the most menial employment. A few turned to prostitution as a source of cash in the context of governmentally-promoted tourism.

Most newly independent African states adopted policies seeking to create 'a hospitable investment climate' to attract import substitution industries, hoping to provide more productive employment opportunities for the growing numbers of urban unemployed. But the transnational corporations made by far their largest manufacturing investments in Africa, not in the newly independent African states, but in South Africa. 29/ There, the ruling white minority denied Africans all political rights. The whole apparatus of apartheid functioned to hold wages of the African four-fifths of the population below the poverty line. 30/ Official doctrine still justified low wages for men, since their wives and families were required by law to live on so-called 'bantustans' ('homelands'), restricted to 13 percent of the national land areas. There, women were expected to produce food to feed the next generation of labor, despite the fact that about 20 percent had no land at all, and most of the rest had infertile scraps incapable of supporting the family. Reliable reports told of chronic malnutrition accompanied by high disease and mortality rates. In one instance, women were depicted as eating only three times a week! 31/

In independent African countries transnational firms limited their investments primarily to last-stage assembly and processing plants to maintain control over local markets behind government-erected tariffs. 32/ They built local plants, frequently partially financed by African governments, in order to sell their advanced machinery and equipment and pre-fabricated parts and materials for last-stage assembly and sale in the African country under a 'made-in-Africa' label. 33/ An electric light bulb factory provides an illuminating example of these firms' limited contribution. It imports the metal base, the glass bulb, and the filament. The only local value added is the vacuum.

These kinds of transnational corporate industries have, for the most part, played a negative role in the development process in the African host countries. 34/ First of all, they do not produce the kinds of tools and equipment at appropriate levels of technology required to increase productivity or process the crops grown either by men or women in the rural areas. On the contrary, they produce sophisticated consumer goods, formerly imported for the narrow high income urban elite, along with a few mass consumed semi-luxury items. Beer and cigarettes provide a significant proportion of the value added.

Production of rayon and nylon textiles -- instead of cotton goods woven from locally grown cotton -- and the assembly of knockdown television sets and private automobiles have become increasingly widespread, requiring the continued import of parts and materials from the associated foreign firm. The African economies have become increasingly dependent on overseas purchases, devoting more and more of their export earnings to this marginally-changed import of manufactured goods produced abroad.

Secondly, factories built in the post-independence era to produce more widely consumed necessities, like cloth, clothing, bread, and bricks, have tended to squeeze out the remaining small scale handicrafts producers, large numbers of whom were women. At independence, a few women in remote rural areas still made and sold clay pots. In more urbanized regions, many women, using simple pedal-driven sewing machines, had earned cash by sewing and selling custom-made clothing. Others baked bread for daily sales in local markets. Still others participated in small-scale and family enterprises making bricks out of local clays for local construction projects.

But urban-based planners and industrial ministries viewed production of pots, clothes-making, brick factories and modern bakeries as potential fields for government promotion of investment to spread modern technologies. These industries do not require much capital or highly advanced skills. The rural industries division of Zambia's parastatal development corporation, INDECO, for example, proclaimed that it was introducing 'modern' bakeries in small towns throughout the countryside. Little attention was paid to the fact that local bakers, many of them women, would no longer be able to sell their home-made produce in competition with these government sponsored concerns. A centralized brick-making factory, using imported machinery, was proposed without regard to the probable ousting of already-existing local, labor-intensive brick-making enterprises.

Thirdly, the new industries tended to be highly-capital intensive. Transnational corporations sought primarily to sell surplus machinery and equipment, designed primarily for their large home markets; they had no intention of retooling to provide technologies more likely to meet the employment needs of third world countries. As a result, the new modern factories furnished relatively few jobs for either men or women. A modern factory to sew clothes might employ a hundred workers; but uncounted hundreds of tailors and seamstresses in remote rural areas might be put out of work. More and more men and women, fleeing rural poverty, found themselves unemployed, competing for low-paid informal sector and service jobs in urban slums. 35/ As urban under- and unemployment mounted, male plant managers and male employees, fearing female competition for the few new jobs created, exercised discriminatory practices to close factory doors to women. 36/ Even clerical and household service work in African cities continued to be done more often than not by men. Increased numbers of women found streetvending, begging, and prostitution as the only ways to earn desperately needed cash.

Only a few African governments sought to attract transnational corporations into 'export-substitution' industries by offering a large supply of low-paid female labor. The highly seasonal sugar industry that pervaded the tiny island economy of Mauritius 37/ created chronic unemployment among men, and almost no jobs at all for women. The government, seeking to emulate Singapore, Taiwan and South Korea, established industrial estates where factories could locate with considerable tax and wage advantages. Women were hired for wages even lower than those men would take.

The poverty level of the Mauritian women factory workers is illustrated by the story 38/ of a U.S. factory manager who complained the women did not produce enough. It was suggested to the manager that the women might be malnourished; if he provided lunch, they might increase output. When he said he would be willing to give the women somewhat higher wages, it was pointed out that their husbands and the rest of the family would probably consume the additional food purchased. The manager finally decided to provide lunches for the women. Their productivity noticeably improved!

Available evidence suggests, in short, that the marginal alteration of the basic institutional structures implanted in the colonial period, combined with renewed attempts to competitively expand crude exports and attract import-substitution industries, tends to further aggravate conditions contributing to the deterioration of the status of women. Inevitably, these factors lead to further impoverishment, not only of the women themselves, but of their entire families. A new kind of vicious circle emerges as their deprivation negatively impacts on their ability to provide for the next generation of labor power, boys as well as girls.

Range of Possible Policies

The above explanation of the deteriorating status of women in Africa suggests that proposals for measures to better their conditions ought to include policies to restructure the national political economies. New institutions need to be developed to implement new patterns of resource allocation capable of providing increasingly productive employment opportunities for all workers, women as well as men, in every sector.

The confines of this brief chapter permit only a summary outline of the kinds of institutions and strategies which might be formulated to provide increasingly productive employment opportunities for men and women in every sector of an increasingly integrated, balanced and self-reliant African economy. The author has elaborated these ideas elsewhere. 39/

First, as experience throughout Africa proves, the issues involved are not merely technical. Narrow elites grasping state power tend to ally themselves with existing national and international institutions perpetuating an externally dependent status quo. The primary requisite for restructuring the local and national political economy is the creation of participatory institutional structures to involve working men and women, together, at all levels of government.

Second, these new participatory state structures need to be directed to ensuring national -- as opposed to transnational corporate -- control of what Tanzania's President Nyerere has called 40/ the 'commanding heights:' basic industries, financial institutions, and export-import and internal wholesale trade. This is essential to ensure that available investable surpluses and foreign exchange earnings are used to implement self-reliant development policies to meet the needs of the majority of the men and women and their families throughout the nation.

Third, a long-term industrial strategy needs to be formulated to ensure that over, say, a 20-year period, the new industries built introduce appropriate kinds of technologies to facilitate the spread of increasingly productive employment opportunities for both women and men in agriculture, manufacturing industries, transport and construction. These will not all necessarily be 'small.' Export processing industries will probably need to be relatively capital-intensive to ensure that nationally processed mineral and agricultural exports can compete effectively on the world market. Only then will they earn the foreign exchange necessary to finance critical machinery and equipment to spread productive employment opportunities into other sectors. Pole of growth industries, those large enough to stimulate the spread of chains of industrial and agricultural growth throughout entire regions, 41/ too, will probably need to be fairly large-scale. A predominant feature of the 20-year strategy, however, must be the formulation and implementation of specific plans to ensure that such large, relative capital-intensive industries are linked to and, in fact, do stimulate construction of essential smaller-scale projects to expand productive employment opportunities for men and women into other sectors of the economy: plants to produce construction materials using local labor and raw materials; small-scale food processing plants to preserve foodstuffs, both expanding local markets and ending the import of processed foods; production of simple, durable, low-cost clothing. Government planners and university and technical institute personnel need to develop participatory research programs 42/ to involve working women and men in considering available local techniques and appropriate new technologies for these kinds of projects.

Fourth, planned long-term financial policies need to ensure that the increasing domestically-produced surpluses are re-invested to ensure fulfillment of the long-term industrial strategy. An incomes policy is important to ensure (1) that credit, taxes, profits and farm incomes are designed to provide adequate incentives to women and men in accord with the work they perform; (2) the gradual expansion of social services -- schools, preventive medicine, low cost housing, etc. -- for all families on the basis of need; and (3) investment of all funds, over and above these planned expenditures, in essential new projects to further expand productive employment opportunities and produce more goods and services to raise national living standards. Implementation of financial policies to attain these goals require critical, participatory evaluation of existing financial institutions -- banks, insurance schemes, and government monetary and taxation programs -- to ensure they plan an appropriate role.

Fifth, working women, as well as men, need to be involved in formulation of a parallel long-term 'personpower' plan, reflecting careful analysis of the kinds of new skills workers will need to implement the industrial strategy; and the ways existing or new educational institutions need to be shaped to enable women, as well as men, to acquire these skills. Education, itself, is a scarce resource in third world nations. It must be planned to enable growing numbers of women and men to manage the increasingly complex technologies introduced into industry and agriculture over the next 20 years and beyond. Attention will need to be directed to avoiding the creation of hierarchical, authoritarian work structures 43/ and elitist 'experts' -- men or women -- who may manipulate new technologies and institutions to their own advantage.

Special attention will need to be directed to helping men, as well as women, understand the need to change working rules and institutions to ensure that women are involved at every level in the new political-economic institutions created, and are trained to participate in the new opportunities opened up by the long-term transformation process. This requires explicit explanation of the impoverization, not only of women, but also their families, when new technologies, introduced in the context of inherited institutional structures intertwined with age-old socialization patterns, relegate women and their work to an inferior status.

The leaders of the liberation movements that freed the former Portuguese colonies, Mozambique, Angola and Guinea-Bissau through more than a decade of guerilla struggle, have re-iterated this point. In Guinea-Bissau, for example, the guerilla forces recognized the vital role of women as the main producers of rice, the national staple food. 44/ Without rice, the guerilla armies could never have mounted the national struggle which ultimately enabled them to declare self-government a year before the fall of the Portuguese dictatorship in Portugal, itself. To ensure the women's support, the leadership convinced the guerilla forces that at least two out of five committee members governing villages in the liberated areas should be women. Over the years, as this rule was enforced, despite the prevalence of strong Muslim traditions in some areas, the peasantry came to understand the value of including women in critical decision-making posts. It would, of course, be over-optimistic to expect centuries of socialization to disappear completely in the span of a few short years. Nevertheless, as a result of this policy, which was essential to win victory against the Portuguese, women gained a new place in the still predominantly peasant society of Guinea-Bissau. They play leading roles, not only on the village level, but also in regional and national decision-making bodies.

When the author interviewed the head of the Guinea-Bissau Women's Commission 45/ -- significantly, she is also head of the national Veterans' Commission -- about factors which should be considered in the possible construction of a necessarily capital-intensive bauxite-alumina project*, her first recommendation was that special provisions be made to ensure that women cadres be trained and given the opportunity to participate at all levels

---

* The total capital required to build the project would exceed the total current national income; but, if successfully planned and implemented, the project might, in five to eight years, end the nation's chronic balance of payment deficit, while enabling them to buy the necessary machinery and equipment to hasten the transformation of their bare subsistence living levels to those more in keeping with the potentials of the 21st Century.

in operating and managing it. She pointed out that experiencing the liberation struggle proved the necessity of continuing concern for the integration of women into all aspects of the national development program. Despite the revolution, she emphasized that past socialization and institutionalized attitudes and practices might still hinder women's full participation unless special attention was directed to overcoming them. At the same time, she underscored the need to ensure that the project itself contributes to restructuring the overall national economy, rather than replicating the enclave type of development typically built by colonial and even post-colonial governments elsewhere. She fully understood the necessity of long-term planning for small scale, more labor intensive projects, built in conjunction with the export-oriented bauxite-alumina project, to spread productive employment opportunities for men and women throughout the national rural economy.

In sum, evidence from the African case tends to support a model exposing the role of technological change in contributing to the deterioration of women's status within the context of what has come to be known as the process of 'development of underdevelopment.' Post-independence government policies, accompanied by only marginal changes in the institutional and resource allocation patterns inherited from the colonial past, foster introduction of enclave-type capital-intensive technologies in agriculture and industry without regard to balanced, integrated national development. They provide few jobs to (primarily male) workers mostly using imported parts and materials to produce sophisticated consumer goods, mainly for a narrow, high income elite. They contribute to the on-going vicious circle of further impoverishment of the majority of women and their families in the context of growing external dependence.

Analysis of the evidence relating to the model suggests the need for further research, especially as to the contradictory impact of stratification on women's status when new technologies are introduced in the context of inherited institutions. The underlying explanation portrayed argues, nevertheless, that, to avoid further deterioration of women's status, new strategies are required to introduce improved technologies within a framework of broader institutional changes restructuring the national political economy to provide increasingly productive employment opportunities for both women and men. Research related to the on-going experiences of recently-liberated Portuguese colonies seeking to implement this type of transformation may be particularly instructive. As the head of the Women's Commission in Guinea-Bissau pointed out, measures to restructure the economy, while necessary, are not sufficient. They need to be accompanied by vigorous educational efforts to overcome inherited socialization patterns and institutionalized practices which traditionally have tended to exclude women from new opportunities created.

References

1. Conference on Women and Development, Wellesley Center for Research on Women, June, 1976 (Wellesley College, Wellesley, Mass.).

2. Cf. Lord Lugard, The Dual Mandate in British Tropical Africa (London: Frank Cass & Co., 1965) p. 614, 43.

3. Harry Johnstone, Trade and General Conditions Report (Nyasaland, 1895-96)

4. R. S. Odingo, The Kenya Highlands: Land Use and Agricultural Change (Nairobi: East African Publishing House, 1969.

5. W. J. Barber, The Economy of British Central Africa: A Case Study of Economic Development in a Dualistic Society (Stanford University Press, 1961).

6. R. Riddell, The Land Question (London: Catholic Institute for International Relations, 1 Cambridge Terrace, London, England, 1978).

7. For description of Bantustans in South Africa, see A. and N. Seidman, South Africa and U.S. Multinational Corporations (Westport, Conn: Lawrence Hill, 1977).

8. N. T. Newlyn and D. C. Rowan, Money and Banking in British Colonial Africa (Oxford: Clarendon Press, 1954).

9. The author has seen ancient iron smelting works, hidden in the bush, away from the eyes of colonial administrators of Northern Rhodesia (now Zambia) because of legal restrictions.

10. The copper mining companies in Northern Rhodesia introduced advanced technologies to enable them to utilize what otherwise would have been ore grades too low to exploit. The sisal estates in Tanzania had up-to-date machinery for operations.

11. cf. S. Young, "Fertility and Famine: Women's Agricultural History in Southern Mozambique," in R. Palmer and N. Parsons, eds., The Roots of Rural Poverty in Central and Southern Africa (Berkeley: University of California Press, 1977) pp. 66-81.

12. Interview with National Archivist, Zambia, 1974.

13. B. Lewis' chapter in N.J. Hafkin and E. G. Bay (eds.) Women in Africa (Stanford: Stanford University Press, 1976).

14. Lord Hailey, An African Survey (London: Oxford University Press, 1957) p. 701.

15. K. Marx, Capital, A Critique of Political Economy (Chicago: Charles H. Kerr & Co., 1906), Vol. 1, p. 189ff.

16. A. Seidman, Planning for Development in SubSaharan Africa, (New York: Praeger, 1974) pp. 62-3.

17. L. Van Horn, "The Agricultural History of Barotseland, 1840-1964" in Palmer and Parsons, Roots of Rural Poverty, op. cit., Ch. 6.

18. Palmer and Parsons, Roots of Rural Poverty, op. cit., passim.

19. As was forecast by M. Blundell in So Rough a Wind, The Kenya Memoirs of Sir Michel Blundell (London: Widenfeld and Nicolson, 1964), pp. 178, 217, 263.

20. Seidman, Planning for Development, op. cit.

21. A. Seidman, "Old Motives, New Methods: Foreign Enterprise in Africa Today" African Perspectives, R. W. Johnson and C.H. Allen, eds. (Cambridge University Press, 1970).

22. See Food and Agricultural Organization, Annual Yearbook, and United Nations, Department of Economic and Social Affairs, Yearbook of International Trade Statistics (annual), for data re increased export crop output and gross domestic product per capita.

23. Reported at Law and Development Seminar, Institute for Development Studies, University of Nairobi, June, 1976.

24. R. Mabeza, field study, Zambia, August, 1978; results to be reported in MA Thesis, Clark University, International Development and Social Change. 1979.

The African Experience 125

25. R. Apthorpe, "Some Problems of Evaluation," in C.G. Widstrand (ed) Cooperatives and Rural Development in East Africa, pp. 213-219 (New York: Africana Publishing Corp., 1970).

26. e. g. Mumbwa district, Zambia, reported by R. Mabeza, op. cit.

27. See discussion in R. Mabeza, Thesis, op. cit.

28. In Zambia, the urban population more than doubled from 25 percent of the national population to 40 percent in the decade after independence was attained. (See Central Statistical Office (Lusaka), Monthly Digest of Statistics re population changes).

29. A. W. Seidman and N. Makgetla, "Activities of Transnational Corporations in South Africa," Notes and Documents, U.N. Centre Against Apartheid.

30. A. & N. Seidman, South Africa and U. S. Multinational Corporations, op. cit., Ch. 2.

31. Cf. Father Cosmos Desmond, The Discarded People (Harmondsworth: Penguin Books, 1971).

32. For discussion of the advantages to business of this type of approach, see Business International, S.A., Prospects for Business in Developing Africa.

33. For discussion of reasons for investing in Africa, see Business International S.A., Prospects for Business in Developing Africa, (Geneva: Business International S.A.)1970.

34. For an analysis of the typical impact, see A. Seidman, "The Need for a long-term Industrial Strategy in Zambia," in Seidman, (ed.) Natural Resources and National Welfare: The Case of Copper (New York: Praeger, 1976) Ch. 22.

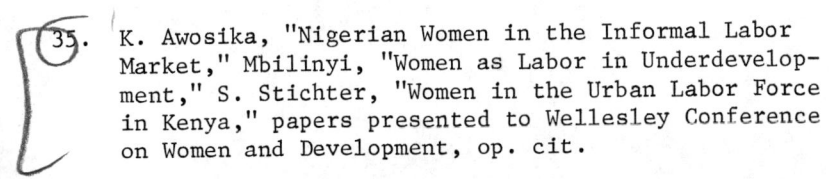

35. K. Awosika, "Nigerian Women in the Informal Labor Market," Mbilinyi, "Women as Labor in Underdevelopment," S. Stichter, "Women in the Urban Labor Force in Kenya," papers presented to Wellesley Conference on Women and Development, op. cit.

36. M. Mbilinyi, "Women as Labour in Underdevelopment" paper presented at Wellesley Conference on Women and Development, op. cit.

37. Studied by author during a week-long seminar on Law and Development with permanent first secretaries of the major ministries in Mauritius.

38. Reported by U.S. Embassy Official to author. 1973

39. A. Seidman, Planning for Development in SubSaharan Africa, (Dar es Sallaam: Tanzania Publishing House, and New York: Praeger, 1974)

40. J. K. Nyerere, A Selection from Writings and Speeches, 1965-67, (Dar es Salaam: Oxford University Press, 1968) pp. 231-250.

41. For discussion of pole of growth concept, see R. H. Green and A. Seidman in Unity or Poverty? The Economics of PanAfricanism (Harmondsworth: Penguin Books, 1968)

42. The importance of developing participatory research involving women themselves, rather than studies of women as 'targets' was re-iterated at the Wingspread Workshop on Women and Development; see the report of that workshop, Women and Development (Racine, Wisconsin: Johnson Foundation, 1976).

43. The prevalence of hierarchical, authoritarian workplace structures was underscored as a problem in the United States at the conference held by the Harvard Graduate School of Education and Change Magazine on Work and Education, April 26-7, 1979.

44. J. Van Allen, "Revolutionary Strategies for Change in Africa," paper presented to Wellesley Conference on Women and Development, op. cit.

45. During a two week mission to Guinea-Bissau to participate in an evaluation of the possibilities and problems of constructing a bauxite-alumina project in August, 1978.

Melinda L. Cain

7. Java, Indonesia: The Introduction of Rice Processing Technology

Introduction

Mechanized rice hullers were introduced in Java, Indonesia, in an attempt to modernize agriculture there and thus to increase rice production. In addition, the use of sickles and scales, and the tebasan harvesting system, were employed towards the same goal (1). However, the introduction of this technology also created labor displacement, particularly among women who traditionally were involved in rice harvesting.

This article will summarize some of the major social and economic impacts stemming from the Government of Indonesia's attempt to modernize agriculture. It serves to illustrate the ramifications of introduction of technology without due consideration to the social context. In particular, the role of women and the impact of technology on them is of importance, because the women were traditional rice harvesters and processors. (It is acknowledged that hand-pounding is not easy work, and was not enjoyed by women. However, it did supply a needed source of income, and therefore, was missed for that reason)(2). One might suggest that women are sometimes "three times burdened" by the problems of development. That is, first, there are problems which are not specific to women, but characteristic of lower incomes compared to middle and upper income groups in general, e.g., insufficient access to resources—land, capital, technology, education, governmental services; longer working hours with lower incomes; lower social status and relatively little influence in the process of decision making in society. Second, lower income women face problems specifically related to their status as women. Special attention to them is required in order to achieve a greater participation in the process of social and economic development. These include an even more restricted access to resources; longer working hours and even lower incomes than those of men in the same social-economic class; the special burden of household tasks and child rearing; and lower status in society than that of males in the same social class, resulting in even less or no influence on community decision making. Finally, the large group of rural women without resident husbands are those who might be called "three times burdened." That is, they experience all the difficulties faced by lower income classes in general and the additional difficulties faced by poor rural women without having an adult male to join them in income earning activity or represent them as household head in the community (3).

Thus, the increase in rice production in Indonesia must be weighed against the loss of income for women. Production goals, in this case, triumphed as they probably should have. However, an effort should have been made to develop alternative sources of income for the displaced women. Thus, it is within this framework, that the situation of women and processing technology in rural Java will be examined.

Background

Indonesia includes more than 13,000 islands, the largest of which is Java. Java covers only 6 percent of the total land area (about the size of New York State) but contains two-thirds of the country's total population of 135 million. (It is interesting to note that in 1870 Indonesia's population was 1.6 million; by 1965 it had reached 69.2 million. Now, in a little over ten years, it has almost doubled.) More than 80 percent of this population resides in rural areas. In contrast, other islands (Kalemantan, Sulawesi, Sumatra) do not have enough labor for production.

Indonesia is representative of the more than one-half of the world's population that depends on rice for a basic food supply. Approximately 90 percent of the world's rice is produced in Asia (4). Sixty percent of the total calories and 65 percent of the protein in the Indonesian diet come from rice (5). Domestic consumption of rice in Indonesia is higher than the country's capacity to produce it, which means that rice must be imported to meet local demand. In fact, in 1978 Indonesia was the world's largest importer of rice.

Obviously, agriculture is crucially important to the Indonesian economy. For example, in 1968 it contributed about 50 percent of the Gross Domestic Product, provided employment for about 70 percent of the total labor force, and produced about 50 percent of all exports (6). In the second five-year plan of Indonesia, REPELITA II, national efforts were defined as being direct to increase productivity and achieve ultimate self-sufficiency in rice production, to expand agricultural exports and to reduce rural unemployment (7). The largest single program in the plan is to increase the production of rice (paddy), of secondary crops (such as corn, sorghum, cassava, soybeans, and peanuts), and of horticulture. The plan outlines increases in rice production from 14.5 million tons in 1973/1974 to 18.2 million tons in 1978/79, or an average annual increase of 4.6 percent, which is about double the rate of population growth. The increase in production is primarily due to the expansion of cultivated land and to increases in per-hectare yields. The governmental program (initially launched in 1968 and revised on several occasions since that time) to support the campaign for increased rice production is called BIMAS, an acronym taken from the Indonesian expression "Bimbingan Massal" ("mass-guidance"). This program is attempting to mobilize the Indonesian peasants in an effort that involves a massive infusion of fertilizer and high-yielding seed varities (HYV). Some reports indicate that the program has been far from successful for a variety of political and administrative reasons (8). Nonetheless, the national goals of increased rice production and self-sufficiency remain.

Since 1971, when Amir Khan of IRRI wrote that most of the rice production in Asia was done with traditional, nonmechanical methods, a strong effort has been made to mechanize rice cultivation. This effect has not been without problems, however, as noted by Khan:

"Mechanization of rice production in the tropics has many problems which still remain unsolved. Attempts to transfer the highly advanced Western and Japanese mechanization technologies have not produced effective results for the small farm holdings in the tropical regions. The overwhelming need today is to develop an intermediate mechanization technology to suit the prevailing set of agricultural, socioeconomic, and industrial conditions of the tropical regions (9).

Traditional Rice Harvesting

Traditionally, Javanese rice farmers did not restrict anyone who wished to participate in the rice harvest. The harvesters were mostly women from within the village and from neighboring villages. The women used an ani-ani (small finger knife) for harvesting. The ani-ani was suitable for cutting local varieties that matured at different times and had varying stalk lengths. The harvesters carried the rice in sheaves, bound in the field, on shoulder poles to the owner's house. This method of harvesting required large numbers of people, and literally thousands of landless families were involved. In fact, one farm survey showed as many as 500 persons employed per hectare (10). The harvester's pay was a share of the crop, with a ratio of about seven to ten for the owner and one for the harvester. The division was made by bundles and not by weight.

The Tebasan Harvesting System and the Use of Sickles and Scales

Traditional methods of rice harvesting in Java have changed significantly partly because of the increased population pressures on land. Individual farm sizes have become smaller as farms have been subdivided from generation to generation, and it has become more difficult for farmers to run a profitable business. The population increase also has meant that a larger number of landless laborers are looking for harvesting work. As the amount received by harvesters has grown smaller, they have tried to obtain larger shares than custom dictates. Furthermore, farmers customarily have felt a social obligation to let all the harvesters participate. Therefore, farmers have found their share of the harvest diminishing.

One way of improving the farmers' share is to limit harvesters. This can be done by the adoption of the tebasan system. Tebasan is a harvesting sytem that enables the farmer to sell his crop to the penebas (middleman) before harvest. This limits the number of harvesters and avoids the problems of supervising the harvest and dividing the shares. About one week before the harvest, the farmer sells his crop to a buyer, who then arranges for the harvest and sells the rice. The penebas may be from the same village or from outside the village. The farmer usually is paid within one week after the harvest if not at harvest time.

The penebas is recognized as a trader, and his right to a profit is accepted. Individual harvesters may benefit from this sytem, especially when the penebas can control the number of participants, thereby ensuring larger returns for each harvester. Based on village surveys, some rice always has been purchased by the tebasan method. However, the system has become more important with the use of HYV, because there are now two harvesting seasons, and thus, more rice to harvest.

A comparison of costs of harvesting with the penebas were estimated from a sample of village surveys. Using the ani-ani rice knife and the traditional system, the estimated harvesting costs were about $30.00 per hectare. Comparing those costs with about $15.00 per hectare that it costs the penebas to harvest, it is evident that the harvest costs can be reduced about 50% by using the tebasan system (11).

Tebasan and the introduction of HYVs have caused an important technical change in the method of harvesting rice: this is the use of the sickle. The ani-ani is more suitable for cutting traditional varieties of rice; the sickle is preferable for cutting the HYV. When the sickle is used, the rice is threshed in the field, then carried in sacks to the penebas's house, where harvesters are paid in cash according to the weight, not according to bundles. Thus, when the penebas began to use sickles, scales became necessary to weigh the shares for the harvesters. Furthermore, harvesters must provide their own sickles, threshing mats, and sacks to carry the rice. With sickles, only about 75 person days are required to harvest one hectare, while with the ani-ani, 200 or more person-days may be needed.

The Introduction of Rice Hullers

Due to governmental initiative, mechanized rice hullers were introduced in 1970 to 1971. The diffusion of hullers occurred very rapidly after 1970, as illustrated by Table 1. By 1978, only about 10 percent was being hand-pounded, mostly for family consumption (12).

An English model by Engleberg is widely used in the Philippines. This machine has few moving parts and is very durable. However, a Japanese model that uses rubber rollers is more common in Indonesia. Pasawahan, a village in west Java, has three milling centers that use the Japanese hullers and polishers.

Rice must be processed through the machine four to eight times. It is first poured into the top of the huller; the hulls and (bran) excess material then travel through a pipe and are discarded outside the building. The hulled rice is then run through the polisher three or four times.

Choice of Technology and Economic Aspects

Timmer has discussed the choice of the rice hulling technology in Indonesia by analyzing the four alternative milling/storage/drying facilities that were considered by USAID/Jakarta and the Indonesian government in order to "modernize" the rice marketing sector. He mentions four efficient alternatives, of which the most capital-intensive required $65,000 investment per worker and the most labor-

Table 1. Number of Sample Farmers Processing Rice with Hullers, and Numbers of Hullers in Sample Villages, 1970 and 1973 (*)

	No. of Farmers in Sample	No. of Farmers Processing Rice with Hullers 1970	No. of Farmers Processing Rice with Hullers 1973	Number of Hullers in the Village 1970	Number of Hullers in the Village 1971
West Java					
Kab. Serang					
Sentul	27	0	0	0	0
Warungjaud	24	0	17	0	*
Kab. Cianjur					
Jati	29	15	29	3	5
Gekbrong	27	0	0	0	0
Central Java					
Kab. Banyumas					
Kebanggan	30	0	29	0	1
Sukaraja Lor	30	0	22	0	*
Kab. Kebumen					
Bulus Pesantren	30	0	27	0	*
Patemon	30	2	25	0	1
East Java					
Kab. Ngawi					
Geneng	29	0	26	0	3
Gemarang	30	n.a.	21	0	2
Kab. Jember					
Sukosari	30	0	26	0	8
Tanggulwetan	28	8	27	n.a.	8

*Farmers from these villages used hullers in neighboring villages.
Source: Collier, "Choice of Technique in Rice Milling: A Comment." Bulletin of Indonesian Economic Studies, Vol. X(1), March 1974. Reprinted by permission.

intensive required only $700 (13). Timmer also points out that beneath the decision to modernize lay a deep-felt bias on the part of Western and Western-trained technicians that "identified capital-intensive with modern, and modern with good (14)." Such value judgments may play an important role in determining technological choice, as shown by the widespread introduction of the Japanese rice mill.

In part due to Timmer and other work, the Indonesian government chose the mechanical but less-high technology alternative because it was economically preferable. Also, loans to buy hullers were available at 1 percent per month interest, whereas regular village credit runs about 5 to 10 percent per month. Therefore, the machines were well subsidized and available to those who could afford them.

Collier estimates the average investment costs of a hulling center to be $3,111 for machinery, buildings, and land. Such a hulling center would have an average capacity of .58 tons per hour. This figure is based on the combined use of old and new equipment. Timmer estimates $8,049 as the initial cost of a hulling center with a capacity of .42 tons per hour (15).

In Pasawahan, the initial cost of a huller in 1976 was Rp 2.5 million (or about U.S. $4,000). The owner of the huller said that operating costs were low except for repair, which did not occur very often. Both the huller and polisher were diesel-powered, using a crude kerosene fuel that cost Rp 30 per liter (five cents per liter, or less than twenty cents per gallon). Ten liters would run the huller for five hours or about one ton of rice. Repair costs so far had been few. The owner pointed out a small part that had recently been replaced for Rp 40,000 (sixty-six dollars).

At this particular hulling center or mill, about two tons of rice could be hulled per day. (This compared to the hand-pounding of forty kilograms per day by one woman.) Two men who operated the huller and polisher could process about 100 kilograms of rice in twenty minutes and were paid Rp 45 for every 100 kilograms. Labor use as estimated by Collier was four to five hand laborers to hull 92 tons per month (average) in contrast to Timmer's estimates of twelve laborers to hull 1,000 tons per year.

In order to compare costs of using hullers and hand-pounding, it was found in one survey that the average cost of hand-pounding was $1.45 per 100 kilograms. In comparison, the average cost to the farmer of using a huller was $.54 per kilogram. In addition, the by-products were kept by the miller while in the traditional harvest, women were able to keep the by-products to use as animal feed (16).

Impact of the Technology

During the last five years, the mill has taken over work traditionally done by women. Two examples illustrate these changes: "A former rice trader, now turned mill owner, stated that he used to employ eight women to hand pound his rice. Four women working five hours could hand pound 100 kilograms of gabah. This rice trader could buy 200 kilograms per day of gabah. The women's wages were 10 percent of the rice they provided, which amounted to just under two liters of milled rice per day. Thus, over the harvest season these eight women earned perhaps sixty liters of milled rice each or enough to feed themselves for four months." "In Kendal, Central Java, a farmer said that in the past there were more than 100 women "hand-pounder" laborers in his village. But now they have no work (17)."

Estimates of jobs lost ranged as high as 1.2 million in Java alone and as high as 7.7 million in all of Indonesia as a result of the introduction of the new technology. Collier estimated that the loss to laborers in earnings due to the use of hullers was U.S. $50 million annually in Java, representing 125 million woman days of labor.

The rice farmer pays less to the mill for threshing and the process is much quicker, but the women have lost a highly remunerative source of income. They are now forced to work longer hours at other jobs, if such can even be found. The shift from a traditional technology to a more modern one has eliminated one of the more important sources of income for landless villagers.

Thus, although the adoption of the use of HYV, tebasan, sickles, scales, and rice hullers has served to increase rice production in Indonesia, it has not helped to solve the problems of unemployment and income distribution in Java. Rather, it appears these problems have been exacerbated. Furthermore, there is little evidence to indicate that the rural unemployed are being taken up by work opportunities in the cities, or have been able to find replacement sources of income in the rural areas.

Concluding Remarks

Indonesia, to state the obvious, is a land of contrasts. Java and Bali are islands with dense populations that create massive unemployment problems. Other island (Kalimantan,

Sulawesi, Sumatra) lack enough labor for production purposes. While the observations made in this case refer specifically to Java, it is important to note the differences within Indonesia and to refrain from generalizing to other islands. This implies that it is possible, if not probable, that regional variations within a country might well dictate the need for several different policy packages vis a vis technology choice or use within a single country. In this case, the policy for modernizing agriculture was applied generally throughout Indonesia, and as illustrated on Java, this caused some unanticipated, negative impacts.

In addition to illustrating the need for region-specific technology policies, this case also shows that technology, itself, is neutral; it is the use of technology that determines whether it has positive or negative effects. It is, therefore, important to consider who will own the technology and who will benefit from its use. On Java, those with a substantial income were able to afford the new technology. Those who were at the subsistence level (mostly women) were not in a favorable position to purchase the hullers and thereby lost access to one source of income. In contrast, I was told that women in W. Sumatra have used the introduction of rice hullers to their advantage. Due to the matriarchical system, women there own land and make agricultural decisions. They were able to form cooperative groups with sufficient access to financial resources to buy the hullers, and use them profitably.

Finally, this case describes a common trade-off in development situations: modernization or mechanization versus labor utilization. It is difficult to call rice mills a "mistake" because the process is more efficient in terms of input/output, and such efficiency is necessary due to national goals of increased rice production. Furthermore, hand-pounding of rice is an arduous task, and it is unlikely that the women were sad to see such hard work be replaced. However, if technology is to be introduced that may have implications for labor displacement, a prudent policy consideration would be to provide alternative sources of income, employment and training for those who might be displaced. One way to deal with these consequences is to promote rural industry based on local materials. For example, in one Javanese village where brick making is a local industry, some women have turned to pounding gravel. Bricks are of higher quality when the women are used, becasue gravel is a better substance for the bricks than the sand that is used when women are not involved. Thus, with some creativity, alternative sources of income can be found.

Notes

1. This case history is relevant to one island--Java. Generalizations suggested here are not applicable to other Indonesian islands.

2. Ben White, et al. "Studying Rural Women in W. Java." Bogor, January, 1979.

3. IBID.

4. Amir U. Khan. "Present and Future Development of the Mechanization of Rice Production." Paper No. 71-06 (Manila, The Philippines: International Rice Research Institute (IRRI), 1971.

5. Personal Communication, Director Tomadias, Social-Economic Division, Nutritional Research and Development Center, Department of Health, Bogor, Indonesia.

6. A. T. Birow, "Pembaugunau Pertanian and Shategi Industrialisasi, "Prisma," (August 1972): 31.

7. Government of Indonesia, Department of Information, REPLITA II, p. 19.

8. Gary E. Hansen, "Indonesia's Green Revolution: The Abandonment of a Non-Market Strategy Towards Chance." SEADAG Papers (New York: The Asia Society, 1971); and Gary E. Hansen, The Politics and Administration of Rural Development in Indonesia. The Case of Agriculture. Research Monograph No. 9 (Berkeley: University of California, Center for South Southeast Asia Studies, 1973).

9. Khan, "Present and Future Development of the Mechanization of Rice Production."

10. William L. Collier, et al., "Agricultural Technology and Institutional Change in Java," Food Research Institute Studies 13 (2): 174.

11. IBID, p. 185.

12. Personal communication, Pudjiwati Sajogyo, Center for Rural Sociological Research and Soesarsono, Food Technology Development Center, Bogor.

13. Peter Timmer, "The Choice of Techniques in Rice Hulling in Indonesia." Harvard University: Center for International Affairs, 1975), p.25.

14. IBID.

15. Collier, "Choice of Technique in Rice Milling: A Comment. *Bulletin of Indonesia Economic Studies* Vol. X(1) March, 1974. pp.113-15.

16. IBID, p. 115.

17. IBID, p. 108.

Grace S. Hemmings-Gapihan

8. Baseline Study for Socio-Economic Evaluation of Tangaye Solar Site

Introduction

In 1978 I conducted a baseline socio-economic study in the village of Tangaye, Upper Volta. The study preceded the installation of a solar unit, the first of its kind in Upper Volta. Research was focused on the three issues affected by the installation of the solar unit in the village. These were: 1) the need for alternative, inexpensive sources of energy; 2) the need for labour-saving devices, particularly for women; 3) most significantly, the means of integrating a highly complex technology into village society. In regard to the third issue, my purpose was to discover, and perhaps activate, the structures within the village that could potentially administer the solar unit. This is to say distributing the services equitably and permanently, as well as providing adequate maintenance.

Description of the Solar Unit

The solar unit consists of two compounds: a solar cell array designed to transform solar energy into electricity and a battery designed to store electricity. This photovoltaic system, as it is so named, supplies the electric energy necessary to power a food grinding capacity of 92 kilograms of sorghum per hour. Millet and maize may also be ground though at a reduced hourly capacity. The pump is capable of pumping 1,457 liters of water per hour. One of the most significant attributes of the solar unit is that it has a battery that stores energy. Although there are other solar energy units in Upper Volta, this system is unique in the country.

Description of Tangaye

The village of Tangaye was chosen as the site for this

pilot project for many reasons, among them the village's accessibility. It is located on a major road linking Ouagadougou, the capital of Upper Volta, to Fada N'Gourma, a semi-urban administrative center. Since most of the technical monitoring of the unit originates from Ouagadougou, ease of access was an important consideration in the selection of a site.

Tangaye is a large village with a population of approximately 2,000 inhabitants. It is located in a high population density rural zone. There are at least 40 inhabitants per square kilometer. Residents refer to themselves as the Zaose and are genealogically linked to the Mossi. According to their accounts, they are sedentarized pastoralists. Most of the villagers combine subsistence agriculture with animal husbandry.

The village is located in the eastern region of Upper Volta within the sudanic zone. Roughly speaking there are two distinct seasons characteristic of this zone. These are the dry season from November to May and the rainy season from June to October.

During the rainy season, farming is practised to the exclusion of all other activities. Farmers cultivate the staples, millet and sorghum. Small quantities of corn, rice, and peanuts are grown in addition to a variety of other products.

Activities during the dry season vary. High population density and poor soil conditions contribute to inadequate food supplies. Since the villagers do not produce the necessary quantity of food to sustain themselves for the entire year, dry season activities are crucial. Villagers must earn money during this season to supplement their meager food supply. They do this by engaging in all forms of small scale business ventures. These include migrant labour, production and sale of crafts, and marketing processed foods. Thus, food processing and water consumption are at their height in the dry season. It became quite clear that this was the season in which labour-saving devices of reduced energy costs, such as promised by the solar unit, would be most useful.

Labour-Saving Devices and the Cost of Fuel

Everyone agrees on the importance of solar energy systems, especially in countries such as Upper Volta, where there are few natural energy resources. Wood is the main fuel utilized by the majority of the population. Suffice it to say that deforestation, in this drought-ridden land, is a growing problem.

When one considers the energy supplies required for powering food grinding mills, the fuel problem in Upper Volta acquires greater significance. Mills are powered by diesel oil which must be imported at rising costs to the millers. In the past the population has seen the cost of milling services increase with the rise in fuel cost. The increase in rate means fewer people can afford to use the mills. A vivid example of this is provided by the case of a milling establishment in the vicinity of Tangaye. When the cost of fuel rose 33 percent three years ago, the miller raised his fees 25 percent. This raise was equal to two American cents (5 francs CFA). As a result of this he lost so many customers that he was forced to open the mill twice a week, on market days, rather than every day as he had done in the past. Few people in the area could afford the 25 percent increase in milling rates. Expenditures for fuel comprise 50-60 percent of the monthly cost of running the mill.

Clearly an inexpensive source of energy is essential if the residents of the area are to have access to labour-saving devices. The limited monetary resources of the people places major constraints on the degree to which they may utilize local labour-saving devices, particularly in light of rising fuel costs.

Use of Commercial Mills in the Area

As forementioned, the villagers have had experience with labour-saving devices in the form of commercial mills. Interviews and observations at these mills revealed the degree to which the population in the village and elsewhere relied on the services of the mill.

There were two such mills in the vicinity of Tangaye. In a village-wide survey it was reported that, though infrequently, almost all families had used commercial mills at one time or another. Approximately 61 percent of the visits were made after 1975. This was so despite the fact that mills had been in the vicinity since 1968. The majority of these visits (55 percent) were made during the rainy season. Large quantities of millet, more than eight liters, were usually ground on these visits.

Most of the villagers did not visit the mills regularly. Those who used the mills regularly were generally vendors who sold regularly in the market where the mill was housed. The majority of the residents of Tangaye availed themselves of the mill only on special occasions.

Daily observations at mill sites revealed that more than 90 percent of the customers utilizing the mill were women. They were for the most part residents of the village in which the mill was housed. They came to grind small quantities of grain for the evening meal. This shows that the services of the mill are still in great demand even for women who do not market as regularly as vendors.

Solar Mill and Pump: Labour-Saving Devices for Women and Herders

The two segments of the population most directly affected by the services provided by the solar unit are women and herders. Women are primarily responsible for furnishing the drinking and cooking water used in their homes. They are also responsible for processing grain for the preparation of all the food consumed in the village.

One of the questions that I set out to ascertain was the degree to which the pump and grinder would be a labour-saving device. Exactly how much labour and how much time was involved? To do this it was necessary to measure as accurately as possible the time consumed in food processing and water procuring activities. This segment of the study was divided in two sections: 1) food processing activities among women and 2) water procuring activities among men and women. In addition, an estimate of daily food and water consumption was made, thus establishing the extent to which the services of the solar unit would meet demands in the village.

Food

It was established that diet, food preparation and level of consumption varied significantly from dry to farming season. Time constraints and available food resources showed marked seasonal variations.

The dry season is the social season. A larger variety of food is available in greater quantities. This is because it is the season immediately following the harvest. Food preparation for feasts, and more commonly for marketing, takes on added importance. Grain is usually ground for the purposes of brewing beer and baking cakes commonly sold on the market. During the dry season it was shown that women spend at least 60 percent of their work day processing food and fetching water.

In the rainy season, however, women had to devote the greater part of their work day to farming. Marketing diminishes. The frequency of consumption of food increases with the expenditure of energy required for farm labour. During this season, food is prepared twice a day. Sometimes large cultivation parties organized for bride service requires large scale preparation of food. The burden of labour increases twofold for women at this time. They must cultivate as well as prepare meals twice as often.

Yet the women employ many labour-saving devices. These, coupled with the greater availability of water due to the rainy season, cut down on the time women devote to processing food and obtaining water. Thus, women spend only 30 percent of their working day processing food and obtaining water. It must be stated that their working day was considerably longer in the rainy season. In absolute terms, women diminished their cooking time by one hour and the time spent in search of water by one hour and ten minutes.

They diminished their cooking time by altering various aspects of their customary food processing methods. This included occasionally cooking whole grains rather than making flour and grinding a coarser rather than a finer flour. A kilo of red sorghum may take anywhere from 20 minutes to one and a half hours to grind depending on the quality of flour desired. Thus women may save up to an hour of grinding time if they are willing to eat coarsely ground flour.

It was established, therefore, that the mill would be a great help to women in the dry season when the volume of food processing was at its height. Women had already found ways to diminish the time spent in food processing during the rainy season. Therefore, the presence of a mill might affect the quality of the food consumed rather than contribute to any great degree to the time saved in processing, especially when one considers the time taken to travel to the mill, waiting to be served, etc.

Water

Villagers' use of wells showed dramatic seasonal variations. People depended entirely on wells for their water supply during the dry season. During the rainy season, however, the wells are almost never used. The population relies on seasonal sources of water provided by the often torrential rains. The earth in this area is not very absorbent. Water slides off the soil and settles in depressions in the earth, thus forming pools. These pools are often more conveniently located than the wells. In addition, the people prefer certain types of water laden with calcium-like deposits. They label this type of water "white water." It is considered to be healthier and more palatable than well water. Hence the water pump will have added importance in the dry season when water is scarce and people must drink, bathe, cook, wash their clothes, and water cattle from diminishing sources of water.

Many wells dry out at this time of the year, rendering the population dependent on a few sources and forcing women to travel long distances in search of water. This is a time of numerous conflicts over the use of water sites, particularly between women and herders. Herders, often the proprietors of the wells, forbid women the use of the wells at certain times of the day when they must water their cattle. Women often have to wake up very early in the morning, before sunrise, in order to obtain enough water to meet their daily needs. Women averaged ten trips per day to the water sites during the dry season. They covered a distance of approximately seven kilometers per day. This distance was covered while transporting heavy containers of water. Herders had to lead animals to the wells and supply them with large quantities of water.

The solar unit provides one pump, located on one of the major wells of the villages. As a labour-saving device, it is quite limited. The pump relieves the effort of drawing water from the well. Clearly, the pump will be much more attractive to herders than it will be to women. The main burden in this case is the necessity to draw large quantities of water. Women, however, must transport water over long distances. Thus, the main effort is in the transportation. I would venture to say that, given a choice, women will utilize the nearest source of water rather than the pump. Herders, however, will simply walk their animals a greater distance in order to utilize the pump which will save them the effort of drawing water. This arrangement may still be advantageous to women, however, since women may find that the wells closest to them have been liberated once the herders are drawn to the pump.

Water technology is an important issue raising many questions above and beyond those raised in the present study. I find that in Upper Volta, as in many other parts of the world, the primary issue is the lack of an adequate water supply. Consequently, the problems most of the villagers are facing are tied to the distribution of a scarce resource.

Development agents raise other pressing issues related to water consumption, health being among the primary concerns. The provision of "clean" water as a means of improving the health of the population is one of the major reasons given for the "necessity" to construct pumps and wells. I suggest that before tampering with the locally available water sources various issues must be carefully taken into account. A study should be made of the various water-borne illnesses known to the villagers and the segments of the population most afflicted. Studies have shown that water-borne illnesses strike infants under the age of five primarily. The rest of the population, i.e., those who have survived beyond this dangerous stage, are uniquely adapted to the water resources available within the region. Providing a "purer" source of water, especially by utilizing technology that the villagers have difficulty replicating or repairing, may interfere with the biological adaptation of the population to the available water resources. If the technology cannot be replicated in the regions, the provision of clean water risks being merely temporary as well as highly localized.

The cultural definition of clean water is another issue that bears scrutiny. In Tangaye the villagers drank well water only when their preferred sources of water were unavailable. The preferred water is labeled "white water" as described earlier and is generally found in ponds filled by the rains.

Another important service developers seem eager to provide is the lightening of the burden of carrying water. Transportation of water is cited as one of woman's greatest burdens. In my original study, "Baseline Study for the Socio-Economic Evaluation of Tangaye Solar Installation," I found a relationship between water consumption and proximity to the water source. I demonstrated that people living closest to the water source consistently utilized greater amounts of water. Since lightening the effort expended in procuring water often results in increased consumption of water, a country of scarce water resources--such as Upper Volta--faces possible disaster if pumps and the like are carelessly installed. Unless one has a means of increasing the local water supply, the above as well as other issues must be responsibly evaluated before embarking on a water amelioration program.

Management of the Solar Unit

Technical aspects of the functioning of the mill are by no means the most important consideration. Most important is the integration of such a system in the recipient society. There are numerous examples of useful technology either being abandoned by the local population or giving rise to social abuses.

It seems to me to be out of the question to expect government agencies in Upper Volta, a country poor in administrative resources, to be solely responsible for the management of the mill and pump. Indeed, if the project is to be extended to other areas it is imperative that the management of the mill be local. My purpose in designing the management plan was threefold: 1) to stimulate personal interest on the part of the villagers in the management of the mill; 2) to make the services of the mill accessible and profitable to all segments of the population; 3) to minimize the possible social abuses in the distribution of the services.

We are dealing with a complex and delicate issue requiring sensitive handling and striking at the very foundations of common procedure at the inception of development projects. Since it was my opinion that the solar unit would be best run by the villagers, I began by investigating traditional means of management of public works within the village. The traditional political system was the first branch investigated. In the past, the chief of the village had the authority to invest certain individuals with the power to administer public resources. However, since the advent of colonialism, the village chief has been divested of the power to administer. In addition, he can no longer tax the villagers and use the revenue, as he once did, for managing public works. In fact, all of his present resources are personal. If he were to manage the mill, it would have to be managed as his personal property and thus run the risk of being used to enrich a minor segment of the population.

The other solution was to open the possibility of management to all segments of the villager population. Villagers show great talent as business managers. I investigated the management of water resources and milling enterprises specifically. There are also, however, numerous examples of entrepreneurship in the villager. All of these, whether water resources or milling enterprises, were privately owned despite the fact that use of the services was open to the community at large.

If the villagers are to apply their management skills to the solar unit, the delicate issue of private management of public property is raised. I devised a system in which the villagers would be able to invest in the mill and share in the profits from the services provided.

The idea of not charging for the services of the mill was dismissed because of potential conflict and monopolization of resources by a certain segment of the population. In addition, if the services were free, it would be impossible to equalize access to the mill without excessive policing. Hence a reasonable price for the services was charged.

Those willing to invest in the mill by providing services and the money for the operating costs would have a part of the monthly profit. Part of the monthly profit has to be put aside for future investments in development projects within the village that the villagers themselves decide upon. In this way, private investors and the entire community will benefit from the profits gained from the milling enterprise.

In order for this system to work, it is absolutely necessary to have input from the population. This requires an intensive information program permitting villagers to criticize the system, detect possible flaws, suggest improvements, or even propose other management plans better suited to their needs.

Even before the mill is installed, it would be necessary to inform the villagers of the implications of housing such a system in the village. They should then be asked if, given the risks, they would want it to be installed. The villagers would then decide, knowing the full implications of housing such a unit.

Although investment in the mill should be open to all villagers, no one should be coerced to invest. Only those who want to participate should do so. Those who have doubts should have the option to see if the system works before committing themselves to an investment.

The villagers should make all the decisions relating to the organization of labour, the repartition of profits, etc. Last but not least, provisions have to be made for maintenance and repairs of the mill. Permanent members of the village, particularly those most concerned with the services offered (women and herders) should be trained in the proper maintenance and reparation of the mill and pump.

Alienation, resulting from the inability to understand the technology on which they are depending, and from the lack of personal investment in the project, must be avoided at all costs.

Too often development efforts of this nature fail because of insensitivity to crucial elements of societal structures available for the integration of new technology in village society. Project designs fail to take into consideration the needs of the population, their resources, and their often excellent suggestions. The knowledge that the recipients are more conscious of their needs, more capable of suggesting adequate solutions than most expatriates or government officials generally divorced from the setting for which they are expected to design development projects, is crucial to the success of any project design.

Bibliography

Carr, Marilyn. Appropriate Technology for African Women. Addis Abba: U.N. Economy Commission for Africa. 1978.

French, David. The Economics of Renewable Energy Systems for Developing Countries. Washington, D.C. 1979.

Jellife, Derrick B. "The Assessment of the Nutritional Status of the Community." In Child Health in the Tropics. W.H.O. 1962.

Latham, Michael. "Human Nutrition in Tropical Africa." F.A.O., UNICEF, W.H.O. 1965.

May, Jacques M. The Ecology of Malnutrition in French-Speaking Countries of West Africa and Madagascar. New York: Hafner Publishing Company. 1968.

Mary Elmendorf

9. Changing Role of Maya Mothers and Daughters

As evidenced by the accumulated data* in a longitudinal study of 13 families in Chan Kom, Yucatan, postponement of marriage among the young women in our sample group began to occur immediately after the opening of a feeder road in 1971, and the trend has continued over the last seven years.1/ Simultaneous inauguration of a regular bus service increased the access of young unmarried women to income-generating activities, to learning opportunities (both formal and informal), and to communication with heterogeneous groups both inside and outside the village.2/ The easily available transportation also allowed them to maintain close contact with their families while enjoying mobility. Even though most of their income-producing labor has been confined to menial tasks paying extremely low wages, it has given the young women a new feeling of independence which, combined with their increased social resources and exchange of ideas with others from outside the village, has enabled them to reject arranged marriages. The result has been a postponement of marriage until a later age.

As these young women continue to delay marriage by work and/or study, the community is redefining the age of solteras, old maids, which until recently was 19. Now, 24 year olds are considered "eligible" but, as with younger members of the group, they are taking more time to weigh the

---

*This study, sponsored by the Research Institute for the Study of Man, was funded by the Office of Population, Bureau for Development Support, Agency for International Development. The field work was carried out in collaboration with Alfonso Villa Rojas.

new option of exercising free will with respect to choosing a mate. At the same time, many older women, as well as the younger, are redefining the roles of wife and mother. Some of the older, premenopausal women are using contraceptives at the encouragement of their younger, unmarried children. However, there has been little change in the use of contraceptives and limitation of births among women who married in the years immediately preceding the opening of the road. Three of our sample group had had five children by the age of 25, and, in spite of wishing to use contraceptives, had problems.

From 1970 to the present, we have been gathering longitudinal data on the roles and status of women in 13 families in Chan Kom. This was a purposive sample of women chosen on the basis of varying marital status: a widow, a young woman and mothers of different ages with from one to twelve children. Most, but not all, are from the elite plaza group. As I said in 1971:

> "Even though most of the women . . . were related to the leading family, and as such held positions where they potentially could claim more 'status through wealth' than others when modernization gives it more importance, I felt a great similarity between them and the other women of the community. They wore the same clothing, ate the same food, drew water from the same wells, had children in the same school, and enjoyed the same communal rights. . . . Even though all of the women I have mentioned have masonry houses, most of their daily life . . . takes place in jacales (thatched huts) built behind the masonry ones. Alfonso Villa Rojas notes that, 'As wives of leaders, as members of the leading family, these women are setting the trend.' They are at the pressure-point of change. <u>Nine Mayan Women: A Village Faces Change</u>, 1977:15

These women, through the freedom they are allowing their daughters to have, and their daughters, in taking their freedom, are setting a new trend in the village relating to women/work/education/marriage and family size/spacing.

Changing Role of Maya Mothers and Daughters 151

In 1976, this sample was increased to 26 families to provide a broader data base and to include some new settlers. We now have information on the entire village population which demonstrates that the trends we have identified are spreading throughout the village. As of November, 1978, the population of Chan Kom was 623 with 95 households.

In 1971, just as in 1930, there was only one unmarried woman over 17 in Chan Kom. Marriage was still the state expected of all adults a few years after puberty just as it had been in 1930 (Redfield/Villa Rojas - 1934:95). And marriages were arranged by families, with little or no participation of the young people and often without their knowledge. (Elmendorf: 1973, 1976).

By 1978, the pressures to marry had decreased dramatically. Of all the women 17 and over in the village there are 25 unmarried in 1978 compared to only one in 1971. Thirteen of these young women are under twenty, eleven in the 20-24 age bracket and one woman twenty-five. We find that from age 15 thru 24 there are 30 unmarried women, or 52% of the total female population in the 15-24 age bracket. From age 15 up there are 46 unmarried men plus one widower of 32, who is actively looking for a wife. In the 15-16 year age bracket, there are six girls and 15 boys, all unmarried. (See Appendix B of Sex Distribution, Married/Unmarried.)

Of the women in the age group of 15-24, there are only 28 married out of 58, or 48%, which means that there are more unmarried women than married, in an age group where nearly everyone was married or promised just seven years ago. This trend is even more pronounced in the 15-19 year old age group, in which there are 19 unmarried compared to nine married. This trend is somewhat reversed in the 20-24 year old category with 11 unmarried to 19 married, but the overall trend is very indicative of change.

There is a similarly marked trend in the figures for the men in this 15-24 age group. There are 15 married men out of 53, or 18% and among the 38 unmarried men there are three times as many aged 15-19 as there are aged 20-24. One interesting contrast between men and women over 24 is that there are 9 unmarried men compared with one unmarried woman.

In our sample, only two of the total of twelve young women had married at age 17, both to local boys chosen by their parents. This is the age suggested as "correct" in traditional Mayan customs and by which age all their mothers had married. (Elmendorf 1976-89,92) In 1978 ten women in our sample, three of whom are over 22, are still single. They do not yet seem worried about not having married, nor do their parents. And, most significantly, they are being given/or have assumed responsibility for choosing their mates, a role traditionally held by their parents.

In 1971 at the opening of the road, the first 17 year old woman who refused to marry her village novio (fiance) in an arranged marriage set for the next day, left on the first bus from the village, after his mother criticized her dancing with a cousin. The significance of the road was immediately apparent. Her behavior was considered scandalous but perhaps she unwittingly served as a model. The young woman later lived with relatives and worked for four years in Merida. At 21 she married a non-Mayan and now has a child and is the only village women known to be learning to drive. Her village novio married a Maya speaking young woman from a nearby rancheria, who has remained in his home, obeying his mother in the traditional way.

During the last seven years, all of the young women in our sample and many others have spent some period of time working or studying outside the village. With the opening of the road in 1971, there were increased occupational opportunities outside the village. Some of the young women found temporary, primarily service type jobs, staying with protecting relatives or as live-in domestics in Merida or Valladolid. There were already existing social networks in these towns, but the use of them by the young people accelerated rapidly after the highway was opened. By 1973 the lure of the tourist area in Can Cun, which had already given employment to Chan Kom men as day laborers, appealed to the young people both men and women, as restaurants and hotels looked for staff. Also, networks of Chan Kom families were formed in the slums around Puerto Juarez, the residential area for the workers in Can Cun. Inputs from "outside" forces tending to increase the rate of changes in the village have been continuous since Chan Kom is still seen as a permanent residence for these "migrant workers" who return periodically for short or long visits.3/

In Chan Kom, communication with heterogeneous groups has taken place during short trips or temporary residence outside the village, especially in the tourist zones, but also <u>within</u> the village, as agency personnel, teachers and anthropologists lived and worked there. Soon after the road opened in 1971, two teachers came -- two young women -- with their Maya-speaking, huipil clad grandmothers as chaperones. These two young women wore mini-skirts and slacks and, as they taught their regular classes, they raised the consciousness of both men and women, boys and girls. After the first two women teachers, many more have come and gone, some married, with their husbands and babies.

One outstanding woman teacher spent nearly three years in the village, teaching her classes and at the same time taking care of her pre-school child in an efficient but warm way. She is probably the model for the two young married women (with children) who are working out of town. She had a great influence on many of the brighter girls and boys and urged the first young women to apply for and get scholarships to the new Escuela Técnica Agropecuaria -- ETA -- when it opened in 1975 as a technical secondary school. Educational opportunities have increased within the village itself, with the expansion of the existing school from grades 1-3 to grades 1-6.

As was the case before 1971, there is still an alarming drop-out rate of girls in the pre-menarche years. However, increasing numbers are completing primary school and planning to go to ETA or other secondary schools. In Appendix E we see that in December 1978 six of the 14 seniors from the village in the 6th grade were girls, 42% of the resident Chan Kom group. Along with these students are seven students, all male, from the INI hostel or <u>albergue</u> 4/ bringing the total of the graduating class to twenty-one.

Two young women in our sample finished third grade before they were ten and have since completed their primary studies. One of them is 24 and graduated from secretarial school in the state capital. She completed her course while employed as a domestic and after working three years in a family store. The other young woman, aged 20, has completed her studies in an external degree program (<u>escuela abierta</u>) in the village, even though she has yet to take her final exams. Also, she has taken several short courses in community health and midwife training given by the Ministry of Health (SSA) and the National Indian Institute (INI) in Valladolid. When she was only ten years old, this young woman was loaned for two years to a <u>compadre</u>, god parent, to work as a live-in maid, <u>nana</u>, for a doctor's family in Mexico City, an experience which greatly influenced her life and vocation.

Both of these young women consider themselves professionals; one is a secretary in the Bureau of the Census in Merida and the other is Health Promoter and Family Planning expert at the SSA Clinic in the village. Both are village leaders. They are models for other young women and are consulted by old and young alike. They both still identify with Chan Kom. On her monthly visits back to Chan Kom, the secretary's advice is sought about practical matters about life in the city as well as counsel about justice, <u>ejido</u> rights and taxes, in the village. And the Health Promoter is called on for all health matters. She has even delivered 13 babies.

But what about the other young women? As of August 1978, 12 or 39% of the 31 unmarried women of Chan Kom were living outside Chan Kom; eleven were in the 15-24 age group and one was twenty-five. Ten are working and two are studying in secondary schools, one in Valladolid and one in Cenotilla. Seven are working as maids; four in Valladolid, two in Merida and one, the 25 year old, in a tourist hotel in Can Cun. Two more are in Merida, one as a salesgirl in a family store and one as a bilingual secretary. One is a cook in a boarding school in Chemax.

Of the 18 unmarried women living in the village, five (one 17, one 16 and three 15) are still attending primary school and nine have "jobs". The nurse's aide, the post mistress and the assistant on the tortilla making machine receive small salaries.[5] Six women (three 18, two 20, one 22) help run their family stores, and call themselves "commerciantes." Of the remaining women three (one 24, one 22, and one 18) consider themselves "artisans" and sell their embroidery on concession to stores in Piste and Valladolid.[6]

As noted previously, when the road was opened in 1971, young women acquired a new freedom to move into the outside world provided by the bus transport and the supportive kinship network. Thus, roles were redefined as women left the village for employment and educational opportunities and delayed marriage. Despite the fact that they are often employed in low-paying service capacities, they are experiencing a personal feeling of importance. Their new roles and status are accepted by the parents, partially because they are all regularly remitting funds to the household economy -- a strong incentive - and are maintaining close social ties with home and family. And the road and accompanying bus service facilitate the continuing communication between parents and children. Moreover, the same process of role redefinition is occurring within the village among the families with young women working or attending classes while living at home.

For women, particularly the young, the road has expanded their opportunities to become traders and "businesswomen" and to continue their education/learning. They view the road as a mechanism for providing liberation from cultural constraints and for giving them more flexibility in establishing economic independence and defining new lifestyles.

Although, for many of the women, employment has been short-term and primarily service oriented, their income has been important to them personally and to their families. Most women are still hoping to be able to supplement family income from the sale of their handicrafts -- hammocks and embroidery. As skilled artisans, who are willing and eager to modify and creatively change their designs, they want information about marketing and purchasing. An increasing number have tried doing piece work for tourist shops, but they are aware of how little they earn.

In discussing marital relationships, all parents agreed that their children have the right to select their own mate instead of having arranged marriages as was the custom. As to age of marriage and size of family, these too are more and more viewed as decisions for the young to make.

One young woman explained that _all_ young men and women in the village could choose their spouses now, but that in their mother's generation, marriages were often arranged by the parents. She related the story about J. and E's marriage. J.'s parents just told her to get dressed to go to church, but when she arrived, E. was waiting for her to get married. Her parents had not even told her. She was 13. The girl said she just stood in the church and cried. Now they are very happy, but they had never met before they got married. The narrator found this very curious and inconceivable for her generation.

Most of the young women say they have no plans for marriage. Nevertheless there is some ambivalence here. They are proud of this new responsibility but seem frightened by the possible outcome of the wrong decision. The young women are asking themselves and others how you can tell what kind of husband a man will be. How will they know if a man has another wife? They mention fear of abandonment and mistreatment. And others speak of being trapped.

The radios and the record players are filled with love songs from modern Mexico, but within the village, and even in the protective village networks of Merida and Valladolid, opportunities for courtship or even friendship with members of the opposite sex are still limited. Ways to meet young men informally and to discuss ideas and plans are extremely rare. Part of the delay in age of marriage may be attributed to the difficulty of choice, but this is an aspect of the new freedom and independence these young women have.

Some say they do not want to ever marry or have children, even though all of their mothers were married and had children by their ages. Some see marriage as a way to become servants, "mothers" to their husbands and children. Others say they are in no hurry. No longer are marriage and motherhood the only option for adolescent girls, even for the young women who have maintained Chan Kom as their home base.

This brings up another fact that perhaps the young women are _only_ saying _they_ don't want to get married because no one has asked them. _7/_ Certainly this is true of a few women such as L. and her 24 year old cousin, whose _novio_ left her for a penniless "widow" with a child to save the

marriage costs, some say. As I try to understand this --
and decision making in this area is hard to define in any
culture -- there does seem to be hesitation about early
marriage from both women and men.

Many of the young men in Chan Kom are delaying their
marriages, some perhaps waiting for local girls to marry.
Some enjoy the free or paid (even by women) sexual encounters in the tourist areas. Some are delaying marriage
while working away from Chan Kom and saving money to send
home for families to build masonry houses or to pay for
labor to work their milpas. Part of the rationale for the
building of separate masonry houses by the young men is to
invest their savings, but partly also it is to define a home
separate from their parents.

But we should look a little more closely at the unmarried men to see how they relate to the women (see Appendix
B, table of married/unmarried population). In the 15-19 age
group there are 31 males compared to 28 females, of whom
only two males and nine females are married. In 1971 we
noted that the marriage age for males was sometimes the same
as for women, but more often two to four years older and sometimes as much as ten or twelve years more.

For both men and women, 62% of the unmarried population falls in the 15-19 age cohort. However, this figure
hides important differences between the two groups. First,
the range of ages of unmarried men (15-34) is greater than
of unmarried women (15-25). Second, with one exception,
there are more men than women in each of the cohorts, with
the greatest difference in the 15-19 year group (10 more
unmarried men than unmarried women). Despite these two
factors, the number of unmarried women in the village
exceeds that of unmarried men. Moreover, there are very few
unmarried men -- four -- remaining in the village within
the age span during which marriages normally occur, 17 to 30
years, compared to (relatively) many unmarried women --
fifteen -- all under 25.

Of the 15 young men aged 15 and 16, only four are
working out of town. Three are studying at ETA (Escuela
Técnico Agropecuaria), two in Valladolid and one in
Cenotillo. Of the eight left in Chan Kom, three are studying in an external degree program on a daily basis hoping to

get a secondary certificate. This leaves five who list themselves as agriculturalists or day laborers. Every male from age 15 is a member of the ejido and can request land to work on his own.

There are 47 unmarried men out of the 104 in the 15 to 34 age group, of whom only nine are in the 20-24 age group where there are eleven unmarried women. This age cohort is very unusual in Chan Kom with only 22 males and 30 females. If we add to these the 25-29 group we have 52 males to 55 females of whom 15 males and 12 females are single plus three more eligible males in the 30-35 group.

But where have all the young men gone?8/ And is that really the reason for this change? Twenty of the twenty-three unmarried men in the 17-24 age group are out of town, nineteen working and one continuing his teacher training at the preparatory school in Valladolid. Three of the men left in town are working as agriculturalists and one is helping part time in the family store.

As D. Merrill noted in August 1978, "The young men from Chan Kom have a larger pool of young women to pick their wife from and the young women have a small pool. The situation is exacerbated by the fact that they (young women) are better educated, have travelled more and probably have more set criteria for choosing their future husband. It is likely that many of the eligible men from the outlying villages don't meet the criteria. It is no wonder some prefer to continue as 'solteras', thus contributing to the new pattern of postponing marriage." (Personal communication, January 1979.)

Returning to a discussion of young women in the village, parental consent/approval of postponement of marriage for their daughters is giving the young women an opportunity to increase their knowledge of other life styles of women working outside the home, women (with children) in professional jobs, and wives without children or with spaced, limited number of children. This parental consent for delayed marriage is probably related primarily to an economic need since the remittances of the daughters, most of whom give their earning to their mothers, add needed cash to the limited household resources.9/ Some daughters, however, are continuing their education, at a double financial loss to the families: no household labor or incoming cash and in a few cases a cost outlay. Some families are making sacrifices for daughters as well as sons to continue their studies outside the village, and younger sisters are discussing plans for what they might do or study.

The decision to remove parental pressure for early marriages for some daughters may be because of the immediate economic contribution they are making. For others it may be an investment for the future, since unmarried daughters may continue to support parents. In any case, roles of parents and children in respect to marriage are changing. Also, young women and men are re-defining the role of daughter-in-law.

The role of daughter-in-law, as defined traditionally, is being rejected by young men and women. This was behind the surprise refusal by a young woman to follow through with an arranged marriage in 1971, when she took the first bus out of the village on the day before her marriage was to take place. Her move was in reaction to her <u>novio's</u> mother's request to her father that he punish her for dancing with her cousin at the village fiesta. In other cases, younger brothers or married men whose mothers are known to mistreat their daughter-in-laws are having trouble finding village wives. Some men go to the more traditionally small communities for "properly respectful wives," but even these aren't always the obedient, hard-working wives the traditional mothers-in-law wanted. Even some of these young wives are resenting the treatment and/or confinement imposed by their mothers-in-law, and one has complained recently to the Mayor, an action unheard of in the past.

Another role that is being re-defined is that of wife. The case of E., the young health promoter, provides an example of the concerns being expressed by young women:

By delaying her marriage three years until she was twenty, E. certainly raised her status and expanded the role of midwife. As a married woman will she be able to continue her "profession" and still fill the role of wife, <u>nuera,</u> and mother?

This process of re-defining the role of wife (and also that of mother) is evident in our sample group of young women. The twelve women come from five families; four of the five mothers are illiterate and all were married by the age of 17 and had their first child by 18. Two mothers had eight children, one 12 and the others 7 and 9; an average of 8.4 children.

The two young married women in the group of 12 say they prefer two children and feel four would be maximum; they discuss contraceptives frankly. One, 22 years old, has two children, a girl four and a boy two years old, and is taking the birth control pill because she does not plan to have more children. The other 18-year old wife has just married a local youth, also 18, after a two-year engagement during which she spent working in Merida. After a few months residence with her mother-in-law in Chan Kom, she has now joined her husband in Puerto Juarez, where they live with her father-in-law in a compound of two thatched huts.

The 10 who are unmarried say they are still not sure whether they will get married, and if they do, how many children they expect to have. As a group, these twelve women are the elder daughters of their respective families, and their sentiments regarding children have been shaped by their perspective on the numbers of children their mothers had.

Concurrently, these young women have had an influence on their mothers. Four of the five mothers, who have not reached menopause, are using contraceptives at the encouragement of their unmarried children. This is remarkable when none of the mothers of these young women ever discussed sex with their daughters or even explained menstruation to them before their first period. The mothers explained to me that it is considered a sin to tell a girl about menstruation before her first period, or to explain to her anything about sex before marriage. They had not instructed their daughters nor had their mothers instructed them.

In summary we see that 52%, or 30 of the 58 women between 15-24 in Chan Kom are unmarried. And of this group twenty-six, or 90% are occupied in some activity outside of the home. By this I mean away from the hearth/laundry

Changing Role of Maya Mothers and Daughters 161

area, in the public eye at least part of the time, even though all of the women in the village and most outside continue to do traditional female tasks in addition to their work. Nineteen are working at paid jobs -- ten outside, nine inside, and seven are studying, two outside and five inside the village. And most of the women, whether married or unmarried, consider themselves artisans and are still seeking ways to earn more from their embroidery. Chan Kom women have not become wealthy, nor have they become permanent slum dwellers. Most of them have maintained their dignity, their respect and their status even as they are redefining their roles, as women, as wives, as mothers.

But there are problems. The women who are having the most difficult times are the young mothers who were married at 14 or 15 just before the road opened and who missed the opportunities their younger sisters and neighbors have had. They do not have the status and respect the older women had in the near egalitarian sex-stereotyped traditional culture, nor do they have the knowledge and communication with their husbands/families the younger women have as they share new information and experiences. With modernization -- water, electricity, and new work patterns -- they have lost status and some are feeling threatened.

Several of these young women had five or more children before they were twenty-five, more living children than their parents had had by their age. But even though they have many years of fecundity ahead, for a complex variety of reasons they have had difficulty adopting contraceptives, despite 1) clear evidence that they would prefer to limit their families; 2) the fact that Chan Kom has one of the highest rates of birth control in a rural Maya area.10/

Since the Ministry of Health started a family planning program in August 1977 as part of the extension of its maternal child health services through the local health post, 25 women, nearly 28% of the 97 "exposed" women accepted contraceptives and 22 are still users. Through private sources outside the village, seven additional women had started using contraceptives, and five continue. This brings the acceptance rate to 32% with continued users at 27% in an 18-month period. (See Appendix G.) 11/

Two young women who married at 17 in arranged marriages to local boys <u>after</u> the road came, one in 1972 and the other in 1976, seem to have much more control over their fertility and their lives than the couples who married in the preceding decade.

The postponement of marriage 12/ by a growing number of young women combined with a growing awareness of alternatives and more open communication between couples is rapidly changing the fertility behavior in Chan Kom.13/ These women, and the 31 unmarried ones, are in a sense symbolic of the direction and pace of demographic change. As this longitudinal study continues, with further analysis of the data on change, it is probable that they will turn out to be representatives of a turning point in the status of Maya Yucatec women in relationship to marriage and the family.

Action Implications

The findings of this study have a variety of action implications which could serve as guidelines to Mexican Government agencies -- national, regional and local. For convenience, they can be placed in the following five categories, (recognizing, however, that there is considerable overlapping between them):

A. <u>Infra-structure</u>

- The evidence suggests the need for the opening of feeder roads into isolated rural villages to provide access to commodities and services which the village lacks.

- It also implies the need for inexpensive bus service to and from the village, with dependability and regularity valued more highly than frequency.

- The provision of basic services could contribute piped water and electricity to enhance the quality of life in the village and particularly with a very major impact on the lives of women and girls, since they can be freed from the endless hours devoted to

Changing Role of Maya Mothers and Daughters

drawing and carrying water and preparing their tortilla masa by hand.

B. Health Services

- The data suggest that health services be designed to operate in harmony with rather than in confrontation with traditional health practices.

- There appears to be a need to assign young women as health aides/promoters in agency field offices, where they can begin to learn on the job and to acquire some sense of pre-professionalism.

- As modest incentives, these aides could be given opportunities to leave the village periodically, perhaps on weekends, for "professional" meetings and refresher courses.

- Make available inexpensive sanitary pads as a health aid which would make it easier for:

    1) Girls to continue in school after the approach of menarche instead of stopping school at age 12.

    2) Women to accept contraceptives which cause bleeding or even their normal menstruation.

- It is clear that such villages would benefit from having more exposure to health facilities, hospitals, clinics, etc., in nearby towns. Periodic field trips for students and parents to such places would remove their fears of the unknown and increase the likelihood that they would later on make more rational use of available services.

C. Education

- Special incentives for women teachers, both married and unmarried, to accept assignments in rural schools. Give them extra pay for working after hours on special projects.

- The encouragement of young people, particularly the girls, to remain in school or to go to training centers nearby to improve their skills could have very positive benefits.

- The establishment of rural hostels, near village schools, where children from still smaller communities could live during the school week, is a strategy which combines economy with community building and the strengthening of human resource development and improvement of selected rural schools.

- Stress needs to be given to skills training as well as formal education, since it is clear from the data that the possession and use of a skill leads not only to increased earnings but also to personal dignity and social stability.

- Include non-formal adult education or external degrees as a priority responsibility for any and all agency representatives present in the village and the result will be growth of understanding, increased willingness to accept change, and more freedom for the younger generation to construct a way of life for themselves and their families in the village, without feeling they must leave to avoid stagnation.

D. Economics

- The evidence suggests that small markets or marketing cooperatives <u>in which the producers participate as policymakers</u> are a priority need for small rural villages with a craft tradition.

- Likewise, the manner of participation of Chan Kom residents in the economic sphere of the tourist trade, Can Cun, Chichen Itza, etc., demonstrates that they will maintain their village identities and roles, when they have access to the money economy at a reasonable distance from home. They do not want to leave, prefer to keep their identity, but need some source of supplementary income.

This fact suggests a policy of deliberately locating small industries in dispersed areas, of creating means of access to the money economy through special transportation schemes or short-term residence facilities where the jobs are.

E. Community Involvement

- Almost all the above suggestions imply community participation of one kind or another in the decisions which shape their lives. Especially important is the need to involve the people in defining their problems and hopes. The data obtained in this study reinforce the essentiality of the principle and lead to the suggestion that time always be taken by Agency personnel to explain, inquire, listen and respond to these felt needs of the community -- both women and men. At the same time, an honest intellectual position on the relationship of change must be maintained, whether it be family planning or improved seeds, to improve the future quality of life of the community as basic human needs are met through different technologies.

Appendix A

Population Profile of Chan Kom, 1978

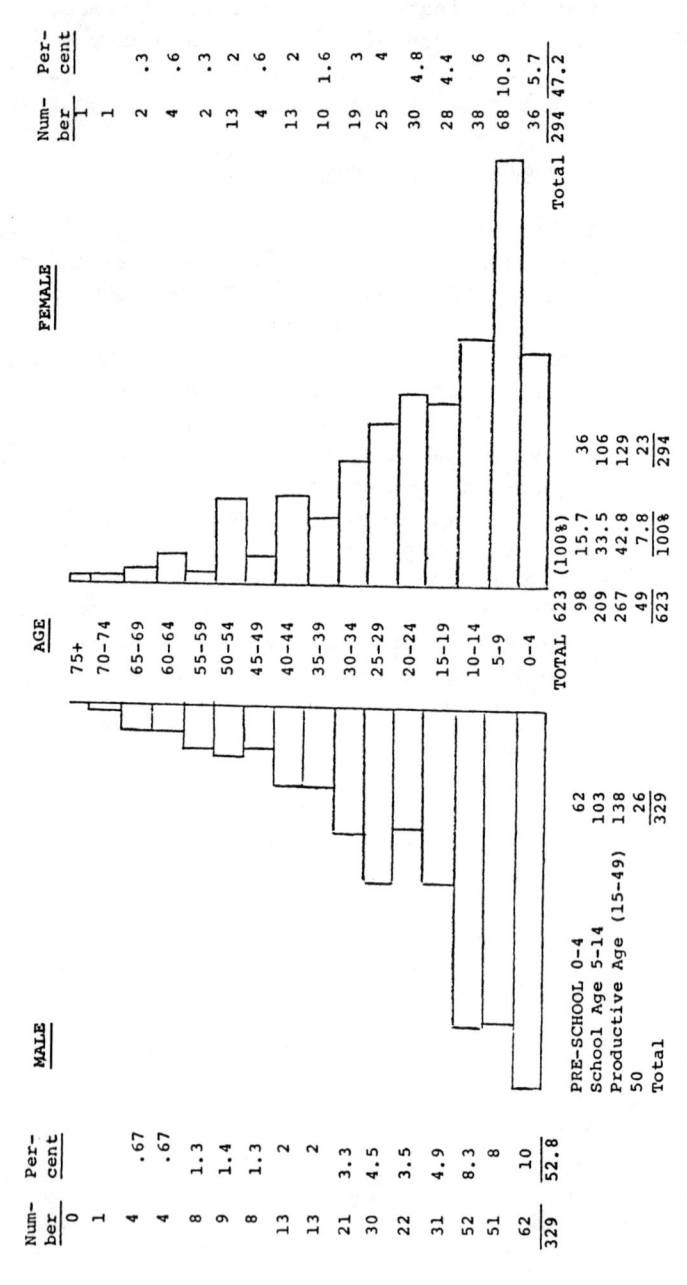

MALE

Number	Percent
0	
1	
4	.67
4	.67
8	1.3
9	1.4
8	1.3
13	2
13	2
21	3.3
30	4.5
22	3.5
31	4.9
52	8.3
51	8
62	10
329	52.8

AGE

75+	
70-74	
65-69	
60-64	
55-59	
50-54	
45-49	
40-44	
35-39	
30-34	
25-29	
20-24	
15-19	
10-14	
5-9	
0-4	

TOTAL 623 (100%)

	98	15.7	36
	209	33.5	106
	267	42.8	129
	49	7.8	23
	623	100%	294

PRE-SCHOOL 0-4   62
School Age 5-14   103
Productive Age (15-49)   138
50   26
Total   329

FEMALE

Number	Percent
1	
1	
2	.3
4	.6
2	.3
13	2
4	.6
13	2
10	1.6
19	3
25	4
30	4.8
28	4.4
38	6
68	10.9
36	5.7
Total 294	47.2

Dependency total: [Age 0-14 plus 50 and over] 356 (57%)

SOURCE: Elmendorf/Merrill Household Survey - 12/78

Appendix B

Sex Distribution by Age and Marital Status, Chan Kom, 1978

MALE					AGES	FEMALE			
TOTAL	WIDOWER	UNMARRIED	MARRIED			MARRIED	UNMARRIED	WIDOW	TOTAL
31	0	29	2		15-19	9	19	0	28
22	0	9	13		20-24	19	11	0	30
30	0	6	24		25-29	24	1	0	25
21	1*	2	18		30-34	19	0	0	19
13	0	0	13		35-39	9	0	1**	10
13	1**	0	12		40-44	13	0	0	13
8	1	0	7		45-49	4	0	0	4
9	0	0	9		50-54	11	0	2	13
8	1	0	7		55-59	1	0	1	2
4	0	0	4		60-64	2	0	2	4
4	1	0	3		65-69	2	0	0	2
1	0	0	1		70-74	0	0	1	1
0	0	0	0		75+	0	0	1	1
TOTAL 164	5	46	113			113***	31	8	152

TOTAL 316

* Looking for Wife.
** Abandoned.
*** Married women reproductive Age (15-49) 97 (75% of Women Reproductive Age).

Sources: Elmendorf/Merrill - Household Survey - 12/1978

Appendix C

Sex Distribution of Unmarried Individuals, Chan Kom, 1978: Working-Studying/Inside-Outside the Village

	MALE					Age	FEMALE				
Inside Work	Village Study	Outside Work	Village Study	Total			Total	Outside Work	Village Study	Inside Work	Village Study
1	2	2	2	7		15	3	0	0	0	3
4	1	2	1	8		16	3	0	1	0	1
2	0	5	0	7		17	4	2	1	0	1
0	0	5	0	5		18	8	3	0	4	1
0	0	1	1	2		19	1	1	0	0	0
Total 7	3	15	4	29			19	6	2	4(B)	5 Total
0	0	1	0	1		20	5	1	0	4	0
0	0	5	0	5		21	0	0	0	0	0
1	0	1	0	2		22	2	0	0	1	0
0	0	1	0	1		23	0	0	0	0	0
0	0	0	0	0		24	4	2 (A)	0	0	0
Total 1	0	8	0	9			11	3	0	5(B)	0 Total
1	0	0	0	1		25	1	1	0	0	0
2	0	1	0	3		26	0	0	0	0	0
0	0	1	0	1		27	0	0	0	0	0
1	0	0	0	1		28	0	0	0	0	0
0	0	0	0	0		29	0	0	0	0	0
Total 4	0	2	0	6			1	1	0	0	0 Total
0	0	0	0	1		30	0	0	0	0	0
0	0	0	0	0		31	0	0	0	0	0
0	0	1(C)	0	0		32	0	0	0	0	0
1	0	0	0	1		33	0	0	0	0	0
0	0	0	0	0		34	0	0	0	0	0
Total 1	0	1	0	2			0	0	0	0	0 Total
Total 13(D)	3	26	4	46 (D)			31 (B)	10	2	9 (B)	5 (B)Total

(A) Both of these young women are continuing their studies partime.
(B) Three more women work as artisans. The other 5 women plus all of of these help with household tasks, cooking, laundry, child care, etc. as do the ones working and studying outside.
(C) Widower
(D) All of these men are members of the ejido and have access to use of communally owned land. Nearly all plant, or have planted, maize, corn, in their milpas. Many have to supplement this with other income producing activity, inside or outside the village.

Changing Role of Maya Mothers and Daughters

Appendix D

Chan Kom: Workers Outside the Village, 1978

Chan Kom is the county seat of a municipality by the same name with an official population of 2,771,*/ including 12 small isolated Maya-speaking rancherias and two larger communities as well as Chan Kom.

Based on a household survey completed in August 1978, the population of Chan Kom was 623, an increase of 97 persons since a similar survey was made in August 1976.**/ The present population is composed of 95 households, comprising an increase of 14 in two years.***/ 40 households have at least one person working outside the village. There are 50 men (36% of the productive (15-49) male population, 138) and 15 women (12% of the productive (15-49) female population, 129) working outside the village. However, there are only eight people 30 or over in this group, so the great majority (88%) fall in the younger age group (15-29).

The demographic picture is complicated by the nomadic behavior of this population, members of which work outside the village but return often (with one exception) to maintain membership in the ejido of Chan Kom.****/ Most

---

*/ Salvador Rodriguez Losa, La Poblacion de Los Minicipios del Estado de Yucatan, 1900-1970, Ediciones del Gobierno del Estado: Merida, Yucatan, Mexico, January 1977.

**/ Elmendorf and Merrill, World Bank Field Study, Mimeo 1976.

***/ 19 of the current households are composed of more than one family; the addition is usually the family of one married son.

****/ "Nomadic" is used here to refer to the periodic movement between Chan Kom and other localities (the selection of which varies with the individual). This seasonal migration is due to various factor, crop failure, inflation, and a foreign invasion "tourism". This fits into the "imbalance" stage. (Lomnitz, Migration and Marginality; Academic Press 1977:30.

of the men continue to prepare, plant and harvest their maize and to participate in fagina (voluntary community labor) and guardia (turns at being village police) in Chan Kom. If they cannot come home, they pay someone */ to do the work. Many have built or are building masonry houses in the village. They return for fiestas, with their families if they have one, and, if they are married, their wives come back for extended visits in the village.

Of the 26 unmarried men working outside the village, 21 are aged from 15 to 21 years. There is no similar cluster among the 24 married men working outside. Of the 15 women who work outside the village, 10 are unmarried. The majority of these unmarried women seven are young, ranging in age from 17 to 20. This is nearly the same cluster tendency as the figures for unmarried men: 70% of the women and 78% of the men working outside the village are aged 15 to 20. In addition, there are few unmarried men (4 aged 17 to 30 years) remaining in the village compared to relatively many unmarried women (15 all under 25 years) who reside in Chan Kom.

Fifteen women aged 17 to 26, of whom five are married, were working out of Chan Kom in August 1978. Several other young women have worked or have started working again as maids in Valladolid. **/ Their parents do not want them to go to Cancun even though they can earn four times as much -- 1,200 to 1,400 pesos every two weeks as compared to 600 to 700 pesos per month in Merida or Valladolid. Three young women, 18, 20 and 25 years of age, worked as babysitters in Mexico City for one to two years when they were pre-adolescents, 10 to 12 years of age.

---

*/ Sometimes cash, but more often reciprocity with village kin.

**/ The highest regular wage earned in the village is the 500 pesos monthly plus a small income from sales of medicines which the nurses-aide receives. Occasionally some of the expert artisans earn more than this in a month but do not average this over a year.

Appendix E

School Enrollment in Chan Kom, 1978

PRIMARY SCHOOL

GRADE	Overall enrollment			Village Residents			Boarding Students		
	TOTAL	BOYS	GIRLS	BOYS	GIRLS	TOTAL	BOYS	GIRLS	TOTAL
1	49	23	26	19	26	45	4	0	4
2	47	24	23	17	19	36	7	4	11
3	38	25	13	22	11	33	3	2	5
4	22	15	7	11	5	16	4	2	6
5	25	21	4	9	3	12	12	1	13
6	21	15	6	8	6	14	7	0	7
TOTAL	202	123	79	86**	70**	155	37	9	46*

*Residents of nearby villages who live in National Indian Institute (INI) hostel in Chan Kom during school week to continue primary education.

**80.5% of the boys and 66% of the girls in the age group 5-14 are attending.

Source: Chan Kom school registration records, 1978

Appendix E. (continued)

	SECONDARY SCHOOL		
	BOYS	GIRLS	TOTAL
Chan Kom - (formal - nonformal)	5	5*	10
Valladolid - (Escuela Agro-Pecuaria) (ETA)	2	1	3
Cenotillo - (Escuela Agro-Pecuaria) (ETA)	1	1	2
Merida (1 Private, 2 Public)	3		3
Progreso - Escuela Tecnica Pescuera	1		1
	12	7	19

*Still in Primary in school but fifteen years and over are included in the Primary figures (page 171).

Appendix F

Changes in Chan Kom, 1971-1976

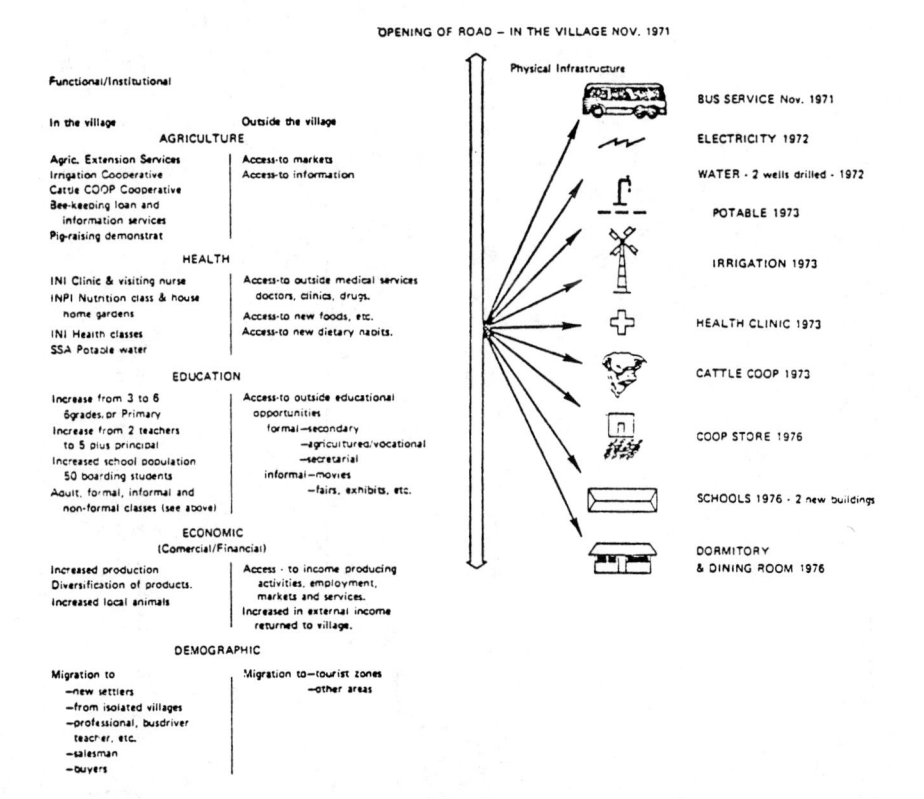

OPENING OF ROAD — IN THE VILLAGE NOV. 1971

Functional/Institutional

In the village	Outside the village
AGRICULTURE	
Agric. Extension Services	Access-to markets
Irrigation Cooperative	Access-to information
Cattle COOP Cooperative	
Bee-keeping loan and information services	
Pig-raising demonstrat	
HEALTH	
INI Clinic & visiting nurse	Access-to outside medical services doctors, clinics, drugs.
INPI Nutrition class & house home gardens	Access-to new foods, etc.
INI Health classes	Access-to new dietary habits.
SSA Potable water	
EDUCATION	
Increase from 3 to 6 6grades, or Primary	Access-to outside educational opportunities
Increase from 2 teachers to 5 plus principal	formal—secondary —agricultured/vocational —secretarial
Increased school population 50 boarding students	informal—movies —fairs, exhibits, etc.
Adult, formal, informal and non-formal classes (see above)	
ECONOMIC (Comercial/Financial)	
Increased production	Access - to income producing activities, employment, markets and services.
Diversification of products.	
Increased local animals	Increased in external income returned to village.
DEMOGRAPHIC	
Migration to	Migration to—tourist zones
—new settlers	—other areas
—from isolated villages	
—professional, busdriver teacher, etc.	
—salesman	
—buyers	

Physical Infrastructure

- BUS SERVICE Nov. 1971
- ELECTRICITY 1972
- WATER - 2 wells drilled - 1972
- POTABLE 1973
- IRRIGATION 1973
- HEALTH CLINIC 1973
- CATTLE COOP 1973
- COOP STORE 1976
- SCHOOLS 1976 - 2 new buildings
- DORMITORY & DINING ROOM 1976

Source: Elmendorf and Merrill, "Socio-Economic Impact of Development in Chan Kom - 1971 to 1976: Rural Women Participate in Change" (World Bank mimeo, 1977).

Appendix G

Birth Control Acceptors in Module VII of the Maternal-Child Health and Planning Program of the Mexican Ministry of Health

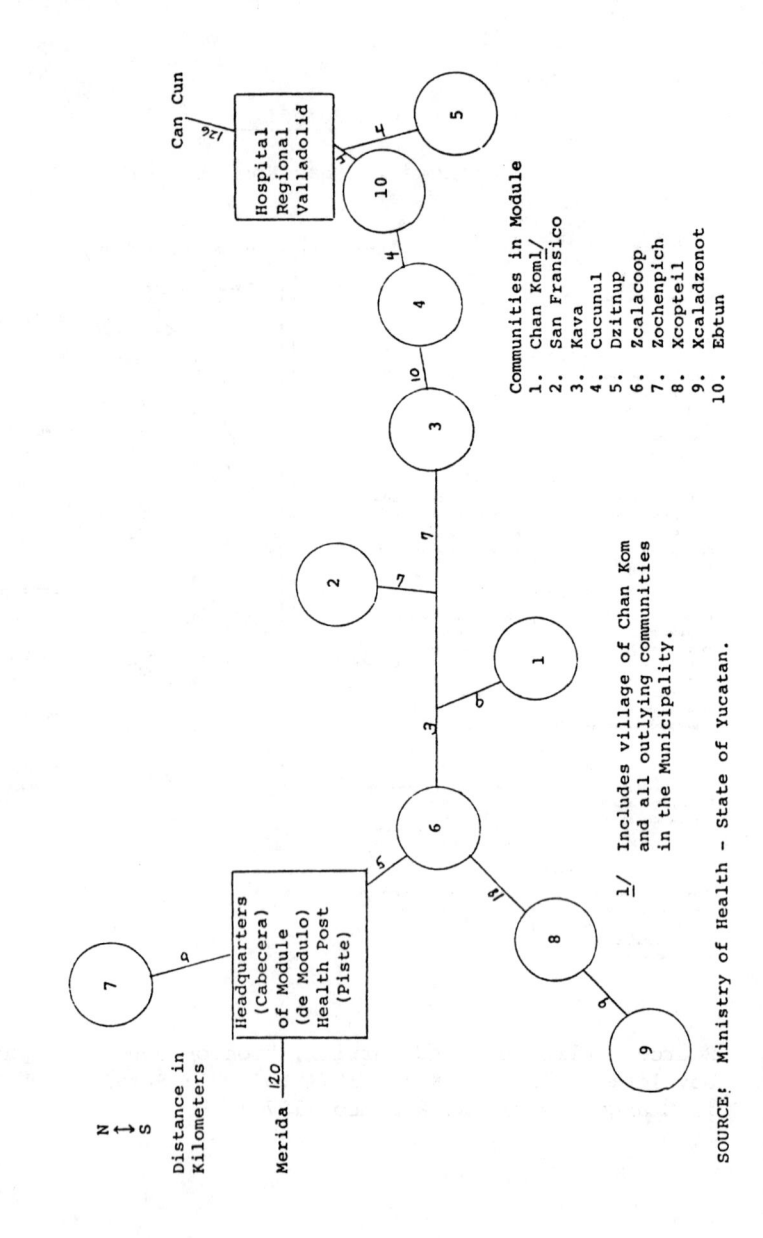

Communities in Module
1. Chan Kom1/
2. San Fransico
3. Kava
4. Cucunul
5. Dzitnup
6. Zcalacoop
7. Zochenpich
8. Xcopteil
9. Xcaladzonot
10. Ebtun

1/ Includes village of Chan Kom and all outlying communities in the Municipality.

N ↕ S

Distance in Kilometers

SOURCE: Ministry of Health - State of Yucatan.

Notes

1/ See Appendix A - Population Profile-1978.

2/ See Appendix F - Chart of Infra-structure changes -- 1971-1976.

3/ See Appendix D for a discussion of the population who work outside but maintain their community membership. "Chan Kom's - Workers Inside and Outside the village - 1978." Key figures in these networks especially women, are discussed in a working paper. "Networks and Role Models" by M. Elmendorf and A. Villa Rojas (in preparation).

4/ The INI students, from near villages without adequate schools, come to live during the week in the alberque in Chan Kom which is set up for 50 students. By December 1978 there were 46 residents, 37 boys and nine girls.

5/ Many of the other women, married and unmarried, earn some money doing embroidery. Every daughter learns to do the traditional cross-stitch before she's twelve and usually makes a Huipil (the cool white shift) which is still worn by many Maya women. Nearly all the women also do intricate embroidery on their pedal sewing machines.

6/ Since July 1978 the women, both married and unmarried, have been trying to organize a sewing cooperative with the Ministry of Agrarian Reform. After many meetings, petitions and planning sessions the women received money for their first order, 45 pesos or $2.00 for a garment which took them 24 hours to make, giving them 8¢ hour or 64¢ a day for their effort. Even the day laborers in Chan Kom get 45 pesos or 2.00 a day. All of the women, including the nurse, help with household chores, cooking, laundry, and child care in addition to their professional or artisan work.

7/ Alfonso Villa Rojas in his December 1978 field notes on Frustraciones Amorosas notes that some early marriages were delayed because of interventions from fathers or brothers. Factors are many but the fact of change is evident.

8/ For further data on men and women working outside of Cham Kom while maintaining their residence there, see

Appendix D -- Chan Kom's workers - Inside and Outside the Village, 1978.

9/ Two consecutive years of poor harvests have given increasing importance to their economic contributions, as have the peso devaluation and the rise in use of consumer items, including food stuffs.

10/ See Elmendorf/Villa Rojas, Quarterly Report, RISM/AID, November 1978. January 1979 - mimeographed.

11/ J. Nagel, Mexico's Population Turnabout, Population Bulletin, Vol. 33, No. 5, December 1978:27.

12/ The age of entry into sexual union has long been recognized as one of the key factors in the process of reproduction. Kingsley Davis and Judith Blake - "Social Structure and Fertility: An Analytic Framework" in Economic Development and Cultural Change, Vol. 4, April 1956.

13/ Such a rapid change is usually related to migration to an urban center, often defined as 100,000 population. Patterns of Urban, Rural Fertility Differentials in Developing Countries, Sally E. Findley and Ann C. Orr. GE-TEMPO/AID, 1978.

Bibliography

Balam P. Dr. Gilberto. Centro Coordinador Indigenista de Valladolid, Yucatan - Realizaciones 1972-1976. Mexico: I.N.I. 1976.

Bastarrachea, Juan. "Family Life Among Mayan Yucatan." Mexico: INAH. 1974.

Boserup, Ester. Women's Role in Economic Development, New York: St. Martins Press, 1970.

Davis, Kingsley and Judith Blake. "Social Structure and Fertility: An Analytic Framework" in Economic, Development and Cultural Change. Vol. 4, April 1956.

Fawcett, James T., ed. "The Satisfactions and Costs of Children: Theories, Concepts, and Methods" -- A summary report and proceedings of a workshop. Honolulu: East West Center. 1972.

Elmendorf, Mary Lindsay. "The Many Worlds of Women: Mexico" - in Women: Roles and Status in Eight Countries, Janet Giele and Audrey Smock, eds. New York: John Wiley Publishing Co.: 1977.

_____ Nine Mayan Women: A Village Faces Change, New York: John Wiley Publishing Co.: 1977.

_____ "Dilemmas of Peasant Women" - in Women and World Development, I. Tinker and M. Bramsen, eds.: Washington: Overseas Development Council: 1976.

_____ "The Mayan Woman and Change" - in Women Cross-Culturally: Change and Challenge, Ruby Leavitt, ed.; The Hague, Netherlands: Mouton: 1975.

_____ La Mujer Maya y el cambio, Mexico: SEP/Setentas: 1973.

Elmendorf, Mary and Deborah Merrill. "Socio-Economic Impact of Development in Chan Kom - 1971 to 1976: A Preliminary Study". Presented at the annual meeting of the Society for Applied Anthropology, Merida, Yucatan, Mexico, April, 1978. Mimeo.

Elu Leñero, Maria Del Carmen. Hacia Dónde Va La Mujer Mexicana?. Mexico: Instituto Mexicana de Estudios Sociales: 1969.

Findley, Sally and Ann Orr. Patterns of Urban, Rural Fertility Differentials in Developing Countries. Santa Barbara, California. GE-TEMPO/AID: 1978.

Garcia Canul, Dr. Antonio. "Information for Development of the Program" State Family Planning Meeting. Merida, Yucatan, October 1978.

Jordan, Bridgette. Birth in Four Cultures: A Cross-cultural Investigation of Childbirth in Yucatan, Holland, Sweden and the United States. Montreal: Eden Press Women's Publications, Inc.: 1978.

Lomnitz, Larissa. Networks and Marginality. New York: Academic Press: 1977.

_____ "La Mujer Marginada En México" Mexico: Diálogos Magazine: 1973.

Nagel, John Jr. "Mexico's Population Turnabout," in Population Bulletin: Vol. 33, No. 5, December 1978:27.

Redfield, Robert. A Village that Chose Progress: Chan Kom Revisited. Chicago: University of Chicago Press, 1950.

_____ Peasant Society and Culture. Chicago: University of Chicago Press: 1956.

Redfield, Robert and Alfonso Villa Rojas. The Folk Culture of Yucatan. Chicago: University of Chicago Press: 1934.

Shedlin, Michele. "Modern Fertility Regulation in a Mexican Community: Factors in Decision Making: paper presented at American Anthropological Association Meeting, Washington: 1976.

Villa Rojas, Alfonso. The Maya of East Central Quintana Roo. Washington: Carnegie Inst. Pub. #559: 1945.

_____ "La Posición de la Mujer Maya ante el Cambio Demográfico." Mexico. Field Report for Research Institute for the Study of Man and AID: 1978.

Linda Y.C. Lim

10. Women's Work in Multinational Electronics Factories

It is frequently observed that the introduction of modern technologies often has detrimental effects on women's economic roles in developing countries. In the industrial or manufacturing sector, more capital-using methods of large-scale production for wider markets typically displace traditional craft production and cottage industries, in which women are predominantly employed. Whereas early industrialization in the now developed countries of the West heavily employed women in labor-intensive industries, most notably textiles, this stage is bypassed when Western manufacturing enterprises are transferred to the Third World and out-compete more labor-intensive, female-intensive indigenous enterprises.

In the industrial development of the West itself, women were eventually displaced by technological development; as industries became more capital-intensive, they increasingly turned from unskilled or semi-skilled female labor to higher-wage skilled male labor. It is these capital-intensive technologies, reflecting the labor-scarce, capital-abundant resource environment of the developed industrial nations today, which multinational corporations have transferred to developing host countries, thereby displacing women's traditional employment activities. At the same time, discrimination against women in both education and employment opportunities systematically excludes them from participating in the growth of wage labor in the modern capital-using industrial sector. As a result, female labor force participation frequently declines with modern economic growth and the use of new technologies.

However, there is an important and increasingly widespread exception to this general observation. In the last ten to fifteen years, the expansion of labor-intensive manufacturing for export from developing countries has created large numbers of modern factory jobs for women. Whereas traditional labor-intensive manufactured exports of textiles, garments and leather goods--industries with relatively simple technologies and stagnant or slowly-growing markets in the developed countries--have until recently been confined to a few small countries, especially Hong Kong, the practice of "offshore sourcing" by multinational corporations in technologically sophisticated industries with rapidly growing markets has spread this source of massive female employment to many more countries in Asia, Africa and Latin America.

Offshore sourcing refers to the location by multinational corporations domiciled in the developed countries of manufacturing plants in the developing countries, producing for export. Semi-finished goods and intermediate components incorporating inputs from the home country are assembled in the offshore location and then returned to the parent corporation for finishing and sale in its home or third country markets. Finished goods may also be returned to the home country, or exported directly from the offshore location to third country markets. Offshore sourcing is concentrated in labor-intensive industries, or in high technology industries with some labor-intensive processes, all of which have traditionally employed women in the home countries of the multinationals, and do the same overseas.

The offshore sourcing industry par excellence is electronics--which makes radios, televisions, digital watches and clocks, cassette recorders, calculators, TV games, CB radios, telecommunications equipment, and sophisticated intermediate products such as integrated circuits and microprocessors which are vital parts of satellites, aircraft and computers. The industry is characterized by rapid technological change which has progressively reduced the material and capital costs of electronic components, resulting in labor costs becoming a very high proportion of total manufacturing costs. While automation is possible, manual assembly using cheap foreign labor is preferred because of the smaller yield losses from manual assembly, and the fact that manual workers can be retrained whereas rapid technological change can make automated equipment obsolescent in a few months. Sophisticated technology in design and manufacture is combined with unskilled or semi-skilled labor in assembly and finishing operations.

In the late 1960's, the dominant U.S. electronics industry, faced with labor shortage and labor control problems in home production and increasing home and world market competition, especially from Japanese imports, began to move nearly 90% of its labor-intensive assembly operations offshore--a move which was rapidly followed by competing European and Japanese firms. By the mid-1970's there were perhaps a million workers employed in the offshore electronics assembly industry in Asia, about 90% of them women. Developing countries which now host electronics assembly plants include Taiwan, South Korea, Hong Kong, Singapore, Malaysia, Thailand, the Philippines, Indonesia, Mauritius, Mexico, Brazil, Barbados, Haiti, El Salvador and the Dominican Republic. The People's Republic of China has just entered the field, and a number of African countries are attempting to attract similar investment by multinational corporations.

To the multinationals, the chief attraction of offshore manufacturing in developing countries is the abundant supply of extremely cheap, industrious and docile labor in these countries, with wage rates as low as less than 5% of that of U.S. workers doing exactly the same jobs, and productivity in many countries as high as or better than that of equivalent workers in the developed countries. In addition, host governments anxious to attract foreign investment for employment creation and foreign exchange earnings through labor-intensive manufacturing for export have offered the multinationals a wide range of very attractive investment incentives, typically including the establishment of Free Trade or Export Processing Zones. These are fully-equipped industrial estates, with all the necessary infrastructural and factory building facilities provided by the government, and with exemption from all import and export taxes granted to establishing firms which are allowed 100% foreign ownership, free movement of capital and remittance of profits out of the country, and corporate tax holidays of up to twenty years. In addition, to guarantee low wages and labor stability, restrictive labor legislation has been introduced, in many cases prohibiting labor organization, unionization, strikes and other labor action in multinational subsidiaries. To permit the employment of women on night shifts, "protective" labor legislation has been removed. The "political stability and labor docility" required by multinational investors has been provided by a variety of politically repressive measures enforced by, in many of these countries, political dictatorships and martial law regimes.

The electronics industry, like the traditional labor-intensive export manufacturing industries such as garments and footwear, overwhelmingly employs women in its labor-intensive assembly processes, in both home and host countries of the multinationals. In this paper I will examine this phenomenon of preferred female employment, and its effects on women, in the two most important offshore locations of the multinational electronics industry—Malaysia and Singapore, where currently about 50,000 women are employed in the industry in each country. The results of my study* corroborate those of similar studies of female employment im labor-intensive manufacturing in other industries and other countries, and may therefore be taken to be broadly applicable to other cases of this most common form of female wage labor in modern manufacturing industry in developing countries.

Why are women almost exclusively employed in the multinational electronics industry? The following quote from an investment brochure issued by the Malaysian government in the U.S. indicates some of the reasons:

> The manual dexterity of the oriental female is famous the world over. Her hands are small and she works fast with extreme care. Who, therefore, could be better qualified by nature and inheritance, to contribute to the efficiency of a bench-assembly production line than the oriental girl? No need for a Zero Defects program here! By nature, they "quality control" themselves.

Manual dexterity and good eyesight are important requisites for electronics assembly work, and it is often asserted that women have a "natural advantage" in such work because they have smaller hands and are used to needlework.

My research indicates that a far more important reason for the supposedly higher productivity of women than men in this industry is their greater docility and willingness to subject themselves to the rigid discipline and tedious monotony of the assembly line. The rare firm which has experimented with male workers in the same jobs finds them to be insubordinate and restless, "unable to sit still for eight hours a day doing one boring repetitive task". Men tend to be "troublemakers" while women are "obedient", no doubt due to their differential socialization and acculturation in patriarchal societies. To further ensure such "obedience", firms hire only inexperienced young women, from sixteen to twenty-two years of age, who have about nine years of formal schooling on average, so that they have been habituated to the rigid discipline and conscientious work habits inculcated in schools and required on the factory floor. Personal interviews screen job candidates to select those with "the right personality"-- defined as co-operative and quiet, and to weed out potential "troublemakers".

---

*See Linda Lim, Women Workers in Multinational Corporations: the Electronics Industry in Malaysia and Singapore, Michigan Occasional Papers No. 9, Fall 1978, Women's Studies Program, University of Michigan, Ann Arbor, for detailed discussion and full references.

Productivity aside, women workers are cheaper than men, and Third World women are the cheapest labor available in the world. Prevailing labor markets wage rates for women in Malaysia and Singapore are one-third less than men's wages, and start at about U.S. $2 a day. Multinationals located in the same industrial estate further collude to keep wages down by discouraging free labor mobility (job-hopping or factory-hopping) through the common practice of blacklisting (refusing to hire) workers who leave one company in search of a better job in another, or hiring them without regard to seniority and experience, at the starting wage rate. Single women are preferred because of reluctance to pay required maternity benefits, and because it is expected that most of them will leave on getting married, to be replaced by newer and therefore cheaper workers.

Since firms try not to compete with each other for labor by bidding up wages, they attract workers by offering fringe benefits tailored to the sex and assumed feminine interests of workers. These include cooking classes, dancing lessons, fashion and make-up classes, and beauty contests, in addition to occasional picnics, outings- dinners, Christmas parties, Western movies and English lessons. The prevention of unionization by both the host government and the multinational employers in Malaysia, and the effective control of unions by the host government in Singapore, also ensure continued labor docility and low wages.

All export-oriented industries in developing countries tend to have unstable employment patterns because of their subjection to business cycle fluctuations in export markets in the developed countries. In addition electronics, though a rapid-growth and high-employment industry, experiences an industry cycle which turns down about every two years. In the highly competitive industry, firms rapidly increase output after a new technological innovation, in order to benefit from the "learning curve" and economies of scale to reduce unit costs and underprice competitors. The expansion of output by all firms leads to overproduction, accumulation of inventories, falling prices and, eventually, output and employment contraction.

These frequent recessions are viewed by employers as a "blessing in disguise" providing a "good excuse" to lay off older and more expensive workers (who have accumulated more wage increases and benefits with seniority), since there is only a short learning curve--each worker reaches maximum productivity within six to nine months in most operations. This periodic shedding of labor serves several useful functions to employers. It keeps labor costs low, with average wages remaining low because of the short job tenure of workers; it depresses the general wage level by increasing unemployment and disciplining workers--there have been instances of workers accepting lower wages for the same work in order to avoid being laid off; and the high labor turnover inhibits worker cohesion and organization and helps to forestall the formation of unions. In addition, employers are provided with the opportunity to introduce labor-saving equipment if wages have risen during the preceding boom.

The instability of employment in electronics and other labor-intensive export industries seems to be more readily acceptable in host countries because it is women, rather than men, who experience the layoffs. One of the industry's reasons for preferring to hire single young women is because there is a "natural" high turnover rate with them leaving to get married and have children. There is a prevailing assumption that women's employment in the wage labor-force is necessarily temporary, and that women's income is only secondary income, optional to the survival of themselves and their families, providing only "pocket-money". This is clearly not true where a second income is required because of the high cost of living (Singapore), or where a high proportion of males are unemployed and women are often important breadwinners (Malaysia). Despite this, there is a tendency to regard women as only a reserve army of labor, which can be easily be absorbed into the home when laid off, and need not even be counted in unemployment figures.

In summary, it is patriarchal attitudes to women's work in both host societies and among multinational employers which justify both the payment of relatively low wages for women and lack of compunction in offering them unstable jobs with short tenure. At the same time it is these easily "exploitable" characteristics of women workers which have led to a massive increase in their employment in labor-intensive factories. In both Malaysia and Singapore, female labor-force participation has risen to well over 40%, higher than in many developed countries. In Singapore, 77% of women in the eighteen to twenty-six age group are employed, while in Malaysia women already account for over half the manufacturing labor force.

The combination of technological, market, social and cultural factors which has created a great demand for the labor of young women in multinational factories has led to considerable internal as well as international (from Malaysia and Thailand to Singapore) migration of these women to the Free Trade Zones and industrial estates where the factories are located. During the period of employment, the women

Women's Work in Multinational Electronics Factories

benefit from the money incomes which they are able to earn for the first time in their lives, and many of them enjoy their new-found independence from home and family, and escape from early marriage. The vast majority of those who work do so out of economic need--their own, and that of their families, to whom they contribute a sizeable proportion of their earnings, perhaps thereby increasing their status within the family.

However, for the individual worker, her chances of becoming laid off permanently or temporarily are very high. Horizontal mobility among firms in the same industry is severely restricted, and she does not learn any transferable skills which might enhance her mobility to other sectors of the economy. Often the only alternative forms of wage employment available to young women are domestic service and prostitution. For the worker who retains her job in the factory, there is no vertical mobility within the offshore plant. Since it is only an assembly facility, 87% of the jobs are for operatives, and there is no internal job-ladder of promotion opportunities. Again, it is assumed that women do not mind such "dead-end" jobs because they have limited career aspirations and financial obligations. It is often stated that "the girls like this routine work because it is not mentally demanding" whereas men are "too impatient" and "too ambitious" for this type of work which has "no future".

The host governments in both Malaysia and Singapore have been encouraging multinational electronics firms to upgrade the skill and technology level of their operations in these countries, in particular to integrate backwards and forwards beyond the assembly stage. If this occurs, the female-intensity of the industry might decline, as labor-saving machinery replaces more assembly workers, while more jobs are created for skilled workers such as technicians and machinists, who tend to be disproportionately male. In labor-scarce Singapore, however, training of females to fill such skilled positions is being encouraged. So far the multinationals have not substantially upgraded their manufacturing activities in offshore locations, given their vertically-integrated production structures and economies of scale in the higher-skill operations which are located in their home countries.

Thus the gains from employment in multinational electronics factories are limited and temporary for the women involved, and not obtained without a considerable welfare cost to the workers. In this high technology, precision industry, the work is intense and meticulous, involving looking through a highly magnifying microscope for eight hours a day, in a rigidly regulated environment. Output goals are constantly raised, and productivity incentive schemes designed by the companies often exact more work from all workers without commensurate monetary reward--for example, in the ubiquitous "competitions" among girls on a line, among different lines, and among different plants, for "prizes" such as a gift of cheap cosmetics for the best worker on a line for the week, or a free dinner for the best production line of the month, or a free trip to the parent company for the best worker of the year.

The nature and pace of work lead to many widespread health problems--of which eye strain and eyesight deterioration, persistent headaches, stomach ailments, fatigue and nervousness are the most commonly reported. Shifts which rotate every one or two weeks have been shown to be hazardous to employees' physical and psychological health in the U.S., but the companies claim that rotating shifts are good because they "give the workers opportunity for day and evening social life". A few factories which employ married women permanently on the night-time or "graveyard" shift say this is a good practice because it "does not interfere with domestic life", permitting the woman to work at night and still do housework and look after her family during the day. Mass hysteria is a frequent occurrence on the night shifts especially in Malaysia, where they have forced several factories to close down for days.

Outside the factory, living conditions are often poor, especially where most of the workers are migrants and have to rent "deplorable" housing facilities at exorbitant prices around the industrial estates, where housing shortages are acute. The women are often crowded into dormitory-like facilities, and rotation of bedspace among women who work different shifts is sometimes practiced. Others may live as far as thirty miles away, and transportation is both scarce and expensive. Given their low wages, heavy family contributions and monopoly pricing of basic necessities around the Zones, many workers can barely survive.

At the same time, relations between the women workers and the host communities where the factories are located are often strained, and even hostile. A major source of friction between the women and conservative local communities in Malaysia, for example, is the change in social and cultural mores, in dress and life-style, which develops as the women work for multinationals which, as part of their fringe benefits, initiate them into the world of modern Western fashion, music, dancing, parties, movies, and even swimsuit beauty contests sponsored by the companies. The "modern" social and sexual behavior of some factory women gives all of them a reputation for "loose" morality, which can sometimes damage their long-run matrimonial prospects.

In general, it seems that modern factory employment in multinational corporations frees young women from some of the conservative strictures of their essentially patriarchal traditional societies, granting them a modicum of financial and social independence. However, it also leads to new forms of exploitation of female labor in the workplace, where low-paid dead-end, unstable jobs provide only small and temporary income gains. New mores functional to the operations of the multinational factory but seen to be disruptive of traditional society create divisions between the women and their local communities, sometimes fuelling religious fundamentalist objections to women's wage employment. While the development of a class consciousness among the female workers is hindered by repressive labor controls, the short duration of employment, and ethnic and linguistic differences within the labor force, there are signs of an emerging individualist feminine consciousness which would be considered "traditional" in the Western home countries of the multinational employers, and is encouraged by their labor practices.

My research and that of others suggest that the successful creation of massive job opportunities for women in the modern manufacturing sector of developing economies does not necessarily mean an improvement in women's welfare, and social and economic position in these countries. Rather, it may merely introduce further exploitation of women and, in some cases, reinforce their inequality in the labor force by confining them to marginal, low-wage, sex-segregated industrial employment.

The lot of female workers in labor-intensive multinational factories can only be improved if host governments intervene to ensure better wages and working conditions, health and living conditions, and job security. But their ability to do so is severely circumscribed by the existence of competitive suppliers of cheap female labor--the large number of other developing countries engaged in or interested in encouraging labor-intensive export manufacturing by multinational corporations. The attempts of any individual government to legislate improvements in the conditions of female employment will only raise the relative cost of female labor in that country and prompt the "footloose" multinational to shift its offshore production to another, cheaper, location. Indeed, as previously mentioned, host governments are more concerned to hold down rather than to raise the cost of labor to manufacturing firms. There is also the ever-present threat of automation and return to the home country should offshore wages rise sufficiently to make these alternatives profitable. The "new industrial protectionism" of developed countries, aimed at restricting through tariffs and quotas the export of manufactures to their home markets from developing countries, further threatens the long-run viability of offshore employment and exerts more downward pressure on wages in the struggle to remain competitive.

Thus, the establishment of industries using "appropriate" technology--labor-intensive and female-intensive--such as electronics assembly in multinational subsidiaries, has not been a panacea for women's employment problems in developing countries. The very employment of women in such industries is based on their inferior labor market status--a "comparative advantage" in offering cheap labor, based on institutionalized discriminatory wage differentials and job segregation based on sex, cultural prejudice, and the lack of equal opportunities for education and training which could provide entry into more stable, higher-productivity and higher-income industries and occupations. Removal of these inequities, while desirable, may wipe out this comparative advantage and the employment it generates for women. Nevertheless, it must be attempted, in conjunction with national development planning to create better employment opportunities for both women and men in developing countries.

Part 3

Implications for Policy

Marilyn Carr

11. Technologies Appropriate for Women: Theory, Practice and Policy

A review of recent development literature reveals a long overdue recognition of the fact that women in the rural areas of the developing countries are responsible for a large proportion of the work.[1] This is an important first step for once rural women are recognized as workers and recorded as such the planners might start planning for them to work more productively. In particular, measures might be taken to see that women gain access to the improved equipment and the credit, training and other facilities they need to do their work efficiently. Implementing the necessary changes will not be an easy exercise and improvements cannot be expected to occur quickly, but at least the trend has started to move in the right direction.

One policy which is now commonly advocated is to give rural women access to more appropriate technologies which can relieve them of many back breaking underproductive tasks on the farm and in the home and help them to increase the productivity of their labour.[2] This immediately raises two questions. First, what are the technologies which are appropriate for women; and second, what measures are needed to ensure that rural women gain access to these?

Appropriate technology has now become such a popular term that it tends to be used without due consideration being given to what it actually means. In particular, the essential question--appropriate for whom--is often left unasked. This can result in a certain amount of confusion since different technologies are obviously appropriate for different types of people in different places and at different times. What we are trying to identify in this specific instance are those technologies which are appropriate for the women currently living and working in the rural areas of the developing countries.

Theory

Theoretically speaking, there are a number of alternative ways in which each daily chore performed by a rural woman can be accomplished. Faced with this range of alternative technologies, it will be up to the woman herself to decide which one is the most appropriate to her specific needs, wants, and limitations. Obviously, the wider the range of technologies available, the more likely it will be that each woman will be able to find a technology which is ideally suited to her particular circumstances.

The idea of widening the range of available technologies was basic to the thinking of the late Dr. E. F. Schumacher.[3] He argued that modern, complex technologies are, for the moment, out of the reach of most rural communities in the developing countries. At the same time, the traditional technologies which are ideally suited in the context of a subsistence economy are usually characterized by low capital and labour productivities which do not generate the surplus needed for economic growth. There is, however, a whole range of technologies which exist or can be developed to fill the technological "gap" between these two extremes. Rural communities could never jump from step one to step ten on the technological ladder--the human, technical and financial means are simply not available. They can, however, progress through the intermediate steps in the ladder if the "intermediate" technologies which are appropriate to their needs and financial means are made available.[4] It was to collect information about these "intermediate" technologies and to make their existence more widely known that Dr. Schumacher founded the Intermediate Technology Development Group (ITDG) in London. Since its formation in 1965, ITDG and its counterparts in other developed countries[5] and in developing countries[6] have shown that a great deal of relevant information already exists; and that when it does not, the technical knowledge required to fill the gaps can be readily found--in universities and polytechnics, in industry, in government research establishments, in the professions and among field workers if their attention and expertise can be focused upon the real need.

In particular, there now appears to be a large and increasing range of technologies available for use in almost every chore in which rural women are involved. Many of these offer the chance of increasing the productivity of the women's labour without requiring large financial outlays, imported materials or highly skilled labour for operating, maintaining and repairing equipment.

For example, with respect to water supplies, there is a whole range of available technologies which can help with the problems of collection and storage of water. Wells can be dug manually near to villages on a self-help basis. Streams can be diverted and water piped to villagers. Locally produced hydraulic rams can be inserted in streams to pump water up to hillside villages. Underground catchment tanks can be built to collect and store rain water, or water can be collected from roofs and stored in various types of containers. Constant experimentation is going on to find more appropriate and cheaper materials for lining wells, constructing pipes and making storage containers. Much work has also been done on the development of water lifting devices which are operated by hand, by pedal power, wind power, solar energy or animal power. All of these provide alternatives to the expensive and usually ill-fated diesel pumps.[7]

To help with the problem of collecting and carrying firewood, there are now many technologies which can reduce the amount of firewood or charcoal needed for cooking or heating purposes. Improved stoves which use only two-thirds of the amount of wood needed with the traditional "3 stones" method of cooking can be built very simply and cheaply from mud and other locally available materials. A whole variety of solar cookers and solar ovens are available which use no source of fuel other than the sun's rays. Solar energy can also be used to heat water for washing purposes. Yet another alternative to wood is to use methane gas for cooking and lighting purposes.

In the field of transport, there are various types of animal-drawn carts, hand carts and wheelbarrows which can be made cheaply from local materials and which can help women to carry more water, fuel and other goods in less time and with less effort. There are also various techniques of constructing rural feeder roads and bridges which can make the women's task of marketing farm produce and other goods considerably easier.

For land preparation, there are improved hand tools, animal-drawn ploughs and small power tillers which are alternatives to the traditional digging implements and the high cost, high powered tractors. For seeding, weeding and fertilizer application, there are many devices of varying complexity and cost which can do the job more quickly and in a less back-breaking way than the traditional methods. For harvesting, scythes and little knapsack reapers which are powered by small diesel engines or by solar power are alternatives to the traditional penknife and the large combine harvester. For threshing and winnowing, there is hand, animal and pedal-operated equipment which is intermediate between the time-consuming and wasteful traditional methods and expensive engine-driven machines. In addition, there is a whole range of relatively low-cost equipment powered in a variety of ways and designed to grind cereals, grate cassava, shell maize, extract oil from fruits, nuts and seeds, shell groundnuts, pit dates and scrape the flesh from coconuts.

To all of this, still further technologies can be added which can help the rural women. Pit latrines, soak pits and sun tables can make the women's tasks of keeping the home neat and hygienic much simpler. Technologies such as kick wheels and improved spinning and weaving equipment can help women to produce their traditional pottery, textiles and rugs more efficiently and raise more income from such work with less effort. Technologies such as improved bee-hives and simple solar dryers can open up new sources of income to rural women through bee-keeping and food processing activities made simpler and less time consuming. Low cost methods of storing rain water and simple water lifting devices can make activities such as poultry keeping and vegetable growing possible for women who could otherwise not afford the time to collect the quantities of water involved.[8]

There is obviously no lack of equipment which would seem to be appropriate for rural women in the developing countries. However, the fact that the equipment exists is obviously not enough. Women walking long distances with heavy loads of water, fuel or other goods on their heads and backs, and women processing crops in the traditional time-consuming ways are still very common sights. Women continue to be overburdened and overworked and unable to engage in income-generating activities to help out with family expenses because they are fully occupied in underproductive tasks.

Why are the technologies which do exist not being utilized to any great extent by the women who need them to quicken the impact of rural development?

Practice

There seem to be three major reasons why rural women in the developing countries are not using new "improved" technologies on a widespread basis.

First, although some technologies may appear to be "appropriate" in the eyes of the technologists and development workers, the people who expect to use them--the rural women--may not think them appropriate at all. This seems to have been the case with much of the research into and development of new cooking technologies which reduce the need for firewood. In the rush to save the fast diminishing forests of the Third World, the technologists seem to have so far proceeded without any due consideration being given to a number of relevant factors such as the needs and wants of the end users of their products. For example, there has been a proliferation of solar reflective cookers which can be used to prepare food without firewood, but which also ignore prevailing customs and conditions in the villages. Such cookers must be placed directly facing into the sun and have therefore to be constantly adjusted as the sun moves. An additional disadvantage is that they cannot support a sufficiently large pot to cook a full meal for a large family. Another objection to these cookers is that the main meal of the day is usually cooked in the evening when the sun has either gone to rest or has lost most of its strength. In addition, village women in many countries are used to cooking indoors and are hostile to the idea of moving their stoves into the open--and especially into the direct sunlight.[9]

Similarly, the proponents of the use of methane gas for cooking seem to have forgotten that production of the gas involves the use of large quantities of water and that in many areas where wood is scarce (e.g., in the Sahel countries of Africa) water is even scarcer. Women are unlikely to see the value of adopting a cooking method which substitutes long walks to collect firewood with even longer walks to collect water and additionally involves collecting animal dung and mixing this with water.

There are other instances of technologies which may appear to be appropriate in the eyes of their designers but are not so in the eyes of the rural women who are the ones expected to use them. For example, attempts have been made in West Africa to introduce scythes to help the women with harvesting the rice crop. These were believed to be much more appropriate than the traditional small knife which the women use in a very time-consuming way to cut each stalk individually. The women, however, were reluctant to adopt these implements since they necessitated cutting much further down the stalk which meant a heavier load to be carried from the farm to the home and caused nasty cuts when they threshed the crop with their bare feet.[10]

Also from West Africa came reports of women demonstrating against the introduction of mills for extracting oil from palm fruits. These mills definitely increased the efficiency of oil extraction but since the whole fruit went to the mill (with the male head of the household being given the money for this), the women were deprived of the by-products of processing the fruit (e.g., the oil-containing nut) which they used to keep as payment for their labour.[11]

Out of such instances has arisen the myth that rural women are resistent to the changes brought about by the introduction of new technologies. This is obviously an oversimplification of the true situation. Women who are working up to 16 hours a day to provide the basic essentials of life for their families are unlikely to reject anything within their access which could improve their situation as they perceive it. If they do reject a new technology, it is almost always because it is one which would make the current situation worse rather than better.

Second, it would appear that some technologies have not received widespread acceptance because they relate to a very low priority need as far as rural women are concerned. This applies particularly to technologies such as pit latrines and soak pits which are related to improving the home environment. In most African countries, for example, the majority of women immediately state that they need help with carrying water, fuel and farm produce and with processing crops. Very few mention a need for better sanitation. This is well-illustrated in the report of a study in Swaziland which pointed out that although the investigators saw sanitation as a problem (with the majority of households using the bush for personal sanitation and disposal of all rubbish) it was rarely mentioned by the people[12] Obviously, very little success can be expected in trying to introduce new technologies for which people see no immediate need. Pit latrines and other sanitation aids are not unimportant, but they will be met with little enthusiasm at the village level while more pressing problems such as provision of water and fuel remain unsolved.

Third, many improved technologies which are appropriate for rural women are not being used by them because--in one way or another--they are denied access to them. In the great majority of cases, rural women are completely unaware of the existence of improved technologies which could help them. When information does filter down to the village level, it is usually the men who receive it, either because the extension workers are men, or because it is only the men who have time to sit around at organized meetings or demonstrations where such information might be given out.[13]

Even when women do learn of the existence of certain technologies, there are further obstacles placed in their way. Women are often denied access to credit facilities because the land and buildings which are needed as collateral are held in the man's name. They rarely have access to advice on how to form themselves into a cooperative and secure a loan through a cooperative scheme.[14] Most rural women could not afford to purchase (even collectively) a grinding mill, an oil-press or a pedal thresher without the help of a loan, and their husbands may see no point in utilizing credit facilities to acquire such devices when there is plenty of "free" female labour to do the work.

Before leaving this issue, it should be pointed out that men often do use their access to credit to acquire new technologies when this offers a chance of making quick and easy profits. Most grinding mills are owned by men who charge their female clientele increasingly high rates for the use of the equipment. It is a bitter complaint of the poorer women in such villages that they cannot afford such rates and that they have no means of improving their situation by acquiring equipment of their own. Making credit available to rural women's groups or cooperatives would seem to be a very plausible way of precipitating the widespread dissemination of improved technologies and of meeting the needs of the poorest of the poor. To back up this argument, it should be noted that in the few instances when women have been given access to credit to buy improved technologies, they prove to be much better at repaying their loans than are men. For example, the Department of Cooperatives in Sierra Leone reported a 100 percent repayment rate on loans given to women's cooperatives as opposed to a rate of nearer 50 percent for men's cooperatives.[15] Similarly in The Cameroons, all loans given to women's groups to purchase corn mills were repaid to the Department of Community Services within a year.[16]

Policy

In the preceding pages, a very complex problem has been dealt with in relatively simple terms so that the basic points being made can stand out as clearly as possible. Implicit in these are several guidelines for action which are now looked at more fully.

Assuming that the major concern is to help rural women in the developing countries by giving them access to improved technologies which are appropriate to their needs and financial constraints, the problem being faced is not a purely technical one since a large range of technological alternatives already exists--as does the technological expertise to fill most of the remaining gaps. Why then do rural women continue to struggle through their work without the help of improved technologies? At the same time, why do so many low-cost technologies designed for use in the rural areas fail to be used on a widespread basis? These two questions are not unrelated. There are three important reasons why both these situations occur.

First, not nearly enough thought has been given to the *exact* wants, needs and problems of rural women when designing technologies or to the possible consequences for women of using the technologies. It would be interesting to know how many technologists in the developed and developing countries actually consult the end users at the design stage whether their inventions are ones which will be culturally acceptable, will result in less rather than more work for rural women, or will lead to a redistribution of income favourable to the women.[17] Much more socio-economic research needs to be conducted alongside the purely technical research if technologies which are both useful and acceptable to rural women are to be developed.

Secondly, not enough thought is given to priority needs in specific areas. However clever, simple or cheap a new technology might be, it will stand little chance of gaining widespread acceptance if it does not meet a priority need. Again, more socio-economic research is required so that technologies can be developed in accordance with felt needs. This is obviously more sensible than developing the technology first and then trying to persuade people that they need it.

Finally, not enough thought has been given to how new technologies are supposed to get into the hands of the people who need them. Much more positive action is required to ensure that information about improved technologies reaches the rural women and that credit/cooperative facilities are made available to them so that they can purchase such technologies. This is obviously much more difficult to follow through than are the previous two recommendations. It requires, for example, the training of many more female extension workers who can inform rural women about new techniques, help them to form and run cooperatives and-- ideally--train women how to operate, maintain and repair any equipment they purchase. This is a fairly long term and far from easy objective.

Several agencies have now started to work along these lines. For example, the village technology programme of the

African Training and Research Centre for Women of ECA is based on conducting socio-economic research at the village level before--as well as during and after--the introduction of improved technologies. Thus, in a project in Sierra Leone, an improved oil-press was designed and produced by the University's Engineering Department in accordance with the needs of the rural women--as related through the field staff of the Ministry of Rural Development. A few of these presses are currently being tested for utility and acceptability in selected pilot villages. Results are still awaited, but it seems certain that these presses will be far more successful than previous ones which have been developed without reference to the potential end user.[18] Similarly, ITDG is now embarking on a major research project which involves assisting national AT centres in developing countries to design improved stoves in accordance with the requirements and preferences expressed by rural people living in specific areas.

With respect to increasing the flow of information and services related to technology, at least a start has been made by several agencies in regard to orienting existing female extension workers. The African Training and Research Centre for Women, UNICEF, and FAO have all been involved in running national workshops in the African region which are aimed at improving the partipants' knowledge and understanding of improved village-level technologies.[19] At a slightly different level, the Overseas Development Ministry of the British Government is funding a six-week intensive course on women and technology for fifteen female government employees in charge of women's programmes in developing countries.[20]

Notes

1. For example, the sources listed in N. J. Hafkin, Women and Development in Africa: An Annotated Bibliography, ECA, Addis Ababa, 1976. It now seems to be widely accepted that women are responsible for 60 to 80 percent of the work in the rural areas of Africa and Asia. In Latin America it is estimated to be 40 percent.

2. For example, in the UN document entitled "A Study of the Interagency Programme for the United Nations Decade for Women: Equality, Development and Peace," it was recommended that ECA/ATRCW, UNICEF, UNDP, FAO, UNESCO, and the World Bank have planned activities and studies for the development, promotion and improvement of village-level, low-cost technologies available to women, in order to enhance their contribution to economic life.

3. See in particular, E. F. Schumacher, <u>Small is Beautiful: A Study of Economics as if People Mattered</u>, London, Abacus, 1974.

4. Although communities with severe technical and financial constraints may be limited initially to step two or three in the ladder, others may well be able to jump straight to step eight or nine.

5. These include VITA in the USA, GATE in West Germany, GRET in France, and TOOL in Holland.

6. These include the Appropriate Technology Development Association in India, the Technology Consultancy Centre in Ghana, and the South Pacific Appropriate Technology Foundation (SPATF) in Papua, New Guinea.

7. Several evaluation studies have shown that the simpler methods of providing water supplies (e.g., hand pumps) are not only cheaper but also much more reliable than methods involving diesel engines. See for example: R. Feacham, et al, <u>Water, Health and Development</u>, London, Tri-Med Book Ltd., 1978.

8. Details of these and many more technologies can be found in the large selection of books and manuals available from Intermediate Technology Publications, Ltd., 9 King Street, London, WC2.

9. Attempts to introduce solar reflective cookers in Ethiopia failed because people believe that standing out in the sunlight causes certain illnesses and skin complaints.

10. See M. Carr, "Report on a Visit to Liberia," ECA, ATRCW, 1976.

11. See P. Kilby, <u>Industrialization in an Open Economy: Nigeria 1945-1966</u>, Cambridge University Press, 1969, pp. 159-165. The fact that the introduction of new technologies can result in a redistribution of income within the household away from the woman towards the man (who is more likely to buy consumer goods such as transistor radios than more nutritious food or basic essentials for his family) has become a subject os some concern. See for example I. Palmer, "Rural Women and the Basic Needs Approach to Development," in <u>International Labour Review</u>, Vol. 115, No. 1, Jan/Feb 1977.

12. Fion de Vletter, "The Rural Homestead as an Economic Unit: A Case Study of the Northern Rural Development Area," University College of Swaziland, 1978.

13. A well-known illustration of this comes from Liberia where a team of Taiwanese farmers were invited to demonstrate the principles of planting irrigated rice. To assure attendance at the demonstration, the government offered wages to the observers. Many unemployed men participated in the experiment while the women (the ones who do the planting) continued their work in the fields. Source: I. Tinker, "The Adverse Impact of Development on Women," Peace Corps Program and Training Journal, Vol. IV, No. 6, 1977.

14. Statistics collected by the African Training and Research Centre for Women of ECA show that of those people having access to training and advice on cooperatives, a maximum of 10 percent are women.

15. M. Carr, Report on a visit to Sierra Leone, ECA/ATRCW, 1976.

16. E. O'Kelly, Aid and Self Help, London, Charles Knight and Company, Ltd., 1973.

17. Part of the problem is that the end users are predominantly rural women and very real difficulties are faced by male technologists seeking to communicate with them or understand their problems. There is a need for many more women technologists.

18. For a full description of this and other technology projects of the African Training and Research Centre for Women, see M. Carr, Appropriate Technology for African Women, ECA, Addis Ababa, 1978.

19. The proceedings of many of these workshops are available in workshop reports published by ATRCW, ECA, Box 3001, Addis Ababa.

20. To be held in July/August 1979.

ODE TO A BUMBLEBEE*

Engineers tell me that
By all laws you should fall flat
Upon your black and yellow face
When trying feats of flight in space.

Louise Fortmann

*The bumblebee is aerodynamically impossible.

Louise Fortmann

12. The Plight of the Invisible Farmer: The Effect of National Agricultural Policy on Women in Africa

As a general rule, national agricultural development policies seem to proceed from the assumption that either agricultural producers are all male or the sex of producers is not a relevant factor. Occasionally the productive role of women is acknowledged at the rhetorical level, but this is rarely reflected in national policy. Rather, planners appear to operate from a world view in which only men are producers. Women are seen as reproducers and consumers of both goods and social services. Both their labor and their production problems are for all intents and purposes invisible.

If there were little or no difference in the roles and resources of men and women, this would be of little consequence. But often the differences are significant. Hence, agricultural development policy which ignores or misunderstands the needs of women producers may have adverse effects on women and/or fail to increase agricultural production.

In order to understand the effect of agricultural development policy on women, it is necessary to identify their roles in agricultural production. In any given country it may be necessary to make this determination separately for women by class, ethnic or religious group, and marital and parental status. Once the relevant divisions have been determined, the following questions can be asked for each group:

<u>What do women do?</u> Do they grow cash or subsistence crops? Are they wage laborers or independent producers? Do they care for livestock or poultry?

<u>How do they do it?</u> What technology are they using?

What are the institutional arrangements that govern their access to land, labor, and capital?

<u>What benefits do they receive?</u> Do women control what they produce? What share of the profit do they get?

Once women's role in agriculture has been determined from the perspective of these three questions, some fundamental questions about policy can be formulated. Again, the policy questions must be asked separately for each group of women, since the general problems of women producers are often magnified in poorer or female-headed households.

a) Are there factors constraining the role of women in agricultural production which fall into a policy vacuum, or are women the subject of policy which has not been enforced?

b) Do policies include women in the target population but fail to reach them because of program design?

c) Do policies adversely affect the position of women?

d) Are policies designed so that women receive the benefit from the labor they contribute?

Using this framework, this paper explores the effect of agricultural policy on women in Tanzania. Tanzania presents a particularly interesting case because equality between the sexes is an avowed government policy. The President has a strong personal commitment to improving women's status and has repeatedly stressed the importance of their contribution to development. Women have been appointed to the highest regional and district political offices. University entrance requirements were adjusted to facilitate the education of women. And women are registered independent of their husbands and fathers as members of their village. The latest policy initiative was the February 1979 announcement by the Vice President that the exclusion of women from mosques was inconsistent with the national policy of equality. As a result, some mosques were open to women for Maulid ([1]).

Women are central to Tanzanian agricultural production. Of economically active women, 97.8 percent are involved in agriculture. Their work is most significant for village and household production. Some women are also involved as wage laborers, but they make up only 5 percent of agricultural employees ([2]). Women traditionally have been responsible for the subsistence production which feeds the family ([3]). Often (but not always) men will help with some of the heavier work, such as clearing and cultivating. Weeding is almost exclusively a women's task. If the household has cows, women are generally responsible for milking them. While cash crops are considered men's crops and men control the money received from them, women do a considerable amount of the work, especially the tedious tasks such as thinning and weeding. Women are also important to agricultural production because they do all domestic maintenance work--food storage and preparation, cleaning, collecting firewood, and hauling water. Thus women not only work more hours per day and more days per year in agriculture than men, but their domestic work also frees men to spend such time as they may choose in agricultural work.

Given this central role of women in agricultural production and the serious effort to promote the status of women, it might be expected that agricultural policy would take account of their needs. This has not, however, been the case in several respects.

Factors in Women's Agricultural Production Excluded from Agricultural Policy

The most critical factor in agriculture is access to land. Access to land in their own right has become increasingly important to women because of the monetization of the economy and the breakdown of traditional support systems. Monetization of the economy has placed women in the position of needing cash to meet both subsistence needs and government requirements such as school fees. Breakdown of traditional forms of social security such as the levirate or the right of return to the household of one's father or brother has left women economically vulnerable in the event of losing (or never obtaining) a spouse.

All land belongs to the nation, and in theory every citizen has the right to its use. But commercialization of agriculture and land pressure in some areas have made land in many instances an increasingly valuable and scarce resource. For the most part, allocation of land to individuals is in the hands of elected village councils. In practice, traditional land rights have considerable influence over the allocation process. The traditional right of women to hold land varies significantly from tribe to tribe. Zaramo and Luguru women have traditionally had the right to inherit or to apply to their clan for land. Arusha widows may continue to cultivate their husband's fields, but upon their death their sons and not their daughters inherit. Haya women do not inherit their husband's land and may be removed by the son who does (4). Village councils have been known to refuse to give land to women and to deny women's groups land for planting permanent cash crops (5).

For a woman, then, access to land often becomes a function of having a living husband. Or she may try to raise money to buy land (6). In theory the policy of ujamaa provides women with independent access to land. But it is only in a very few places that ujamaa production has reached a level that meets the subsistence needs of the members.

The inability to hold land not only reduces the production potential of women; it keeps them economically powerless and forces them into master/servant relationships with their husbands or fathers. Because a women's need for land is not perceived as a problem (or is perhaps perceived as a threat), there are no procedures by which she can enforce her theoretical right to have it. The establishment of such procedures and clear-cut rights to land for women involves extremely complex issues--residence rights, cultivation rights, and resolving conflicting systems of inheritance. But this lack constitutes the single greatest gap in Tanzanian agricultural policy in terms of women.

A second difficult policy area is that of legal rights over children. Children are economic assets in rural Tanzania because they provide a supply of labor (7) and are relied upon for support in their parents' old age. Children are traditionally the estate of the husband (and, often, his male relatives), and he may take them after the age of seven (roughly the age at which they cease being only consumers and can be useful in herding, weeding, and so on). Thus a divorced or separated woman, even if she has land, may be left without the assistance of her children in her fields and their support in her old age.

A third issue concerns the failure to define the women's domestic activities as an enabling function for agricultural production. Women spend a great deal of time in drudgery which directly or indirectly contributes to production. A case in point is the provision of water, which has most frequently been defined in terms of social welfare. In fact it is properly a matter for agricultural policy. Not only is water directly necessary for the utilization of many improved agricultural technologies (water for irrigation, water for mixing with chemicals, water for livestock and poultry), but a significant part of most women's day is spent in carrying water--for both domestic and agricultural needs--time which might otherwise be applied to more productive activities. Tanzania does, in fact, have an ambitious village water program, but its importance in relieving a constraint on agricultural production, particularly subsistence production, goes basically unrecognized.

Agricultural Policies Implemented so as to Exclude Women

Some agricultural policies are intended to affect all cultivators, but because of women's special problems of access they are excluded. The extension service is a prime example. Because the system is designed as if women did not do most of the work, extension agents and agricultural information rarely reach them. Data from a study of the National Maize Project (NMP), a production project, are presented in Table 1.

Table 1. Comparison of male and female information contact scores† (by region and participation in the National Maize Project)

	Males	Females	t
Arusha			
Participants	4.08	3.54	0.68
Nonparticipants	2.16	1.24	2.27*
t	4.33***	5.73***	
Morogoro			
Participants	5.18	2.87	2.52**
Nonparticipants	2.75	1.51	2.60**
t	4.66***	2.89***	

N = 485

* Significant at .05 level.
** Significant at .01 level.
*** Significant at .001 level.

†The information contact score consisted of the following items: knows the extension agent's name, visited by extension agent in the past year, attended a farming demonstration in the past year, knows there is a demonstration plot in the village, listens to the agricultural radio program, reads the agricultural magazine, has seen a film on maize.

Data from (8).

On the whole, women scored significantly lower than men on the information contact score. This reflects the prevailing norms about appropriate behavior for women and the staffing pattern of the extension service. Most of the extension staff are male. There are social constraints on male/female interaction which reduce the likelihood of a male agent's talking directly to a female farmer. Further, the conventional wisdom that women cannot reason as well as men reduces any incentive for working with women. The result is a system under which women must rely on a man to relay the information second hand from the extension agent. (In Morogoro Region, for example, extension agents visited 58 percent of the men participating in NMP but only 20 percent of the women [9].) Reliance on indirect communication runs the risk that the information may not be transmitted accurately. This is particularly important because women actually implement the decisions their husbands may make on the basis of the extension agent's advice. Further, female heads of households (roughly 25 percent of the population) may have no channel of information at all. There is a clear need for female extension agents or some other means by which women can obtain equal access to the technical information they need.

The extension service is primarily male, because women have not been admitted to agricultural training in large numbers. In 1975 only 25 percent of the graduates of Agricultural Training Institutes (the source of extension agents) were women, and 25 percent of these were studying nutrition, not agriculture (10). Very few women were sent to the (now defunct) farmer training courses. Women's child care responsibilities constrain their ability to attend training courses. The current Folk Development Colleges do not always have facilities for child care or nursing mothers.

Access to relevant new technologies also tends to be a problem for women. Although Tanzania has a vigorous food crop research program, the majority of agricultural research is directed toward cash crops, which are controlled by men. Some of the cash crop technologies could be utilized by women on their subsistence crops. The ultra-low-volume (ULV) sprayer, for example, developed for use on cotton, could as easily be used on maize. However, most cash crop inputs, including sprayers, are distributed through the cash crop authorities to their growers; hence women tend to be excluded.

In general, credit and input supply programs seem not to reach women producers. Only 8 percent of the participants in the National Maize Program in a sample of 27 villages were women (60 percent of these being female heads of households).

In two villages there were no women participants at all, reportedly because the men refused to allow them to buy inputs (11).

It is not altogether clear why women did not participate. It is, however, clear that the answer is not that they are inferior farmers. As the data presented in Table 2 clearly show, women who participated in the program were as progressive as the males, while male nonparticipants were as traditional as female nonparticipants. It may be that discrimination against women by program administrators was not limited to only two villages. Since female-headed households are often the poorest, they may not have been able to afford the inputs or to risk taking credit for them. In the case of a wheat credit program, farmers with small acreages (often the case with female heads of households) could not afford to put their land into wheat production. In order to include women in production programs, the constraints under which they operate must be considered.

Policies with Adverse Effects on Women

Some policies have adverse effects on women by increasing their work load, which already averages over ten hours a

Table 2. Comparison of male and female good maize practice scores (by region and participation in the National Maize Project)

	Males	Females	t
Arusha			
Participants	9.88	9.88	0.00008
Nonparticipants	4.09	4.17	0.125
t	9.38***	7.39***	
Morogoro			
Participants	6.81	5.83	0.856
Nonparticipants	4.08	3.55	0.896
t	4.07***	3.34***	

N = 485

*** Significant at .001 level

Data from (12).

day. Nonagricultural policies can have this effect by luring men away to wage labor, leaving the women to run the household farms completely alone. Other policies emphasize technologies which require additional labor--usually women's labor. It is the women who must carry the forage and extra water required by exotic breeds of cows and poultry. Women carry the water for backpack insecticide sprayers. Women do the extra weeding that follows the use of fertilizer. Women harvest, thresh, and sometimes carry to market the extra produce from high-yielding varieties. Sometimes ujamaa falls under this category. In some places villages were forced to cultivate an ujamaa farm. It was not an uncommon response for men to send their wives to work on this farm as the token family members. These women then had ujamaa field work added to their regular work load, often without much return.

A second set of policies may adversely affect women by driving them out of agriculture or significantly reducing their income-generating capacity. In the past few years the Tanzanian government has indicated increasing interest in production on large mechanized state farms. These parastatals often utilize so much land that they create a land shortage in their immediate vicinity. Land shortages can be expected to aggravate the problem of women's access to land. This is not compensated for by access to jobs. The high-paying nonmanagerial jobs on such state farms--driver, mechanic, foreman--are reserved for men. For some crops--sisal, for example--only men are employed. In other crops the proportion of women workers is minute. Regulation of markets, including the imposition of market fees, may have the effect of precluding women from selling their own produce. Relatively few women in Tanzania actually sell in the market. Those who do tend to be smaller operators who can least afford these fees (13).

Ensuring That Women Benefit from Their Labor

President Nyerere has said, "Women who live in villages work harder than anybody else in Tanzania." Often they fail to get the benefit of all this hard work.

The early settlement schemes, for example, were planned in terms of male settlers and their families. In some schemes, settlers left their wives at home to tend the family fields and picked up a female companion along the way. These women did most of the work but, having no legal status, had no right to the fruits of their labors (14). Ujamaa policy, which gave women individual membership, provided a partial solution to this problem. But even women with the legal status of wife have no guarantee that their husbands will share with them the profit from the cash crops which they helped to grow. Finding a means of protecting women's interests, particularly in the latter case, is highly problematic.

Tanzanian agricultural policy has been shown, despite the best intentions of the government, to ignore or run counter to the interests of women on a fairly regular basis. Access to land, the extension services, inputs, improved technology, and credit are inadequately provided them under existing policy implementation. The production-enabling significance of their domestic activities remains unrecognized.

One might speculate that women farmers are invisible because there are no women on the planning staff to look for and look out for them. There are no women in senior policy positions in any of the organizations dealing with farmers—the Ministry of Agriculture, the Tanzania Rural Development Bank, the National Milling Corporation, or the cash crop authorities.

Solving the problems of female farmers is no simple task. Family power relationships and negative attitudes do not lend themselves to simple solutions. But an agricultural policy which ignores women is in a real sense not an agricultural policy at all and is doomed to be ineffective. Women producers must have secure rights to land and labor; must have access to information, inputs, and improved technology; and must benefit from their own labor. Without these, to the detriment of national production, their yields will remain low and their potential wasted.

References and Notes

1. Daily News (Dar es Salaam), 7 February 1979.

2. C. Koley, "Agricultural data," pp. 149-155 in The Population of Tanzania, Census Volume 6, B. Egero and R. A. Henin, eds. (Bureau of Resource Assessment and Land Use Planning, University of Dar es Salaam, and Bureau of Statistics, Dar es Salaam, 1973).

3. There is relatively little class formation in Tanzania; hence it is possible to speak generally of Tanzanian women as a whole. Some differences between ethnic groups are described in this paper. Problems are almost invariably aggravated for female heads of households.

4. R. Young and H. Fosbrooke, Smoke in the Hills (Northwestern University Press, Evanston, Ill., 1960), p. 61; M. L. Swantz, Ritual and Symbol in Transitional Zaramo Society (Gleerup, Uppsala, 1970), pp. 96-97; and M. L. Swantz, "Strain and strength among peasant women in Tanzania," BRALUP Research Paper No. 49 (Bureau of Resource Assessment and Land Use Planning, University of Dar es Salaam, 1977), pp. 6-7.

5. Planting permanent crops is sensitive, since, for example, the person planting an orange tree retains possession of that tree regardless of who owns the land.

6. Contrary to government policy, land in some places is openly bought, sold, and rented. The only businesses readily open to village women are brewing beer and, less frequently, petty trading. In a few instances, women become prostitutes, using their earnings to buy land.

7. Universal Primary Education presumably is reducing the amount of such labor.

8. L. P. Fortmann, "Women and Tanzanian agricultural development," Economic Research Bureau Paper No. 77.4 (University of Dar es Salaam, 1977), p. 14.

9. L. P. Fortmann, "An evaluation of the progress of the National Maize Project at the end of one cropping season in Morogoro and Arusha Regions," prepared for USAID/Tanzania, 1976, p. 30.

10. L. P. Fortmann, Eastern African Journal of Rural Development, Special Issue, 101 (1976).

11. Fortmann (9), p. 29.

12. Fortmann (8), p. 4.

13. A. Fleuret, "The role of women in rural markets: Lushoto, Tanzania," paper presented at the First Women and Anthropology Symposium, Sacramento, California, March 1977.

14. J. L. Brain, "Less than second class: Women in rural settlement schemes in Tanzania," in Women in Africa, Nancy J. Hafkin and Edna G. Bay, eds. (Stanford University Press, Stanford, Calif., 1976), pp. 271-273.

Hanna Papanek

13. The Differential Impact of Programs and Policies on Women in Development

The goal of "integrating women in the development process as equal partners with men" has been accepted by member governments of the United Nations since 1975 and has affected the national policies of some of them. But the <u>diagnosis</u> of women's special needs and the <u>design of policies</u> to meet these needs have continued to face many obstacles.

In this paper, I argue that serious commitments to diagnosis and policy design have not yet been made in international agencies and national governments to the extent required by the goal that has been accepted. Both diagnosis and policy design require a differentiated view of the women in a particular country, one that takes account of distinctions of income and class in the context of economic, political and social factors. The present undifferentiated view, underlying much development planning, often takes a curious "as if" stance--as if women were like men, as if all women were alike, or as if women did not exist at all.

I argue further that problems of diagnosis and remedy exist at many levels, from local community programs to national development policies and the policies of aid-giving agencies. Lack of effective linkage between local and national levels, or between specific programs and macro-policies, usually prevents the achievement of women's integration in development. The most significant problem remains the failure to recognize that women--like men--are affected by <u>all</u> development policies. The gains achieved by a local project can be wiped out by a policy change at the national level. Women are not an isolated group in the population of any country but are integrated into every institution, from the family to the state, even if that integration takes different forms for women and men. Because women are already integrated into their societies, already participating in economic and political activities, albeit usually with less power than men, the integration of women in development requires specific measures appropriate to their particular situation. The idea that the benefits of development will automatically "trickle down" to the poor has already been challenged in many quarters. Why should we then assume that the benefits of development, once they reach men, will automatically "trickle over" to women?

Diagnosis and policy design also depend on accurate research, even if policy decisions are ultimately made within the fairly narrow constraints of resource availability and national or international political considerations. With regard to the importance of research, it has already become clear that the large investments made in development-oriented economic research have paid off in terms of effective policy design. For this reason, I argue that some investments must be made in research on women in the context of the same broad frameworks of analysis also used in other types of development research on economic, social, and political issues. Until now, research on women and development has largely been the province of individual committed scholars in many countries.[1] Occasionally, this research has been supported by public or private resources, but the scholars themselves tend to remain in isolated positions in universities or national and international agencies that do not recognize the value of their work. In other words, little has been done to date to create the scientific competence to carry out broadly based policy-oriented research on specific problems of women and development, so that understanding gained in one region or academic discipline can be applied to the solution of problems encountered elsewhere. Without this body of scientific competence, it remains difficult to plan and evaluate programs, projects and policies affecting development and women. Yet attempts to create this broader understanding often run into persistent obstacles.

These obstacles to research also stand in the way of effective policy regarding women; both sets of problems deserve more detailed discussion. The most significant obstacle to both research and policy design is the existing emphasis on isolated "women's projects" or programs or "women's components" in development projects. Many of these undertakings are excellent in themselves and may meet the pressing needs of women in many communities. But they are not enough. An analogy may make this point clearer. In South Asia, regional development programs to benefit less developed regions of undivided Pakistan were common before Bangladesh became independent, but the benefits of these remedial programs were usually wiped out by the effects of national policies, such as the exchange rate that favored import-substituting industries (mainly located in West Pakistan) over export-oriented activities (mainly located in East Pakistan, now Bangladesh). In other words, excellent local programs may benefit women in the short run, but the effects of such programs can be wiped out by policies at the national level that appear to be unrelated to women but actually affect their interests in many ways.

In the second place, an emphasis on isolated "projects" or "components" reflects an approach to women that hampers their integration in the development process rather than advancing it. Of course, it is well known that the "project approach" is characteristic of many national and international agencies concerned with development. In the United States, for example, the Percy Amendment (no. 574 to the Foreign Assistance Bill of 1973, S.2335) states that the major provisions of the Foreign Assistance Act "shall be administered so as to give attention to those programs, projects and activities which tend to integrate women into the national economies of foreign countries, thus improving their status and assisting the total development effort."[2] Other examples of the project approach can be seen in the procedures and criteria used by many international and national bodies in the field of development.

While the project approach may be the most feasible for the implementation of certain kinds of solutions to problems of development, it should be kept in mind that--in the case of women--this approach perpetuates certain conceptual and institutional barriers to women's integration in the development process. For example, in the case of India it has been pointed out that "the national consensus to keep the women's question out of the sphere of political controversy has resulted in "projecting it as a purely social issue of long-term changes in attitudes, through education and development."[3] Under such circumstances, it is not surprising that development planners and researchers tend to focus on remedial programs for women and on education, rather than on possible direct changes in economic, political, and legal structures as they affect women.

An institutional consequence of this view of women's needs--which is widely shared by other nations besides India-- is the location of most women's programs and projects in educational and social welfare agencies. But remedial agencies are not at the center of power in any nation. Major policy decisions about economic and political development are made elsewhere. Of course, there have been many important positive outcomes from programs undertaken by social welfare and educational institutions that have greatly benefited women. This makes it even more difficult to contemplate changes in the structure and location of agencies concerned with women's needs and interests. In many countries, social welfare ministries may be the strongest advocates for women; they are often staffed by the most committed supporters of development programs for women. Perhaps as a result, there may be few supporters in other parts of the government in many nations. Women's interests have not yet been accurately perceived to matter politically or to be important to the effective functioning of other public and private agencies. For example, while women may often be effectively mobilized around issues such as legal reform, their support is often dissipated in struggles between other interest groups instead of being organized around specific issues that may unite women's economic or social interests. For another example, it should be recognized that, in many instances, the effective integration of women into specific aspects of development may spell the difference between the success and failure of a development program, such as the introduction of new agricultural techniques.

The mistaken idea that women are always the dependents of men usually accounts for the notion that public agencies can only intervene when the family has failed and the policies directed toward men will automatically benefit women. In actual fact, of course, women contribute as much as men to family earnings, particularly among the poor, whether this contribution is reflected in national income statistics or not. Furthermore, many families are supported entirely by women, as when men have died or disappeared, or when they are ill, disabled, or incompetent. There are significant distinctions between cultures with regard to women's participation in the paid labor force, but these differences are often overshadowed by the importance of class and income. Research on these distinctions will be of great significance for development policies, since many stereotypes and preconceptions obscure the true facts and lead to false prescriptions.

The conception of women as a "backward" group whose needs can be met by scattered programs and projects not only undermines the formulations of adequate development policies but also affects the building of an accurate data base and relevant frameworks of analysis in research. There is often a divergence between the kinds of research produced by scholars and those that policy-makers consider important. This divergence is particularly severe in the case of research on women and emphasizes the importance of building scientific capacity for work in this area. Many kinds of research management are, of course, employed to bridge the gap between the research priorities of policy-makers and those who actually carry out research, particularly if they are independent scholars. These methods range from the selection procedures of private and public agencies in awarding research grants to the processes by which national and international agencies select research consultants and subcontractors. Women are not well represented on most of these bodies. Research on women, moreover, is often not taken seriously by those who set research priorities, either because the field is relatively new or because of generalized prejudice.

Furthermore, the requirements of institutions for certain kinds of information are more likely to set the terms of reference for research than the perceived needs of the group to be studied or the interest of individual scholars. The problem-solving needs of a concrete enterprise usually determine the framework within which research is formulated and the "language" or approach to be used. While some perception of the needs of a particular group may contribute to the formulation of the problem to be solved, members of that group rarely influence the ways in which research is carried out and used in arriving at solutions. Individual scholars are often closer to the population to be studied and may be more aware of the terms of reference the "target group" would like to see applied to them. The possible divergence between these two sets of interests must be resolved between the researcher and the institution interested in her results. The possibility of this divergence, sometimes anticipated in the selection processes of development agencies, may lead many such agencies to prefer commissioned research or the collection of information by their own staff. This problem is particularly acute in research on women and development, for several reasons, and has a bearing on the development of the field as a whole.

First, the new scholarship on women does not yet have the great variety of clearcut theoretical frameworks typical of established intellectual traditions, even though important beginnings have been made. As a result, it is often difficult to integrate the findings of other relevant research into the framework used for a new study. Second, many scholars interested in women and development tend to conceptualize their concerns for women in more generalized terms than development agencies may find acceptable, especially since they are often coupled with advocacy for women. Although intervention programs with profound consequences for local populations are often supported by development agencies, there seems to be wide-spread tendency to be much more cautious with respect to women's programs.

In this situation, two kinds of responses seem to be very common. One is the practice of demanding particularly strong documentation that a program for women is really needed.[4] Simultaneously, the claim may be made that "nothing is known" about women. This is usually not the case, even though it may be quite true that nothing is known to the individual making the claim. The proliferation of publications about women in several countries has been accompanied by a tendency to relegate them to a special "women's corner" or as irrelevant to the development of knowledge, even where these publications are demonstrably relevant to broad economic, social, political concerns. The argument that little is known about women must also be taken with another grain of salt--development planners must often make many of their decisions on the basis of inadequate information because of a poor data base or underdeveloped data-collecting institutions. The same considerations should be applied to data on women as are used for other types of needed information that may be hard to obtain. On occasion, there have also been attempts to condense data on women into a single index figure, such as "the status of women in country X," possibly as a result of the Percy Amendment's reference to the goal of improving women's status. A single status indicator, however, is not a good substitute for more complex data on women. Aside from the analytical problems of developing a single index for a highly differentiated population, status is a construct involving comparisons. Should a status index reflect the position of women relative to the men of their society, or relative to women in other societies? What about class differences? Almost inevitably, such an index is both invidious and inaccurate. Whenever a single status indicator is demanded, in lieu of more complex information on women, this should be seen as an immediate warning signal that the need for accurate information on women is not taken seriously. It may reflect the same vision that relegates women, regardless of education or class, to a single category of the disadvantaged--a view of women as a backward tribe, living far up in the hills.

A more fundamental problem for researchers is the general inadequacy of social science theories and methods for the study of women. Social science might be seen as reflecting the life experience of its makers--and it is obvious that the theories and methods based largely on the life experiences of middle-class men from highly industrialized societies are not adequate to understand the problems of other kinds of people. This is particularly serious for categories of persons, such as women, whose interests are not well represented among social scientists themselves but who figure large in their personal lives. As a result of personal familiarity and scientific ignorance, research on women is often considered both superfluous and unnecessary by individuals and institutions.

Integrating Research on Women's Work in Development Analyses

The key issue in most women's projects is the micro-level has become "income generation" or, more simply, paid work. Particularly in the poor countries of South Asia, local projects to improve women's capacities to earn have proliferated in recent years under both private and public auspices. In Bangladesh, for example, women's credit cooperatives have been developed as part of the Integrated Rural Development Programme.[5] Women have also been trained as para-medics in rural health delivery programs, where young unmarried village women provide health and family planning services for other villagers.[6] Earning opportunities are emphasized in all these programs, even where non-formal education is the stated major goal. In both India and Bangladesh, several very ingenious projects have been developed to provide earnings for poor women in rural and urban areas.[7] A special project for self-employed women has been developed by the Textile Labour Association founded by Mahatma Ghandi.[8] In all these efforts, special stress has been placed on providing paid work for poor women.

The development of these work programs for women in South Asia is closely related to major social trends, demonstrated by research on women but still not widely appreciated by analysts and planners. These trends are of crucial importance to the integration of women in development and indicate the complexity of the problems to be faced by planners. In India, the long-term trend in recorded economic participation of women in the paid labor force shows an overall decline. Since 1921, the proportion of women in the total labor force has dropped steadily, as has the percentage of gainfully employed women in the total population.[9] At the same time, education has expanded in the post-independence period, although more slowly for women than for men, especially at the primary and secondary levels. By comparison, higher education for women has expanded more rapidly than at other levels, although this expansion is practically confined to the urban middle and upper classes.[10] The educational expansion has been coupled with a slight increase in women's participation in white collar and professional occupations; higher employment rates for women with technical degrees than in non-technical fields have also been recorded.[11] The women's programs already mentioned have found that the illiteracy of poor women presented barriers to their employment, particularly in non-agricultural work and in new occupations for women. But, as these research findings also show, "While illiteracy drives many out of employment, education does not necessarily lead to their employment."[12]

Findings of this sort require explanation in terms of large-scale systematic factors at the macro level most relevant to national policy formulation. Local projects to increase the employability of women may remedy immediate local problems; such projects can be set up and evaluated without large-scale research on the causes of the decline in women's labor force participation. However, these local programs will not affect the general trend. National, macro-level policies to deal with a general trend of this sort must be based on an analysis of the systemic causes of the special relationship that appears to obtain among women between education, employment, and socio-economic class. Yet such a general analysis of this sort is unlikely to be undertaken as long as women's needs are defined purely as a "social issue" in terms of traditions, attitudes, and social norms. To be sure, generalized attitudes about the individual's place in society are bound to affect the position of women of specific classes, regions, ethnic or language groups in any particular society. The causes of the decline in labor force participation of Indian women, for example, must be sought not only in terms of these highly differentiated factors but also in larger aspects of the Indian economy and the relationships between India and other nations, through trade, aid, and politics.

The phenomena described above for India are not unique; other nations have experienced similar relationships between women's education and their participation in the paid labor force. Since these relationships appear to differ from those obtaining for men, some explanations must be found in terms of a women-specific model. What needs to be explored is the variation between women's responses to education and employment opportunities at different levels of income and socio-economic class. How and why these patterns differ for women and for men also needs to be explained for specific times and places. An overly general explanation, referring only to stereotyped notions of men's and women's work or to "the status of women" will not serve the purpose. The most useful kinds of explanations are probably those linking both education and employment to the class position of the women's families—both those in which they were born and into which they have married. Attitudes toward women's proper social roles held by families at different class levels are likely to be very important in explaining patterns of education and paid work. In other words, research that differentiates among women according to class and income, at a level of analysis that takes account of economic, political, and social structural factors over a period of time, is needed to explain the observed facts. This must be coupled with a critical examination of the methods used to collect data and the categories used in data collection (as they vary over time) since serious problems in these areas are characteristic of research on women.

A similar type of analysis is also needed to explain another set of findings that again stresses class distinctions. These paradoxical findings, contradicting the conventional wisdom, are noted here not only for their intrinsic interest, however. They are also intended to support the point that <u>an integrated approach to research on women and development</u> is as necessary as an integrated approach to women's programs at the local level. In Indonesia, data from the 1971 Census indicate an unexpected relationship between schooling and mean number of children ever born. Fertility increases with schooling in both rural and urban areas, falling off only for the very small number of women with the highest levels of schooling. This inverted U-shaped relationship between schooling and mean number of children ever born exists in every age group in both rural and urban areas.[13] The same study also found support for this relationship in micro studies. For example, in a single rural community in central Java, researchers found that upper-income women over thirty had from one-fifth to one-fourth more births than poorer women, even if only currently married fertile women without marital disruption were considered.[14]

While these findings are undoubtedly interesting in themselves, they can, however, be distinguished from the paradoxical findings on women's education and employment in that an analytical framework is available to understand their broader significance. Studies of fertility and family planning have not reached a point of development where a further integration can be attempted, in terms of an "analytical framework sufficiently flexible to accommodate explanation of the wide variety of historical and ongoing trends, fluctuations, and differentials in the shift from premodern to modern fertility levels."[15] This has been made possible, in part, by the huge investments that have been made over the past three decades to understand a recognized world-wide problem with social, economic, and political implications. An enormous research infra-structure has been developed to which both policy-relevant and project-related studies can be linked.

Such a framework of analysis is not now available to understand some even broader issues involved in women's changing relationships to the processes of economic development. There is no comparable research infra-structure, consisting of a body of data, interpretations, institutions, publications, conferences, and funding agencies. It remains an open question whether the need for developing analytical frameworks and research infra-structures on the subject of women has even begun to be understood by the consumers or research in national and international agencies concerned with development. It goes without saying that such efforts cannot be developed in isolation. Indeed, the primary re-requirement for the development of a scientific capacity for dealing with questions of women and economic changes is that it must be integrated into existing systems and structures of development-related research and planning.

For example, in the single most important area--women's work--existing tools of data collection and analysis may tell us something about who is in the paid labor force, but rarely what women do and when they do it, in the course of a day, a month, or a lifetime. We may know something about women workers but very little about women's work. The difficulties of diagnosing the problems of women's integration in development become most apparent in this gray area of what constitutes women's work and its rewards. In the absence of a clear understanding of the problems, it becomes almost impossible to develop suitable remedies at the macro and micro levels except in the cases of most pressing and obvious need.

The conventional assumptions of economics and sociology do not suffice, for a good historical reason. The methods of data collection and analysis developed in western countries at a time when industrialization was relatively new and the separation between home and workplace was very salient in people's lives. As economic analysis became more sophisticated, it was applied to cases where information was most readily available, namely in firms large enough to need precise data as part of their mode of operation. Very precise data have never been necessary to subsistence farming or to small retail operations. It is only under the conditions of resource scarcity that development planners in poor countries and aid-giving agencies in rich countries have found it necessary to develop more precise data on agricultural production, human fertility, and the composition of the labor market. Since housework in all its complexity has never depended on precise information either, and since the separation between home and workplace precluded the inclusion of domestic work in conventional analyses (except insofar as it involved paid labor or production for sale), there has been even less concern with developing measurement techniques and analytical concepts for the work done by most of the world's women for most of their lives. Indeed, much of this work has been overlooked or mistakenly classified as "leisure" or "non-work." Nothing could be farther from the truth, as can easily be shown by the paradox that while the work of "non-working women" is considered to be without much economic significance, all substitutes for it are very expensive.

The recent upsurge of interest in women's relationship to the development process has resulted only in the most superficial sense from changes in the "consciousness" of planners, scholars, and politicians. Instead, I am convinced, it has resulted from the more general pressures generated in resource-poor countries by the need to utilize all available human resources in order to survive. Since these pressures have been generated, in the first instance, by political institutions concerned with economic development, I also believe that the agencies most closely concerned with development planning at the macro level must be convinced to implement the commitments of International Women's Year where it really counts. Women must be integrated into the development process not only symbolically, and through concrete local projects, but in the most central processes of resource allocation in development planning. This is a key issue. It must be made clear that this is not only in the interests of women themselves but is, in fact, indispensable to the process of development. In resource-poor nations, agricultural growth cannot occur without a more precise and rational allocation of existing resources. Although "everyone knows" that women have always worked hard on the land, whether their work was publicly visible or not, knowledge about the nature of women's work has now become important to the complexities of allocating resources for development.

Attention must be paid to the work of women not only because that is good for women. Those who plan development policies must also realize that it is good for development.

References and Notes

[1] The classic example is, of course, Ester Boserup, *Woman's Role in Economic Development* (New York: St. Martin's Press, 1970). Collections of articles and papers by academics and policy-makers include: Irene Tinker and Michele Bo Bramsen, *Women and World Development* (Washington: Overseas Development Council, 1976); Wellesley Editorial Committee, *Women and National Development: The Complexities of Change* (Chicago: University of Chicago Press, 1977); Margery Wolf and Roxane Witke, *Women in Chinese Society* (Stanford: Stanford University Press, 1975); June Nash and Helen Safa, *Sex and Class in Latin America* (New York: Praeger, 1976); Nancy Hafkin and Edna Bay, *Women in Africa: Studies in Social and Economic Change* (Stanford: Stanford University Press, 1976); Ruby Rohrlich-Leavitt, *Women Cross-Culturally* (The Hague: Mouton, 1975); Lois Beck and Nikki Keddie, *Women in the Muslim World* (Cambridge: Harvard University Press, 1978); Rounaq Jahan and Hanna Papanek, editors, *Women and Development: Perspectives from South and Southeast Asia* (Dacca: University Press, 1979).

Individual scholars have also compiled bibliographies of materials on women, notably Meri Knaster, *Women in Spanish America: An Annotated Bibliography* (Boston: G. K. Hall, 1977); Mayra Buvinic, *Women and World Development: An Annotated Bibliography* (Washington: Overseas Development Council, 1976); Carol Sakala, *South Asian Women: A Reference Guide* (KTO Press, 1979, forthcoming).

Another landmark book, making data on women widely available, is Elise Boulding, Shirley Nuss, et al., Handbook of International Data on Women (New York: Sage Publications-John Wiley, 1976).

[2] U.S. Congress, Senate, *Congressional Record*, S.18423, October 2, 1973.

[3] Vina Mazumdar and Kumud Sharma, "Women's Studies: New Perceptions and the Challenges," *Economic and Political Weekly* (India), January 20, 1979, 113-120.

[4] Florence McCarthy, Taherunessa Abdullah and Sondra Zeidenstein, "Programme Assessment and the Development of Women's Programmes: The Views of Action Workers," in Jahan and Papanek, 1979.

[5] McCarthy, Abdullah and Zeidenstein, 1979.

[6] Shamima Islam, "Strengthening Non-Formal Education for Women in Bangladesh," in Hahan and Papanek, 1979.

[7] Ruth Dixon, *Rural Women at Work* (Baltimore: John Hopkins Press, 1978).

[8] Ela Bhatt, "Organizing Self-Employed Women Workers," in Jahan and Papanek, 1979.

[9] *Towards Equality: Report of the Committee on the Status of Women in India*, (New Delhi: Government of India, Department of Social Welfare, Ministry of Education and Social Welfare, December 1974), p. 152.

[10] *Towards Equality*, p. 216.

[11] *Towards Equality*, p. 220.

[12] *Towards Equality*, p. 222.

[13] Terence H. Hull and Valerie J. Hull, "The Relation of Economic Class and Fertility: An Analysis of Some Indonesian Data," *Population Studies* 31(1), p. 43-57.

[14] Hull and Hull.

[15] Richard A. Easterlin, "The Economics and Sociology of Fertility: A Synthesis," in Charles Tilly, ed., *Historical Studies of Changing Fertility* (Princeton: Princeton University Press, 1978), p. 57-133, citation on p. 120.

NGO Task Force on Roles of Women,
Mildred Robbins Leet, Chairperson

14. Roles of Women: UNCSTD Background Discussion Paper

<u>Women in Science and
Technology for Development</u>

The <u>basic premise</u> of the NGO Task Force on the Roles of Women in Science and Technology for Development for UNCSTD is that technology is human knowledge applied to human needs. It is not gender-related, but affects all people and all needs, from the most humble to the most sophisticated. Social and economic development cannot be successful without the participation of women, who make up half of humankind. All elements of society must be involved in the choice of science and technology for development; all must understand its limitations, and all must enjoy its benefits.

<u>Our further premises</u> are:

• that the subject of the Conference is people--not technology for technology's sake. Therefore, an agenda must be designed to deal with issues addressing human needs in order to enhance the capacity of both women and men to create, control, and use technical knowledge, capital, and natural resources.

• that women are not a target group or a special problem, but equal partners in seeking solutions to the problem of development which exists in every country, not just those classified as underdeveloped. Women are an essential, integral part of the development process. The Conference should proceed at all stages in full consciousness of this fact. To do otherwise would be inequitable, unjust and self-defeating.

• that it is essential to think about technology in the context of the cultural and socio-economic environment in which it will operate, since this environment will influence the lives of women and men, and their families. Not enough attention is given to the link between technological choices and this environment, between specific economic goals, such as increasing agricultural export, promoting industrialization, or providing employment, and the impact these choices will have on people, especially women.

• that the issue at hand is not only the transfer of science and technology per se, but more importantly, the <u>sharing</u> of science and technology. The Conference is more than a dialogue on technological transfer between givers and receivers. Rather, it is a common meeting ground for people concerned with a common goal, namely socio-economic development to meet basic human needs. To transfer often implies imposing different values on peoples and institutions. To share implies a mutuality of interests and greater fulfillment and productivity for all.

• that any discussion of science and technology, especially regarding the need for research and development must begin with the end-user, who is often a woman. The more that potential users are involved in identification of their own needs and the choice of technology, the more appropriate the technology is likely to be.

• that the concept of development must be broadened to include all parts of the Third World without reference to politico-military considerations. Significant resources should be committed by all nations to non-military technology benefiting non-military interests.

The above premises are shared by both men and women. However, there is a wide gap between their acceptance in theory and their implementation in practice. As the ILO Background Paper states:

> "Women and technology as a dimension in the development process has remained virtually an unexplored territory. That the subject is important as an 'issue' may be gathered from the fact that for the first time, this item is appearing on the Agenda of a Preparatory UN Meeting, with a view to further investigation in UNCSTD in 1979."

The following issues of concern to women are offered as a contribution and stimulus to such further investigation:

<u>Stereotypes about the role of women in science and</u>

<u>technology, held by women and men alike, prevent women's full participation in socio-economic development.</u>

Science and technology suggest masculine images. Science in particular has been a male preserve. Names of women are notable by their absence in any listing of important personalities in science. The reluctance of girls to study science, as well as their "math anxiety," has been noted by many educators. Technology conjures up a "machismo" image--men tending giant machines or men climbing into space capsules to perform feats of daring. More often than not, a technologist connotes a man.

In both developing and developed countries, local customs and values powerfully discourage women from moving into what is perceived as a male province. So deeply ingrained are these values that women themselves often subscribe to them and play a subservient role in society. It took the International Women's Year to bring to world attention the full impact of this attitude and to create an atmosphere in which women could begin to see themselves as equal, and men could perceive the benefits of this equality.

<u>Technology can perpetuate inequality between women and men.</u>

In fact, it often makes it worse. New forms of technology, like any gift of power, tend to exacerbate inequalities. Although women have their own traditional technologies, there is ample evidence that women have not benefitted proportionately from technological advances, that indeed they have often been harmed by the introduction of new technology. Science and technology are not socially neutral. They do not necessarily serve the goals of equality and development unless they are consciously designed to do so. Technology is a two-edged sword. It holds the potential for eliminating the significance of differences in muscular strength between women and men. Most women could equal a man's accomplishment on a tractor, providing both had the same training and experience. On the other hand, technology unevenly distributed can multiply small differences in productivity between women and men. If <u>only</u> men are taught to use the machines or given the means to buy them or the rights to use them, women are at a clear disadvantage.

A classic example of the negative effect of technology on women is the agricultural setting in which plowing (men's work) is mechanized, but the processes of cultivation, such as hoeing, weeding, and transplanting (women's work) are not. Women must work harder and longer than they did before mechanization in order to keep up with the expanded plowing capacity. The development of simple technological aids for rural women has been recognized as essential in order to reduce the time they must spend in arduous, low-productivity labor, and to prevent the deterioration of their status as their male counterparts modernize.

Forty to eighty percent of Third World agricultural labor is female, although most often it is men who own the land. Depending on the traditions and customs of a particular country, they plant the seed, haul the water, till the soil, harvest the crops, market the produce, tend the animals, spin the wool, weave the cloth, and make the clothes, all the while striving to keep their families alive by growing their home vegetable gardens. This is not to deny that in many countries some women are also traders and money-makers.

<u>Women are being displaced by men and machines even in areas traditionally within their sphere of economic activity.</u>

The introduction of labor-saving devices threatens to separate women altogether from many of their traditional functions, or to leave them with only the drudgery. Pottery-making in Ghana, for example, was largely the work of women, but with the introduction of the potter's wheel, men took over the industry. Due to lack of funds of their own, as well as lack of training in the new methods, women were unable to take advantage of the mechanized process. The spinning of yarn and preparation of looms traditionally done by Muslim women in Kashmir was threatened by a project which would have mechanized spinning completely and displaced some 20,000 women for whom no other suitable employment was available. The widespread use of chemical sprays in agriculture in one province of India deprived women of an important source of income since the majority of women of working age were employed four hours a day weeding the fields. We recognize that certain trade-offs must be made in choosing technologies and that some of these may have an adverse effect on women, but these should be anticipated and specific alternatives considered and built-in.

<u>Intermediate or "appropriate" technology is not necessarily beneficial to women unless they are actively involved in its choice.</u>

The concept of appropriate technology is surprisingly

controversial for a concept with such obvious benefits for women. The dispute centers on the possibility that making "women's work" easier for women to do will press them ever more firmly into a stereotyped mold in which their opportunities will be further limited, while keeping "high technology" a male preserve. The short-term benefits of improved hoes and scythes are undeniable, but they will not improve women's relative status if men are being taught to operate combine harvesters. Women do not wish to be equated automatically with the more primitive forms of technology. Whether high or low technology is involved, women should be included. It is essential for women to assume their full share of responsibility for technical choices. There is growing evidence that male-dominated, excessively competitive, and profit-oriented technology which fails to take into account human and social consequences is a major factor in accentuating socially-disruptive and resource-depleting forms of industrial production and GNP-measured economic growth.

Most women's work is left out when nations calculate their Gross National Product (GNP).

This statistic is widely used as the indicator of economic growth, but does not take into account the distribution of the benefits of such growth or in-kind productivity. No nation, developing or otherwise, calculates the contributions made by women outside the so-called "productive" labor force. No economic value appears to be placed on the nurturing, supportive, and maintenance services performed by women. Women are "the hewers of wood, the drawers of water," as well as the caretakers of children--services without which no nation could survive. But none of this is reflected in the GNP. Thus, economic projections for the Third World are based on an inadequate index of socio-economic performance, with consequences that are detrimental to women and men alike. To reflect more fully the contributions of women to national economies, new and more inclusive ways of measuring development and growth are essential.

Women are excluded from planning and decision-making, even when decisions have a direct impact on their lives.

In some parts of the world this has been a relatively recent occurrence, which needs to be reversed. The exclusion of women from planning and decision-making has made women economically invisible. Hence, development economists and rural specialists literally do not see that most farmers are women. Training programs, modern technology in the form of seeds, fertilizer, irrigation, and machinery, as well as credit and access to markets, are far more readily available to men than to women farmers. The result is a modern agricultural sector geared to export, co-existing with a domestic subsistence sector in which women predominate, but have no effective voice in the decisions which affect their lives. Also it is important that urban and rural women, rich and poor, collaborate with each other in the decision-making process.

It is especially important to include women in planning and decision-making as technology moves closer to where they live, and directly affects their lives. In the area of cooking fuel and energy in general, for example, women can and must play a central role. The high proportion of fuel that goes for cooking in the developing countries suggests that immediate attention be given to this area, specifically to improved methods for making use of wood and grass. In this regard, pilot training programs have been started in remote villages in Honduras and Guatemala, where women are being directly involved in the building of specially designed stoves of indigenous materials that will decrease the amount of firewood needed, encourage the boiling of water, and eliminate smoke in the home. In addition, there is a need to explore use of bio-gas converters as well as mixed systems which use wind, water, or solar energy, when feasible.

That same exclusion of women holds true in professional positions and academic posts. Statistics on the proportion of women in top-level planning jobs make it evident that even in developed countries, women are not fully and equally involved in planning, decision-making and implementation. A stream of data suggests that key institutions of business, government and education have a disproportionately small proportion of women in top positions.

<u>Education and training in fields related to science and technology are not made available on an equal basis to women.</u>

Even when women gain the necessary education or training, they do not have equal access to career opportunities in scientific and technical fields, including the social sciences. If technology transfer is to be successfully implemented, opportunities for appropriate education and training must be made available to women. In many developing countries, access to education at all levels is more readily available to males than to females, and the difference increases with the increasing educational level. Where family resources for education are limited, they are often allocated primarily to male children. Quality of education may also differ for males and females. There is much evidence that the stereotypes regarding male and female roles in many countries lead to different types of education for girls and boys, and these differences often result in female children receiving education which is less likely to prepare them for technical, scientific, social and professional careers. Particularly neglected is training in analytical thinking, setting of goals and priorities, and making choices. It is important, therefore, that any specific assistance, either for general education, or for specialized technical and scientific training, be given under conditions which will maximize the participation of women and girls.

When women do obtain an appropriate education, they should have an opportunity to use it. Discrimination against women scientists has been extensively documented in developed countries, and the available evidence suggests that the problem is equally severe in many developing nations. To avoid contributing to this problem, certain steps should be taken:

- Women should be included in leadership positions on international, national, and local boards, commissions, and advisory groups which make decisions concerning current development projects and plan new, non-traditional ones;

- Women should have equal opportunity with men for employment and advancement on the staffs of technical and scientific institutions;

- Women scientists should share equally in access to research opportunities, including equal access to funding and facilities. They must have the same opportunities to publicize their work, and their work should receive the same consideration afforded to that of male scientists and professionals;

- Women should have equal access with men to technical employment in all development projects, whether funded by governments or privately; and

- Monitoring procedures covering all aspects of the employment of women scientists and professionals should be part of all development projects, and appropriate measures should be taken to insure compliance.

Conclusion

Research in preparation for the International Women's Year and now for the United Nations Decade for Women amply demonstrates that women play major social and economic roles in society--as family members and mothers, as agricultural producers, as traders and marketers, as community leaders, as educators of children and young people, and as professionals. Indices such as the Gross National Product fail to take most of these roles into account. It would be unrealistic for the Conference on Science and Technology for Development to disregard the findings of IWY and the Decade for Women if it is to set realistic guidelines for the betterment of the urban and rural poor, since women are a major segment of that population.

At the same time, the Decade for Women needs human-scale planning by the Conference on Science and Technology for Development to achieve its goals. Therefore, the vision of progress with equity will be realized more quickly and effectively if both groups share their energy and experience.

The great danger is that the Conference could so concentrate on technology, on engineering, on design, and on material aspects that their effects on people--on their lives, on their ways of living, and on their human relationships--could be overlooked. And so, what we stress is the need, in considering all aspects of science and technology for development, to take into account what happens to people, to young and old, to those in the informal as well as the formal sector, to women and men.

We therefore urge that methods and policies which actively and equally involve and benefit women be fully integrated into the World Programme of Action of the Conference on Science and Technology for Development.

Roslyn Dauber

15. Applying Policy Analysis to Women and Technology: A Framework for Consideration

Because of the enormity and complexity of the problem of getting women in developing countries to have equal access to new and appropriate technologies, change can be frustratingly slow. Development is not a linear process. Rather, it is a kind of social experiment that has never before been conducted on such an enormous scale, having technology at the focal point. Technology is an essential ingredient in all economic development, and how we use technology is a policy question.

In the next few pages I am going to discuss the role of technology, actual and potential, in improving the lives of women in developing countries. I will look at this from a policy perspective, discussing how policy analysis can be applied to the selection of technology and why and how it must be linked to effective work in the social reality to which it is directed.

Because policy analysis is an activity which tends not to be well understood, its important impacts tend to be overlooked. This is unfortunate, because policy analyses are the feeder roots for national and international policies. Hence I want to digress briefly to make clear just what policy analysis is and what impact policy analysts can have.

Policy Analysis

For our purposes there are three types of policies that should be distinguished: (1) those that improve the incentive operating in the choice of technologies; (2) those that will expand knowledge of technological alternatives particularly suited to developing countries; and (3) those that lead to institutional changes for improving and lowering the cost of disseminating technical information. (1) Technology assessment, as will be discussed, addresses these three types of policies.

Policy analysts are those people who work in support of decision-makers by considering all possible means to achieve a desired goal. They work at all levels of government--nationally and internationally. To understand the policy environment in which they work, we must consider the policy process. The process can be broken down into four parts:

1. Policy demands: that is, demands for action arising from both inside and outside the political system.

2. Policy decisions: the authoritative rather than routine decisions by the policy authorities.

3. Policy outputs: what the system does. Goods and services are the most tangible outputs--that's why we speak in terms of technological choices. The concept is not restricted to purely tangible items; it includes broad social purposes like equality for women.

4. Policy outcomes (or impacts): the intended or unintended consequences of political action or inaction. (2)

Policy analysts must consider the impact of their recommendations at each stage of the policy process, as well as impacts outside of the formal system. They must consider whether their goal is policy maintenance or policy change and how their plans can be implemented. Obviously, in development we are concerned with politics to create substantial change. (Policy analysts should be especially sensitive to item four. There have been many instances in development where unintended consequences have worked to the detriment of women).

For some, the purpose of policy analysis is not so much to account for the messy and irrational world that exists, but rather to design the ideal system and to see how it can be matched up to the actual world. (3) This is the approach when the goal is to redistribute political and social power more equitably by establishing women as equals. When the policy sphere is dominated by men, then men must somehow be encouraged to reformulate their views of the social order and legislate a world that provides greater opportunities for women. After policy establishment comes implementation, and, one hopes, the expected social progress. The World Plan of Action for Women set down at the 1975 UN Conference on Women is one yardstick nations can use to measure their social progress. Yet there are discrepancies between these sorts of commitments and their implementation. Formal governmental decisions are only way stations along the path to action, and the opportunity for slippage between decisions and action is substantial. Effective action requires the support and commitment of many individuals. For women to benefit from technology requires that planners be dedicated to employing technologies suitable for women wherever possible and that women be given the opportunity to master those technologies that produce the socio-environmental changes that they want and need. Let us now consider what "development" means for women.

Development Theory and Related Policy

Development can be considered to be the process by which social, economic, and technological improvements are planned and implemented so as to raise the standard of living in a local area, nation, or entire region.

Traditional development theory acknowledges three constraints pertinent to women:

1. Society is not a single organic unit. As a result, changes in one sector will not necessarily generate compatible changes throughout the society; new technologies intended to raise productivity may remain encapsulated in one sector; and development programs addressed to men most often fail to spin-off benefits to women. (As will be discussed, technology assessments can help solve this problem.)

2. There are contradictions in the process of social change. Thus, policies to increase women's employment may only increase exploitation if wages and working conditions are not improved at the same time (see chapter 10).

3. External forces and national leaders play a key role in producing social change. Most importantly, strategies for change involve change in power. This phenomenon is conveniently ignored by outsiders who wish to assist in another country's development but do not want to interfere in "local" matters. Technical assistance personnel who insist that technologies are neutral fit into this category.(4) Lucille Maier, Secretary General of the 1980 U.N. Conference on Women, addressed this problem by emphasizing that women must be integrated into all levels of the development process and must not be separated out as a "special problem area" apart from the mainstream of all development projects.

These are the constraints on development strategies affecting women within a region planning change. We must also analyze the many constraints on development strategies that come from international forces. For example, the Marxist interpretation of development suggests that women are relegated to the domestic economy and denied the opportunity to participate in the production of goods for exchange in the larger society because the household serves an economic function. It maintains women as a reserve labor force available to join capitalist production when required, thus enabling capitalism to survive its chronic cycles of inflation and depression. (5) Yet in developing countries, where the majority of the population are functioning at a subsistence level, women cannot operate as this kind of safety valve, nor are the majority of men actually the kind of responsible household heads that fit the traditional Western model. In fact, this dependency theory only provides a convenient rationalization for why women lack focus in developing theories.

On the other hand, Western development theories have often created their own image of a world quite different from the reality experienced by the people living in it. This has had tragic consequences, and a new theory of development is needed which redefines women's roles and options in development. This new theory of women and development should incorporate the following factors:

1. Evaluation of women's work by production outputs, not by the presence or absence of technical or monetary rewards;

2. Examination of the political role of women with a realistic and expanded notion of what constitutes politics;

3. Explanation of change or lack of change in women's roles over time. If a social change has not benefitted women, is this a failure of development or an indication of a need for a deeper understanding and reformulation of social goals to meet human needs? (6) If new technologies exclude women, where is the breakdown that prevented the technology transfer?

Redefining traditional political theory is also important. One view holds that world markets are such that national economies create an environment where at each lower level of the system there is less autonomy for decision making. (7) Yet, one can also say that women have more freedom from centrally sanctioned norms because of their exclusion from paid work and other public institutions of modern life. One should note in passing that "liberal" political parties have not necessarily encouraged emancipation for women. In fact, it is hard to restructure any society to bring women into the political mainstream. In developing areas it might be more immediately productive to reach out to women in unorthodox, non-institutionalized and non-traditional ways (see chapter 6 for a discussion of Appropriate Technology International). From the outside, a kind of freedom seems to go with a marginal existence at the periphery. Thus, if the periphery is the point of access, appropriate technologies and local decision-making strategies may be most productive. Policy analysts who build these ideas into their recommendations can create a positive influence for women in the development process at all levels of society. However, they must realize that the communications process is fundamental in producing the desired social change.

Communications Strategy: Key to Policy Implementation

Communications networks are a powerful social technology and make a crucial difference at any level of organization. (This notion was developed by Mallica Vajrathan in <u>Women and World Development</u>.) Communications strategies can maintain or remove barriers that permit one group of human beings to dominate, manipulate and exploit other human beings. Changing the social structure to achieve a balanced distribution of social, political and economic power between men and women requires a revolutionary change in basic attitudes of the majority of the people in any society. This change in attitudes will not come about without a systematically planned program of supporting communications. Thus policy analysts must plan for communication support programs designed to teach women the specialized technical and administrative skills needed to participate in modern economy. The communication path must allow flow in both directions--up from person to community to officials, and then from officials to community to individual persons. A top-down mode only is not sufficient.

A communication strategy for improving the position and roles of women must have two main objectives:

1. The behavioral objective of breaking down myths and realities of male supremacy and bringing about the acceptance of women as independent persons.

2. The development objective of improving the quality of life for both men and women. (8)

To achieve the first objective, women can be motivated to see themselves as equal partners to men, and appropriate mechanisms should be programmed along with training courses for women. To achieve the second objective, technology assessments performed <u>in conjunction with</u> training courses would allow communities to anticipate changes facing them. The quality of life, especially for rural women in less developed countries, can be enhanced through improved communication services, for these are the key to producing improvements in fertility, nutrition and health education.

Change and Policy

Development change agents tend to be rural health personnel, agricultural extension officers, teachers and family planning workers. Change agents can also be policy analysts and decision-makers either in the developing countries or in international organizations dedicated to improving the quality of life around the world. The World Plan of Action that came out of the UN Conference on Women is symbolic of the universal agreement that women must be fully equal in national affairs, that this is the only way to create a just and peaceful world, and nothing can be done if the agents of change do not support the policies of change. Specifically, to improve living conditions for Third World women, three policy-related changes are necessary:

1. Women must become more visible and be valued as persons.

2. Domestic policy-makers in both North and South must realize that development means the enrichment of all aspects of life for all people.

3. The international, political and economic order must be structured so that each nation has an effective voice in decisions and is assured of just treatment in the world order. (9)

Technology and its Role in Development

The introduction of new technologies into developing countries affects every sector of the society. The active and reasoned choice of a technology effects the ability of the society for technological adaptation. That is, technologies should be chosen that can be smoothly and advantageously incorporated into the development effort. The introduction of a new technology affects employment patterns, income distribution, consumption patterns, and the relations among the three. Markets are created or changed, and the economic class structure affected. Sometimes new jobs are created that benefit the nonskilled, at other times the introduction of a technology works mainly to benefit the already prosperous classes. The industrial structure and factor prices are changed by new technologies. Even the social and political structures (10) of a country are altered by the introduction of technology. In spite of these many effects, technology itself is less the cause of development than a part of an interactive process.

Technology may be a major resource to create new wealth; an instrument that allows its owner to exercise social control in various forms; a tool that decisively affects modes of decision-making; and/or a force that relates directly to the patterns of alienation found in affluent societies. Technology brings power to effect great social and economic change; resources that lead to tangible products; and new processes or ways of doing things, which are internalized by individuals. This powerful force has effects on women which must be carefully considered.

Modern technologies tend not to fit neatly into developing economies. Technology problems clearly differ between the large-scale modern sector and the rest of a developing country's economy. The technology system in the modern sector has greater scope for use of new capital than for the use of additional labor, restricting especially the opportunities for least skilled. Incentives for implantation of foreign technologies are not contiguous with incentives for adaptive innovations of the indigenous technology. In most developing countries there is no policy agreement on the extent to which, for technological or growth reasons, the modern sector should be promoted, nor agreement on the extent to which its promotion would be to the detriment of less privileged sectors. Indeed, it is not known how these sectors respond to the entire policy environment nor what their ramifications are in terms of economic, social and institutional measures which affect the diffusion of technology in these sectors. Their total effect on women is hardly understood at all.

Even though open questions are unresolved on a societal level, it is possible to use technology assessments of individual technologies to predetermine the impact of a particular technology on the society, especially with regard to its impact on women.

Technology Assessment

Technology assessment (TA) was designed to produce the broadest possible policy analysis. What distinguishes technology assessment from systems analysis is its emphasis on the social consequences that are likely to be precipitated by the contemplated innovation. TA also emphasizes appropriate intervention by policy-makers and decision-makers. TA originated in developed countries for complex technologies, but it can be successfully applied to developing countries because of its broad social orientation. If seriously and more conscientiously used, technology assessment could significantly reduce the adverse and unintended consequences of newly introduced technologies. It can be applied at different policy levels, from introducing a specific machine at the village level to building a new road system in a nation or across a continent. Technology assessment can be "technology driven," constructed around a specific technology, or "problem driven," constructed around a social problem that may be alleviated through technological means. Technology assessors tend to take a broad view of the term technology and include social technologies, such as management systems or educational systems, as well as hardware in the scope of their analyses.

There are ten elements to technology assessment, which are performed cyclically and concurrently as a means to amplify each step. (11) The ten elements are:

1. A statement of the problem, which often changes, and a broader restatement or recasting of the problem is done after analysis is underway.

2. Definition of the system (or technology) and specific alternatives which could accomplish the same objective--micro-alternatives.

3. Identification of potential impacts--a creative undertaking requiring imagination and speculative thinking. Futures methodologies are often employed at this stage.

4. Evaluation of potential impacts--a mixed effort of firm-handed analysis and information judgment necessarily conducted on speculative ground. This is a key step. Evaluation research and creative speculation can be combined for interesting results.

5. Definition of the relevant decision-making apparatus --a step often neglected, but essential in developing countries where decision-making patterns are fluid.

6. Laying out options for the decision-maker--new inventions and imaginative development of options are usually needed.

7. Identification of parties of interest--potential winners and losers; overt and latent interests; most important for women.

8. Definition of macro-alternatives--broad system alternatives, such as the use of solar energy vs. imported oil.

9. <u>Identification of exogenous variables</u>--larger events which may disturb an entire social system, e.g., birthrate and food consumption.

10. <u>Conclusions and policy recommendations</u>--the more specific and concrete the better. (12)

    This ten-step process can be bounded by time or it can be allowed to continue as long as a new technology is being developed and/or introduced. In cross-cultural settings, wherever social systems are mixed, it is especially important to look at the <u>state of society assumptions</u> that the policy-makers, policy analysts and policy and service recipients operate with. That means that technology assessments should also include an examination of women's roles under state of society assumptions and an imaginative treatment of potential impacts on and systems alternatives for women.

    Specifically, one should ask, how would the introduction of the technology being considered be affected if women completely controlled the technology and/or the environment in which it was used? This has not usually been considered in technology assessments and would certainly provide a refreshing change of pace for the predominately male legion of technology assessors. This is an extremely important point. It is essential that men learn to think about what the world will be like when women are participating fully as educated, economically viable and independent individuals. Technology assessment, along with a redefinition of development, can provide a new theoretical framework for policy analysts as women enter the development process vis-a-vis the introduction of new technologies.

Technology, Women and Employment

    Employment patterns require special consideration in any technology assessment concerned with the impact on women of a technology in developing countries. A major rationale for introducing new technologies in developing countries is that new income and new jobs are an expected outcome. But women's jobs reflect women's opportunities--or lack thereof--and this is especially true in relation to technologies which promote development. For instance, activities now open to women are mostly in the pre-industrial sector, with agriculture employing more than one-third of the female work force. Moreover, when women do gain access to the so-called modern sectors, the types of work they perform are almost always preindustrial. They work as domestic servants or as unskilled or semi-skilled workers in food-packing plants and textile factories. Weaving, sewing, packing sardines and vegetables in boxes after washing and drying them have traditionally been designated feminine tasks and, therefore, are accepted by the "patriarchal" society. Worse still, the performance of these traditional tasks in the modern sector does not in any way require those responsible to train women to acquire new skills that eventually would allow them to claim a decent place in the economy of a country that is undergoing deep-rooted changes. Moreover, the fact that women--most of them illiterate and unskilled--are trapped in subordinate positions of only a primitively industrial nature generates the same atmosphere in the factory or office that exists in the home: the men give the orders, make the decisions, and have the "important" roles. The access of women to only the most rudimentary extra-familial activities hardly constitutes an upgrading of their situation in the family, especially considering that most women fall into the lowest wage-earning category even in those tasks which they do perform. This is especially true in Moslem countries. (13)

Ester Boserup has shown that industrialization tends to intensify the differences in the roles of the sexes in the developing economies and that it has produced a distortion in the relation of the sexes at the economic level. She has shown that the change from a subsistence economy to a money economy has dealt a serious blow to the value of goods traditionally produced by women, such as handicrafts, and that it restricts women who do gain access to renumerative activities to non-skilled, subordinate and underpaid jobs.

Women's self-perceptions are affected by their ability to earn in the economy. Women have not recognized themselves as producers of goods and services, although they produce some of the most important goods and services in every society. Unfortunately, most of their goods are invisible and the prime victim of entropy. No one understands this concept better than the housekeeper/mother, doomed to reassert herself each day against the forces of inevitable disorder. Women tend to discount their production because society discounts it. Two changes are necessary: (1) society must recognize and credit women's capabilities as producers of visible goods, and (2) their invisible services must become visible. (14)

Unfortunately, at present women's traditional subsistence activities continue to be both important and difficult during technological development _and_ their work loses prestige because it exists outside of the new market economy. Clearly, one must question the value of the Western model being transferred when we consider that the jobs available to women remain at the most menial level and, in urban areas, women are only marginally able to maintain themselves and their children. We must look for major system alternatives, and this means paying much more attention to the regions in which women do operate. Technology can work for women, but it must be introduced directly and informally in developing countries.

Women and Technological Development

Even in the developed countries, the role of women has not been one of equality of either opportunities or expectations. In the past decade, however, the United States has in its own internal political process begun to consider the role of women in economic development and the use of technology for improving life both domestically and internationally. U.S. internal policies designed to expand the opportunities of women have led to affirmative action requirements and significant changes. A grass-roots demand ultimately became a top-down decision-making strategy. This section will consider briefly U.S. policies toward women in Third World countries. It will also consider possible universal applicability of an action agenda concerned with appropriate technology and how it affects women.

In response to the 1975 World Conference on Women, congressional hearings considered issues related to women in development. Because the Agency for International Development is the largest governmental body devoted to development, legislation directed change in that agency. The legislative result of the hearings was the Percy Amendment to the Foreign Assistance Act which mandates that the impact on women of all AID programs must be considered in all AID allocations. Policy has been established but it will not be truly effective until two conditions are met:

1. More AID personnel in the field must become sensitive to the issues, as made clear in this volume. AID officials have complained that few good proposals are submitted from the field, but this judgment might be different if AID had more women in decision-making positions.

2. Women all over the world must become aware of the problems associated with aid programs as presently structured, whether they derive from U.S. initiatives or those of other developed countries.

Equally important are the policies adopted by the developed world with regard to negotiations aimed at restructuring current global economic relationships. It is essential that women have a voice in any restructuring of the economic order--a voice that recognizes the relationship between the world order and human needs. (15) Establishing that voice will not be easy. It must be planned for; it must be actively worked for; and, most importantly, women must be willing to accept responsibility, learn new things and relinquish old behavior patterns.

The NCAT Plan for Action

In the United States, some community organizations have become actively involved in promoting the participation of women in issues of technological development. While it is true that women in the United States have led quite different lives from those of their Third World sisters, women in both worlds share in being excluded from the power centers of the economic and--especially--the scientific and technological mainstream. As Marilyn Carr points out in chapter 11, appropriate technology has come to mean a philosophy which advocates the use of resource-conserving technologies. In practice, however, these are small-scale technologies appropriate for community development and equally appropriate in many instances to the developed as well as the developing world. Thus, I believe an examination of one advocacy group, the National Center for Appropriate Technology (NCAT) in Butte, Montana, may be instructive since some of the strategies it advocates could be adapted for use by women in developing countries.

The NCAT plan of action, designed to involve women in issues of science and technology, includes two priorities:

1. To educate people about and to eliminate sex-role stereotyping; NCAT believes that all policy groups need to develop a stated commitment to a future in which all people are treated as individuals and not as sexual stereotypes.

2. To recognize that, since women as a group have historically had a restricted and less valued role, women must now actively participate in the new technologies to change that role assignment.

To accomplish these ends, NCAT recognizes that a conscientious effort must be made to develop female expertise. This can be done by setting up training programs specifically for women, including the establishment of apprenticeship programs for women to learn such basic skills as the use of tools or machinery. Educational programs must include female instructors and women should be encouraged at every step to take positions of increasing responsibility and to involve themselves in decision-making. And, of course, child care must always be a consideration when employing women.

To further social change within the United States, policies must expand rather than continue to restrict women's opportunities. On the domestic level, NCAT advocates the end of a sexual division of labor; the sharing of housework by all who live in a household; the recognition of housework as a skilled and therefore remunerative job; and the development and/or improvement of technologies that increase women's autonomy (e.g., contraceptives; labor-saving home technologies). On the governmental level, NCAT advocates that government programs seek to remove all barriers to women in scientific and technical fields, including loan and grant programs and special-skill learning programs.

The NCAT Plan for Women should be considered by planning groups in countries which are struggling to create a strategy for coping with technological change. Because men and women often lead more segregated lives in developing countries than in the United States, women in the Third World should be encouraged to work with men as equals--not as subordinates. (16) A beginning will be made if women are incorporated into the policy process at all levels, as is necessary for effective policy implementation.

Conclusion

The integration of women in public life will not solve all the world's problems, nor even all of women's problems, but it will broaden the area of legitimate public concern by moving "women's issues" from the margin of societal attention into the mainstream. The integration of women into public life will be one step toward establishing cooperation among all people--men and women--in building a more just world. The practical goals of adequate water, food, shelter, as well as the more subjective goals of personal freedom and equality, constitute a value system that transcends national boundaries. What the achievement of these goals will look like in practice will necessarily vary from culture to culture. Whether we can achieve them is also in question.

I believe that the kind of world in which we and our children wish to live can be created, but only if women become more visible and vocal at every level of society and government. Women must maintain an idealistic yet tough perspective, as set forth in this volume in particular by Hazel Henderson, Elise Boulding, Marilyn Carr, Melinda Cain, Louise Fortmann, and Hanna Papanek.

Finally, to create the world in which we wish to live, we must be able to imagine it. And here lies the fundamental responsibility of the policy analyst: to be the visionary, the designer of society as it can be. Decision-makers need that vision as well as courage and stamina to bring about a more positive future. This will require a sustained effort, and one which is enriched by a continual process of scrutiny and reevaluation. It is in part what I hope we are accomplishing with this book.

References

1. Richard Eckaus, <u>Appropriate Technologies for Developing Countries</u>. Washington, D.C.: National Academy of Science, 1977, p. 16.

2. W.I. Jenkins, <u>Policy Analysis: A Political and Organizational Perspective</u>. New York: St. Martin's Press, 1978, p. 19.

3. <u>Ibid</u>., p. 21.

4. Carolyn M. Elliott, <u>Signs: Journal of Women in Culture and Society</u>. Vol. 3, No. 1, August 1977, p. 3.

5. <u>Ibid</u>., p. 6.

6. <u>Ibid</u>., p. 7.

7. <u>Ibid</u>., p. 10.

8. M. Vajrathon, "Toward Liberating Women: A Communications Perspectus," in I. Tinker and M.B. Bransen (eds.), <u>Women and World Development</u>, p. 95.

9. AID, <u>Agenda</u>. Department of State, vol. 1, no. 3, March 1978, p. 5.

10. OECD, <u>Choice and Adaptation of Technology in Development: An Overview of Major Policy Issues</u>. Paris, France: Development Center of the Organization for Economic Co-Operation and Development, 1974, pp. 13-14.

11. This complements Axinn, "The Development Cycle;" see especially with regard to development theory <u>I.D. Review</u>, vol. 19, no. 4, 1977, p. 9.

12. S. Arnstein and A. Christakis, <u>Perspective on Technology Assessment</u>. Jerusalem, Israel: Science and Technology Publishers, 1975, p. 13.

13. F. Mernissii, "The Moslem World: Women Excluded From Development" in I. Tinker and M.B. Bramsen (eds.), <u>Women and World Development</u>, p. 36.

14. J. Smith (ed.), *Something Old, Something New, Something Borrowed, Something Due: Women and Appropriate Technology*. Butte: NCAT, p. 21.

15. AID, *Agenda*. Department of State, vol. 1, no. 3, March 1978, p. 5.

16. *op. cit.*, J. Smith (ed.).

Roslyn Dauber

Concluding Remarks

This collection of essays pools the collective experience of a wide variety of researchers and policy analysts. Our perspectives are as all-encompassing as the topic covered. As pointed out in the International Labor Organization paper (Chapter 3), women, technology and development have not often been thought of together. It is interesting to note that without being assigned specific points to address, similar observations emerged in all of the papers in this collection. All agree that women have tended to be adversely affected by the introduction of technologies in the rural area and by the industrialization process. All agree that the developed world's standards and modes of operation are not what the developing world needs and often have adverse impacts. All agree that development planning, at the program and policy level, nationally and internationally, has tended to misperceive the current role of women and their potential as a most powerful indigenous resource.

Further, it has been shown that women have been denied access to new technologies and the training required to learn the technical skills necessary to adapt to these technologies, creating the false impression that women are by nature resistant to modernization and technological change. The case studies address this point, showing that where women have been resistant to change, it is because they are not benefitting and often are harmed by the change. Their response is geared to survival in a world where women tend to lose status and autonomy through modernization.

We find in program designs that the new technology has not often been evaluated as to its cultural acceptability. We recommend technology assessments and community-initiated evaluations of proposed changes.

If we accept Elise Boulding's evidence, we find ourselves to be in a world not settled at a steady state status quo, but in entropy as far as women's roles in many traditional cultures are concerned. She makes the point that women in developed countries cannot be pointed to as successful models. In the United States, the dollar earnings of women are steadily declining in relation to men's earnings. Women are only allowed into the market economy as the lowest wage earners. (Even in the bureaucracies that do development work we find that women employees lag behind men in job responsibility and wages.) Integration of women in development often means providing women with so many helping services that they become dependents of the modern nation state. Too often women become pawns in someone else's development scheme. In agricultural activities equitable economic partnerships are destroyed through the introduction of technologies. Most interesting in terms of drastic social change is the widely reported perception on the part of women that relationships between men and women are disintegrating and that women are being increasingly left to their own resources to provide subsistence for themselves and their families.

The most sensible way to make policies respond to the needs of women is to base them upon what women want. This means going directly to the village level and making sure that national policies, geared to increased production and economic development, do not conflict with local needs. Marilyn Carr (Chapter 11) points out graphically why "appropriate technologies" are unusable unless the users set their own priority needs. It may sound like a truism that meeting the basic needs of women in their role as nurturers will help not only the women and children, but the vitality of the entire region. Louise Fortmann (Chapter 12) suggests that four policy questions be asked: (1) What are the factors constraining the role of women in agricultural production which fall into a policy vacuum and so have not been handled? (2) Are women the subject of policies that are enforced? (3) Are women included in the target population but left out of the program design? (4) Do the policies ensure that women receive benefit from the labor they contribute?

Another major theme that emerged from this book is the relation between research and policy. All agreed that there is a paucity of data collected with which one can address a specific women-and-development problem. The International Labor Organization, UN agencies, and universities could be directed to do more research. Often there is a divergence between what research scholars think important and what policy-makers consider important, but we hope both the case studies and the policy studies in this book can show how research concerns can be related to immediate policy problems.

A number of important points emerge in a careful examination of the course of technological development as it has so far been carried out: (1) the dynamics of technological change continually displace women with low skill occupations. (2) Technological change is often female-labor-specific in that it absorbs male labor at the same time it disemploys female labor. (3) Those women who leave a rural lifestyle to escape displacement find only a marginal existence at a city's periphery, outside the market economy. (4) Because much of female work is unpaid, development planners disregard the fact that women in developing countries work much longer hours than the men. (5) Women often suffer restricted access to tools, resources necessary to improve the quality of life, land, and information. (6) Women must be integrated into development, not just in specific projects and symbolically, but in the central process of a resource allocation in development planning.

It is the thesis of this book that traditional development strategies must be revamped to radically restructure the ways in which human resources are used to benefit society. Women must be allowed to define their own needs. Moreover, western notions of equality between the sexes cannot be imposed upon the third world. Cultures vary, as do behavior patterns between social classes. If the developed world wishes to act as a partner in development, it must learn to listen to those who traditionally have had the least access to sources of power.

Melinda L. Cain, Roslyn Dauber

Annotated Bibliography

Observations on Annotated Bibliography

Many studies describe negative impacts of the introduction of specific technologies. That is, due to failure to involve women in the planning and choice of technologies or even to recognize their current activity, they are negatively impacted by losing access to income activity or by being put in a situation of having their workload increased.

A second trend appears to be toward an investigation into intermediate or appropriate technologies to help rural women. This includes manuals and descriptions, field work to help women organize and use simpler technologies--and a general plea from all to development planners to direct and adapt modern technology for women. From this case study information, a strong message is presented to planners for policies to avoid technology directed for men only.

The citations included here are only a sample of the growing literature on women and development. We have tried to single out those contributions with specific reference to technology and women, particularly those with an insightful eye to crucial issues highlighted in this book. We encourage a combined focus on this aspect of women and development literature to build on the collection of knowledge in this area, in order to further analyze the issue and direct such information to policy circles.

Alabastro, E.F. "Filipino Women in Science and Technology: Their Training and Employment," paper presented at the ASEAN Conference of Women Engineers and Scientists, 19-21 July 1978. (Available from Denver Research Institute.) University of Denver, Denver, Colorado.

The author, an associate professor at the University of the Phillippines, is a chemical engineer by training, and is currently working in the Department of Food Science and Nutrition. She points out the relatively high status of Filipino women in comparison with other Asian women in terms of access to educational opportunities. However, career options for women are more limited and it is here that cultural biases are seen. In particular, in the traditional fields of engineering and technology, only 7.8 percent of the students are female, caused, in part, by the limited employment opportunities for women engineers. Dr. Alabastro cites two important reasons: the protective labor laws for women that make the hiring of women more expensive than men, and a social prejudice that men are more adept at jobs requiring managerial skills and the use of machinery. She concludes by stating that it is futile to encourage more women to pursue careers in science and technology unless more employment opportunities are generated for women. However, such strategies for expanding career opportunities must consider cultural setting, including accepted practices and taboos.

Billings, Martin H. and Arjan Singh. "Mechanization and the Wheat Revolution, Effects on Female Labor in Punjab." Review of Agriculture, Economic and Political Weekly. December 1970, pp. 169-174.

The employment pattern of women in India is largely determined by social values and status derived from economic and caste differences. Thus, ways in which farm tasks are shared between men and women vary among subcultures. However, with the application of the new technology in agriculture, the structure of agricultural production processes and employment patterns are undergoing rapid change. While there are wide inter-regional and inter-district differences in the female work participation rates in agriculture in the Punjab, these differences have been largely associated with three factors, in the following order of importance: 1) proportion of workers engaged in agriculture; 2) literacy among women; and 3) gross value product per worker. A correlation analysis of the geographical differences supports the hypothesis that, with the economic development of an area, participation in farm work by women declines. While the immediate impact of the Green Revolution has been on the gross value product per worker, the extent to which the Green Revolution will affect the female work participation rate is uncertain in the absence of a detailed study--which is, therefore, called for. (Review abstract) (Annotation from Development As If Women Mattered, Overseas Development Council, 1978.)

Boserup, Ester. <u>Women's Role in Economic Development</u>.
New York: St. Martin's Press. 1970.

A pioneering study which surveys women's participation in various economic sectors in developing and developed countries. Women's activities in different farming systems, <u>the impact of modernizing agriculture on their labor and productivity</u>, concepts of land ownership and other influences resulting from Western contacts are examined in selected African and Asian countries. Similarly, migration and the consequent change from an agricultural to a non-agricultural means of livelihood, as well as the emergence of more trade, industrial, and professional work opportunities, are analyzed in terms of their effect on women's social and economic status. 283 pp. (Taken from "Selective Bibliography on Women," The NFE Exchange, Issue No. 13-1978, Institute for International Studies in Ed., Michigan State University.)

Carr, Marilyn. <u>Appropriate Technology for African Women</u>.
Addis Ababa, Ethiopia: UN Economic Commission on Africa. 1978.

"Agricultural, rural and national development will be a slow and difficult process if the women, who form half of the population and, in some countries, represent up to 80% of the agricultural labor force, continue to be denied access to knowledge, credit, agricultural extension services, consumer and producer co-operatives, labor-saving devices and income-generating activities."

This latest book from the UNECA briefly looks at the reasoning behind the relevance and application of AT in countries in Africa in the first of the three chapters. The second section examines the role of African women in the development effort and attempts to show how important it is that improved technologies reach these women as well as men. Finally, the book describes some of the village-level technologies which are currently available to help African women. It also provides a look at the work being done by various organizations in Africa with respect to approaching development through both AT and women. Annex I contains an annotated bibliography and Annex II gives a selected directory of people and organizations.

Carr, Marilyn. "Appropriate Technology for Women."
<u>Appropriate Technology</u> 1:4-6. 1978.

The author points out that rural women in Africa, Asia and Latin America may work as long as 16 hours a day. For the most part, modern equipment aimed at men has resulted in more, rather than less, work for women. Recently, several UN agencies and many African governments have become interested in the important role of village technologies to ease the workload of the women, making it more productive and thereby improving rural family life. In particular, the Training and Research Centre for Women established by the UN Economic Commission for Africa has been increasingly active in this field since 1975. Carr describes the four types of projects undertaken by the Centre: national surveys of traditional technologies; socioeconomic studies of the introduction of new technologies; pilot projects aimed at introducing new equipment with in-depth study of the social, economic and technical problems and benefits involved; and study tours and workshops aimed at increasing the understanding of extension workers and government officials with respect to village technology.

Chaney, Elsa M. and Marianne Schmink. "Women and Modernization: Access to Tools." in June Nash and Helen I. Safa (eds.), Sex and Class in Latin America. New York: Praeger Publishers. 1976.

Reviews the negative impact of "development" and "modernization" on women--especially women's access to the tools of technology, here defined as those skills and materials pertaining to economic activities. In agriculture, where women play a preeminent role, their access to technology is denied in favor of men, thereby aggravating the production and income gap between men and women. The modernization of production in the industrialization process revolves around goods that were once produced in the family unit by women. When specialized enterprises assume production responsibility, it is men who move into the factories in large numbers; although women perform low-paying, low-skilled jobs, they quickly reach an "upper limit" beyond which they rarely go. Women's preponderance in the tertiary sector is discussed as well as women's participation in politics; both reflect the difference between the controllers of the tools of modernization and those permitted only limited access. Contains a good reference list. (Annotation from Development As If Women Mattered, Overseas Development Council, 1978.)

Dixon, Ruth B. Rural Women at Work: Strategies for Development in South Asia. Baltimore: Johns Hopkins University Press. 1978.

This book is based upon interviews with dozens of women and men in international agencies, governments, foundation offices, population institutes, family-planning clinics, rural community development programs and producer cooperatives involving village women in Bangladesh, India, Nepal and Pakistan. The author suggests that women's productive activities should be moved from the traditional household and subsistence agricultural sectors to income-generating employment outside the home. She contends that nonagricultural employment that expands the range of social and economic rewards to women outside the home can raise the status of women and alter their reproductive behavior. It can promote rural development as well, probably more effectively than would similar programs aimed primarily at men. As one way to promote employment, Dixon proposes the establishment of rural producer cooperatives, owned and operated by women. She recognizes that such cooperatives are no panacea and, indeed, would represent only a small piece in the population-poverty puzzle, but she offers evidence to suggest strongly that it would be a key piece and one worthy of a thorough test.

Dixon concludes that what are needed now are concrete proposals for action and for additional research. Her book provides both.

Goode, P.M. "Village Technology for African Women," Appropriate Technology 3:16-17. 1975.

The author discusses the long working days of Ugandan women and gives three examples to illustrate ways in which simple and inexpensive techniques have been introduced to the work of women in Uganda. These include the use of the "ddebe" oven, the introduction of kitobero or additional food mixture for young children and the growing of vegetables. It is pointed out that "development in the rural areas of Africa may well depend to a large extent upon the part played by women. They are hard working, eager to participate in new approaches and are often more realistic then men."

International Women's Tribune Centre. "Women and Appropriate Technology." Newsletter #7. July 1978. (Available from IWTC, 305 E. 46th St., New York, NY 10017.)

This special issue of the IWTC Newsletter is particularly helpful in introducing the reader to the many activities and publications in the field. Issue #7 includes an annotated listing of resource materials, information on technical assistance groups working in the field and a summary of UN news and conferences.

Islam, Meherunnesa. Food Preservation in Bangladesh (A Manual for Instruction). UNICEF Women's Development Programme. 1977.

This manual consists of recipes and instructions that have been tested in Bangladesh for over a decade and a half. We include this report to illustrate how technology can substantially benefit families by simple food preservation techniques. How to bottle native vegetables and fruit and recipes for preserves are presented. This manual was revived to support UNICEF's women's program. It is a simple how-to book, meant to be experimented with and improved upon. The food training program booklet was initially developed for AID home economics classes. This program could provide seasonal employment for women, bottling surplus fruits and vegetables for sale. Growing more food to feed people will be of no value unless one is also able to preserve it.

O'Kelly, Elizabeth. "Appropriate Technology for Women." Development Forum. United Nationa: CESI/OPI. June 1976.

A key goal of the International Decade for Women and the World Plan of Action from the 1975 International Women's Year Conference is the development of modern rural technology and energy-saving devices so as to help reduce the heavy workload of women and facilitate their full participation in community, national and international affairs. However, the author points out that prejudices still exist against women infringing upon technology considered as man's territory. Yet, especially in developing countries, "the women are the ones most in need of technology, and the ones most likely to be progressive enough to use it, given the chance to do so. In the areas of farming, food processing and storage, and cottage industries, intermediate technologies to reduce drudgery and increase productivity are suggested." Examples include simple irrigation or drainage schemes, hand-operated hulling machines, locally constructed food storage containers, Smokelen cooking stoves, aquaducts, hand pumps and hand-operated machines for cottage industries.

O'Kelly, Elizabeth. Rural Women: Their Integration in Development Programmes and How Simple Intermediate Technologies Can Help Them. (Available from the author, 3 Cumberland Gardens, Lloyd Square, London WC1X 9AF. $4.00 plus postage.) 1978.

This book is a finely distilled condensation of the many drops of personal experience of the author in Asian and African countries. In it she discusses rural women in different societies and the particular technologies that are suitable to them--or not suitable--and why. She brings together a great many details about rural women's work, attitudes, physical surroundings, resources, that should be part of the consideration of new interventions. There are also descriptions of the Corn Mill Societies in the Cameroons and of the Women's Institutes in Sarawak as examples of the use of intermediate technologies to gain women's confidence and of the resultant growth of women's groups and activities.

Appendices contain very practical lists of: 1) names and addresses of organizations concerned with intermediate technology and/or rural development overseas; 2) manufacturers, and their addresses, of some of the equipment suggested; and 3) useful books on different kinds of technologies, such as biogas, fish culture, food preservation and soap making, as well as more general publications and bibliographies.

O'Kelly, Elizabeth. Simple Technologies for Rural Women in Bangladesh. UNICEF Dacca Women's Development Program. June 1978.

This monograph makes explicit the wisdom of using simple technologies, easily adaptable to the Bangladesh culture. After briefly describing the typical work life of rural women, the author shows what types and how time saving technologies can be introduced to improve women's lives. A technology resource list is included. This comprises a piece of O'Kelly's larger work on the topic. (See the above citation for a good typology for analysis.)

O'Kelly, Elizabeth. "The Use of Appropriate Technology to Help Rural Women." Appropriate Technology 2:20-21. 1977.

A major problem, from this author's perspective, is that rural development program administrators have apparently forgotten the technologies of the past, thinking instead in terms of the transfer of current technologies often too costly or complex to be practicable in developing countries. Furthermore, administrators fail to distinguish between savings of "manpower" and savings of labor; they also fail to appreciate that the division of labor between the sexes is very different than in Western societies. The author uses a discussion of subsistence and cash crop farming to illustrate how various intermediate technologies can be introduced to permit less arduous and more productive work for women. In particular, the author describes an effective way to get new ideas across to women--the formation of clubs or village-level associations that serve to gain their confidence and to be a useful focal point for extension and medical workers.

Petty, Irene M. "The Role of African Women's Organizations in Identifying Needs for Labor Saving Devices." Prepared for the AAAS Workshop on Women and Development for UNCSTD. Available from AAAS.

The author illustrates her premise that African women's organizations represent a cross-section of the population and should be recognized as a rich national resource, by examining three women's organizations: the Federation of Senegalese Women's Organizations, The National Union of Togolese Women and the Association of Ivorian Women. She suggests that such organizations provide an effective role model to women at other levels and can be used to compliment national (public) development efforts. Further research is suggested in order to better understand the real contribution that women's organizations are making. She recommends that male/female teams be used in doing such research in technical assistance activities and project planning minions.

Ritchie, Jean A.S. "Impact of Changing Food Production, Processing and Marketing Systems on the Role of Women." Proceedings of the World Food Conference. Ames: Iowa State University Press. 1977.

This chapter examines the inter-relationships between changing agricultural patterns and food use and the roles of age and sex groups in some societies in Africa. The author points out that the goals described in the 2nd UN Development Decade and Decade for Women depend greatly upon the introduction of economic and technological changes in the production, processing and marketing of food and other agricultural produce since the economies of Africa are based on the efficiency of the farmer. Increased productivity will depend not only on agricultural inputs but on an efficient use of all human resources, women as well as men. The present roles and relationships assigned to women form a barrier to such progress, as illustrated by the neglect of the subsistence economy, largely in the hands of African women, with the result of a slower growth of food production and a low family cash income. She concludes that the failure to look at society as a whole and to establish an equitable balance between food production and cash crops has been a major obstacle to development in many countries.

Rogers, Barbara. "What do Women Want?" Appropriate Technology 4:8-9. 1979.

The article addresses the failure to consider women's needs for technological innovation in an appropriate form, pointing out that such "forgetfulness" causes development efforts to be "sadly incomplete, and in some cases counterproductive." The author uses examples of well digging and forestry in Upper Volta and agricultural production in Zambia, to illustrate that women's "expertise" in the field should merit consideration in development efforts. Unexplored areas where appropriate technology would particularly benefit women include tools for cultivating the fields and harvesting produce. A preferable situation would be where everyone is considered equally eligible for introduction to appropriate technology, asking the question "What do people want?"

Smith, Judy, Jan Zimmerman and Ilene Wright (eds.). Something Old, Something New, Something Borrowed, Something Due: Women and Appropriate Technology. Butte: National Center for Appropriate Technology. Vol. 1, no. 1. August 1978.

Although this journal is concerned strictly with the domestic appropriate technology movement in the United States, it is the first piece we've seen on how women can take charge of their lives through careful thought, familiarity and understanding of useful technologies. An excellent philosophical discourse on how women can enhance their autonomy through careful selection of technologies is included. Also included is a concrete "plan of action" on how women can fruitfully relate to technologies. The spirit of this journal can be easily applied to technologies in developing countries.

Tinker, Irene. "The Adverse Impact of Development on Women." In Irene Tinker and Michele Bo Bramsen (eds.), Women and World Development. Washington, D.C.: Overseas Development Council. April 1976.

Criticizes the Western model of development not merely as being inadequate, but as having a negative impact on women. The model exports a Western, middle-class value judgment of what is appropriate for women which undermines traditional occupations that give them status in society. Modern technology, created and exported by men, implies a preference for male employees. The author contends that a close inspection of real economic activity would reveal that women play a larger and more unrestricted role in pre-developed economies. The gap in male/female earning power is widening. Women's roles and jobs in a number of societies are briefly described as are the changes in these roles as a result of colonialism, modernization, education and urbanization. The author calls for a more comprehensive understanding of the impact of the development process on women. (Annotation from Development As If Women Mattered, Overseas Development Council, 1978.)

U.N. Economic Commission for Africa. "Africa's Food Producers: The Impact of Change on Rural Women." Focus, Vol. 25, No. 5. Addis Ababa: Women's Program Unit of the Human Resources Development Division, UNECA. January-February 1975.

A very useful paper demonstrating the diminished importance of African women's role in agriculture with the advent of modernization. In most of traditional Africa, women were the backbone of rural farming. Their role was crucial, as they were responsible for growing family subsistence crops. With modernization, women have been left behind and are often ignored when the cash economy and farm machinery are introduced. Rural women's work doubles when men migrate to the cities. Most women in rural areas are engaged in market trade, but as the marketing sector is modernized, women suffer; modernization tends to increase the importance of bulk buying arrangements and decrease that of the marketplace. This change in the importance of a woman's role in rural Africa has had impact not only on their agricultural role but also on the rural community as a whole. The paper's most interesting point is that modernization makes women's tasks increasingly burdensome and relatively less productive than in traditional societies. (Annotation from Development As If Women Mattered, Overseas Development Council, 1978).